Gender Myths and Feminist Fables

Development and Change Book Series

As a journal, *Development and Change* distinguishes itself by its multidiscipli-nary approach and its breadth of coverage, publishing articles on a wide spectrum of development issues. Accommodating a deeper analysis and a more concentrated focus, it also publishes regular special issues on selected themes. *Development and Change* and Blackwell Publishing collaborate to produce these theme issues as a series of books, with the aim of bringing these pertinent resources to a wider audience.

Titles in the series include:

Gender Myths and Feminist Fables
The Struggle for Interpretive Power in Gender and Development

Edited by

Andrea Cornwall, Elizabeth Harrison
and Ann Whitehead

Blackwell
Publishing

© 2008 by The Institute of Social Studies

First published as Volume 38, Number 1 of *Development and Change.*

BLACKWELL PUBLISHING
350 Main Street, Malden, MA 02148-5020, USA
9600 Garsington Road, Oxford OX4 2DQ, UK
550 Swanston Street, Carlton, Victoria 3053, Australia

First published 2008 by Blackwell Publishing Ltd

Library of Congress Cataloging-in-Publication Data

Gender myths and feminist fables: the struggle for interpretive power in gender and development/edited by Andrea Cornwall, Elizabeth Harrison. and Ann Whitehead
    p. cm. – (Development and change book series)
``First published as volume 38, number 1 of Development and Change."
Conference papers.
    Includes bibliographical references and index.
    ISBN 978-1-4051-6937-0 (alk. paper)
1. Women in development. 2. Feminist theory. 3. Feminism–Political aspects. 4. Sex role–Sociological aspects. I. Cornwall, Andrea, Institute of Development Studies.
    HQ 1240.G45446 2007
    305.4209172'4–dc22

A catalogue record for this title is available from the British Library.

Set in 10pt Times by Aptara, New Delhi, India

The publisher's policy is to use permanent paper from mills that operate a sustainable forestry policy, and which has been manufactured from pulp processed using acid-free and elementary chlorine-free practices. Furthermore, the publisher ensures that the text paper and cover board used have met acceptable environmental accreditation standards.

For further information on
Blackwell Publishing, visit our website:
www.blackwellpublishing.com

Contents

Notes on Contributors

Andrea Cornwall is a Fellow of the Institute of Development Studies at the University of Sussex, Falmer, Brighton, UK (e-mail: a.cornwall@ids.ac.uk), where she is the Director of the DFID-funded Research Programme Consortium Pathways of Women's Empowerment (www.pathways-of-empowerment.org). Her publications include *Dislocating Masculinity: Comparative Ethnographies* (co-edited with Nancy Lindisfarne, Routledge, 1994), *Men and Masculinities: Politics, Policies and Practice* (co-edited with Sarah White, *IDS Bulletin* 31(2), 2000) and *Readings in Gender in Africa* (James Currey, 2004).

Judy El-Bushra developed her current interest in the overlaps between gender and conflict as themes in research, policy and practice while working with ACORD over twenty years. She currently manages the Great Lakes Programme of International Alert, 346 Clapham Rd, London SW9 9AP, UK.

Anne Marie Goetz is a political scientist and Fellow of the Institute of Development Studies, University of Sussex, currently on leave and working as the Chief Advisor on Governance, Peace and Security for UNIFEM, New York (e-mail: anne-marie.goetz@unifem.org). Her research interests are in gender and good governance, with a particular focus on gender-sensitive accountability systems.

Mercedes González de la Rocha is a Mexican social anthropologist who has carried out extensive research on poverty and household social organization. Since 1981, she has been affiliated to CIESAS (Centro de Investigaciones y Estudios Superiores en Antropología Social), where she combines research and teaching activities. She is the author of *The Resources of Poverty: Women and Survival in a Mexican City* (Blackwell, 1994). Since 1999, her research has focused on an analysis of the impact of social policy programmes on the well-being of poor families. Her most recent publication – *Procesos domésticos y vulnerabilidad. Perspectivas antropológicas de los hógares con Oportunidades* (CIESAS, 2006) – provides an in-depth study of poor households' vulnerability and the extent to which social policy programmes enhance their options for survival. Contact: CIESAS Occidente, Avenida España 1359, Coloñia Moderna, Guadalajara, Jalisco, 44190, México.

Elizabeth Harrison is an anthropologist at the University of Sussex, Falmer, Brighton, UK (e-mail: E.A.Harrison@sussex.ac.uk). Her work has been broadly within the anthropology of development, with a particular interest in institutional dynamics and in the deployment of policies for gender justice. She has conducted research primarily in sub-Saharan Africa and, more recently, in Europe.

Cecile Jackson is at the School of Development Studies, University of East Anglia, Norwich, UK (e-mail: cecile.jackson@uea.ac.uk), where she researches and teaches on gender and development. Her current work centres on a

DfID–ESRC funded project 'Marriage, Power and Well-being' in southeastern Uganda, predominantly Bagisu.

Melissa Leach is a social anthropologist and Professorial Fellow at the Institute of Development Studies, University of Sussex, Falmer, Brighton BN1 9RE (e-mail: M.leach@ids.ac.uk), where she leads the Knowledge, Technology and Society (KNOTS) team and is Director of a new ESRC Research Centre, Social, Technological and Environmental Pathways to Sustainability (STEPS). Her current research interests include science–society relations, environment and health issues.

Bridget O'Laughlin is an Associate Professor of Population and Development at the Institute of Social Studies, PO Box 29776, 2502 LT The Hague, The Netherlands (e-mail: brolaughlin@iss.nl). Her current research interests are the politics of AIDS policies in southern Africa and the ways movements for land reform address the diversification of rural livelihoods.

Ann Whitehead is Professor of Anthropology at the University of Sussex, Falmer, Brighton, UK (e-mail: a.whitehead@sussex.ac.uk). A contributor to foundational debates on feminist engagement with development and on theorizing gender, she has had a wide engagement with national and international feminist politics. She was co-founder of the first UK Masters course on Gender and Development at IDS and the University of Sussex in 1987. Building on research on agrarian transformation and changes in rural social and gender relations in Northern Ghana, her work addresses changing gender relations under the impact of economic processes and development policy discourses on gender and economic change.

Gender Myths and Feminist Fables: The Struggle for Interpretive Power in Gender and Development

Andrea Cornwall, Elizabeth Harrison and Ann Whitehead

INTRODUCTION

Gender and development has become, over the course of recent decades, a distinctive and plural field of enquiry and practice. Gender and development is a recognized sub-discipline and 'gender' has gained official status within the discourse of mainstream development. It has become institutionalized in numerous ways: in advisory posts in donor agencies and non-governmental agencies, in masters courses in universities, in ubiquitous training programmes and in women's national machineries. Diverse and differently located groups of feminist gender advocates have created a body of academic research and initiated many changes within development institutions.[1] In these processes, a key site of innovation has been the creation and evolution of new languages — languages of representation, languages of analysis and languages of policy discourse — and debate over these. The contested nature of the language of gender and development, its uses and contexts are central themes of this collection.

This volume arises from contributions to a conference entitled 'Beyond Gender Myths and Feminist Fables', hosted by the Institute of Development Studies and the University of Sussex,[2] which brought together activists and academics from the South and the North and representatives from bilateral and multilateral development agencies and international and national non-governmental organizations (NGOs). The impetus for the workshop was widespread disillusionment among feminist gender and development innovators with what had become of 'gender' in development, including frustration with the simplistic slogans that had come to characterize much gender and development talk.

1. Key contributions to the analysis of the emergence of this field and the dilemmas faced within it include Baden and Goetz (1998), Jackson and Pearson (1998), Kabeer (1994), Marchand and Parpart (1995), McIlwaine and Datta (2003), Miller and Razavi (1998) and Razavi and Miller (1995).

2. A number of papers from this conference, addressing themes ranging from the pragmatics of mainstreaming 'gender' to the contemporary politics of feminist engagement with development, were published in a special issue of the *IDS Bulletin* 35(4); see Cornwall et al. (2004).

The chapters collected here focus directly on locating particularly resonant ideas about gender within the field of development discourse and practice. Taking pervasive popularizations of notions such as 'women are less corrupt than men', and images of women as 'closer to the earth' or 'inherently peaceful', contributors seek to situate the deployment of these notions and images within development narratives. Their analyses illuminate how the languages through which knowledge is produced and deployed within feminism affect the representation and strategic employment of that knowledge. Together, they raise broader questions about the relationship between research and policy and the difficult task of feminist advocacy within the domain of mainstream development practice, which can be indifferent or even hostile to gender issues.

A central question for us is why bowdlerized, impoverished or, for some, just plain wrong representations about gender issues have become embedded in development. The contributions explore this in the multiple sites in which such knowledge is created and put to use, tracing the genealogies of influential ideas and the contests that have accompanied their inscription in development narratives. Beyond this, many of the pieces are also self-reflexive, asking hard questions about feminisms' own political and narrative practices. To what extent has feminist development advocacy and mobilization relied on essentialisms in its own imaginaries? One of the biggest challenges for feminism was to set loose the association between identity and identification that served to mobilize the category 'women' as a politically salient interest group. Yet many pressures conspire to bring us to powerful but unhelpful default positions.

Women often appear in narratives of gender and development policy as both heroines and victims: heroic in their capacities for struggle, in the steadfastness with which they carry the burdens of gender disadvantage and in their exercise of autonomy; victims as those with curtailed choices, a triple work burden and on the receiving end of male oppression and violence. Embedded at least in part in our own self-conceptions, these rallying calls have the power to move, but they are also — our contributors suggest — very far from the complexity of women's and men's lives. Our critical self-reflection extends to the use of the term 'gender' itself which, some would go as far as to argue, has become part of the problem rather than part of the solution.

In this introduction, we comment on the issues arising from these dilemmas and on what they suggest about the relationship between feminist knowledge and development practice. In doing so, we also interrogate the ambivalence that underpins feminist engagement with development. Our aim is to go beyond homogenizing versions of the development enterprise and of feminism, and to situate representations of gender issues in the everyday discourses and practices of gender and development.

TALKING DEVELOPMENT AND DEVELOPMENT TALK

Development and feminism share philosophies of transformation and as such have political objectives that are hotly and continuously contested. A critical area of such contestation is in the struggle for interpretive power — what languages and images, representations, narratives and stories, should be used to plan or mobilize for change. Issues of representation and the politics of discourse have become subjects of widespread debate within development studies in general, moving from the widely quoted work of Escobar (1995) and Ferguson (1990), to attempts to present the discourses of development in less monolithic terms (Crewe and Harrison, 1998; Grillo and Stirrat, 1997; Mosse, 2003, 2005).

Some of this work is centrally focused on the production and reproduction of development discourse and narratives; on the 'framing, naming, numbering and coding' (Apthorpe 1996: 16) that underlies development policy. For example, Arce (2003: 33) argues that struggles over meanings are central to understanding development institutions and their outcomes: 'the language of development frames our understanding of contemporary problems'. The reason that this is important is because language representations are deeply implicated in positions concerning what constitutes knowledge; in turn, this provides a basis on which to map out and legitimize interventions.

The making and shaping of development policies can thus be understood as a terrain of contestation in which particular framings of the problem and the solution — what Maarten Hajer (1995) calls 'story-lines' — come to gain purchase. Such 'story-lines' rely for their effectiveness on being mobilized by advocates and used as a basis for enlistment of actors who span different sites of engagement (Hajer, 1995; Latour, 2005). The representations that come to shape development practice are a reflection of institutional and individual power. Recent work by Mosse (2005) draws attention to the disjuncture between the representation of policy as a technical matter, arising primarily from an assessment of evidence, and the complex ethnographic realities of the political nature of policy formulation. In particular, Mosse proposes that 'policy primarily functions to mobilise and maintain political support, that is to legitimise rather than to orientate practice' (2005: 14). His ethnographic case is that of a development project in rural India, but the arguments have a wider relevance for analyses that seek to understand the ways in which policy making can create different rules as to the status and production of knowledge. For example, King and McGrath (2004) have recently drawn attention to the ways in which development agencies are positioning themselves as 'knowledge agencies'. In the case of the World Bank, being a 'knowledge bank' arises out of its avowed interests in local sources of knowledge, participatory approaches, and the recognition of a plurality of voices. The extent to which this results in better or more effective aid is a moot point; some argue that it has made the Bank 'more certain and arrogant rather than less' (King and McGrath, 2004: 93).

These discussions have great relevance to our understanding of how representations of gender come to be mobilized in development policy and practice. In a powerful analysis of development, written almost forty years ago, Albert Hirschmann (1967) drew attention to the role that myths play in animating and motivating the actions of development actors. He argued that in order to contend with the otherwise insuperable obstacles that such actors face in transforming conditions of misery and inequality, they need something to believe in, something that will guide and sustain them, something that would both lend them moral conviction and a sense of purpose. Development, he contended, needs to create, and sustain belief in, its own myths.

Many development players would find unacceptable any idea that policy directions are inspired by belief rather than fact. The commonest use of the term 'myth' in development discourse is to invoke it as a device to emphasize the falsity of taken-for-granted assumptions and as a basis for designating what ought to replace them. But if development practitioners and researchers find it hard to accept that their behaviour may be based on myths, they might be persuaded by the work of a number of twentieth century political theorists who stress the relationship between myth and action. Hirschmann draws on the work of Georges Sorel (1908) to contend that development needs its own myths to guide and motivate action; mistaking these heroic stories of change that inspire intervention for actual, given realities of development work is to miss the point, Hirschmann argues. He cites Sorel, who argues; 'myths are not descriptions of things, but expressions of a determination to act... A myth cannot be refuted since it is, at bottom, identical with the convictions of a group' (1908/1941: 33).

For Sorel, the epistemological status of myth, its relationship to truth or falsehood, is beside the point: what matters is the power that myths have to make sense of the inchoate flux of life, and provide a sense of purpose and conviction. It is, as Doezema's (2004) work on trafficking in women has shown, drawing on Laclau (1996), when myths take on a political dimension and are put to use to serve political agendas that their potency becomes apparent. Myths work for development by encoding 'truths' in narratives that nourish and sustain convictions. And development's myths gain their purchase because they speak about the world in ways that lend political convictions the sense of direction that is needed to inspire action.

GENDER MYTHS AND FEMINIST FABLES

As 'gender' has been taken up in development policy and practice, story-lines, fables and myths have been created that have emphasized some aspects of feminist agendas, and pushed others out of the frame. Reflecting on the uneasy outcomes of the transformation of feminist knowledge into development agendas, participants at our workshop expressed concern about the consequences. They had become wearily familiar with the constant repackaging of ideas. They were becoming punch drunk with the reassertion of key axioms under different labels such as 'poverty reduction', 'empowerment', 'rights, 'exclusion' and 'citizenship'. Contributors to this volume explore some of the dynamics of the rendition of feminist ideas in the narratives and story-lines that have come to be used in the development mainstream. These are adopted for a range of purposes. They include, of course, tactical moves to bring about policies that can change women's lives for the better. Getting gender concerns onto the mainstream development agenda requires pragmatism. In order to capture resources for policies to tackle gender injustice and disadvantage, discursive strategies need to be adopted that will forge alliances with many different kinds of development actors in a plethora of development institutions. Some of the contributions also explore the role that gender myths play in galvanizing and inspiring feminists to undertake the hard slog of change.

Some of our authors find the notion of myth useful — as Hirschmann did — for making sense of how and why certain ideas gain purchase with diverse development actors and of the work that these ideas do in motivating development interventions. But they invoke different aspects of myth's potential range of meanings. For Mercedes de la Rocha a myth is a popular dogma, a useful thing to say: it takes the form of a sacred narrative (something that is uncontestable), that can be acted out or reproduced in rituals in 'fora where members of academic institutions, governments and international agencies meet to discuss social policy and poverty issues' (this volume, p. 46). Other authors centre their analyses less on myths than on 'received wisdoms' in gender and development (El Bushra) or 'powerful assumptions' and 'generalizations' (Jackson). Jackson highlights the taken-for-granted and self evident character of myths, focusing on ideas that form 'part of the unquestioned. . . dispositions of thought which may be reproduced over generations of scholars' (this volume, p. 108).

In some cases, the images deployed by gender myths are less textual and more visual, as is the case in Melissa Leach's account of the way in which particular images of women's relationship to the environment became 'visual development icons', encapsulating 'powerful and appealing messages'. Her chapter offers an example of feminist fables. In this case a powerful set of narratives about environmental degradation had come to be harnessed to gender myths about women's inherent propensity to act as conservers of resources, and guardians of nature. As in de la Rocha's chapter — where a myth becomes 'a fable (or a fairy tale?)' (this volume, p. 46) when charged with a key moral message — the women and environment fables occurred at the height of global moral contestations about the environment. Feminist fables work, as Emery Roe (1991) has so effectively described, to set up the overcoming of a problem by heroic intervention that results in a happy ending. Their persuasive power comes in defining the problem as well as the solution. By presenting policy actors with actions that find their resolution in a desired set of outcomes, such fables also offer them a place within the story,

requiring, as well as justifying, their intervention. The feminist fable here —
the story of the brave heroines who rescue the environment — was potently
coupled with essentialized notions that have a broader mythical appeal.

Cornwall argues that feminist attachment to certain ideas about women
and about what is needed to improve their lives needs to be analysed in terms
of the affective power of the deeply held beliefs about women that come to
be encoded in gender myths and feminist fables. She draws upon Cassirer to
emphasize the emotional qualities of myth: 'Myth does not arise solely from
intellectual processes; it sprouts forth from deep human emotions. . . it is the
expression of emotion . . . emotion turned into an image' (Cassirer, 1946: 43,
emphasis in original). Myths, Cornwall suggests, are narratives that do more
than tell a good story. They are composed of a series of familiar images and
devices, and work to produce an order-of-things that is compelling precisely
because it resonates with the affective dimensions of values and norms. It
is the mythical qualities of narratives about women evoked in gender and
development policies, then, that gives them the power to spur people into
action.

The contributions to this collection highlight a number of links between
knowledge and power in the field of gender and development that myths
contribute to making. For some, myths are 'out there' and the province of
powerful development others, as in de la Rocha's chapter where myth's crucial
function is 'to provide justifications and/or to legitimize social oppositions
and tensions', or in the account given by O'Laughlin for whom the people
who repeatedly recite the simple story are those 'with powerful voices'.
For others, myths are what feminists make when they seek to influence the
powerful. For yet others, myths and fables are what feminists live by in order
to act for social transformation.

The remainder of this Introduction looks in more detail at the different
ways in which the political nature of knowledge production is elaborated
through different kinds of gender myths and feminist fables. We begin by
exploring further the ways that the nature of development intervention affects the production of knowledge within gender and development and the
language in which this knowledge is communicated and debated.

POWER AND THE INSTITUTIONAL CONTEXT: IMPLICATIONS
FOR GENDER AND DEVELOPMENT

The different institutional sites dealt with by the contributors to this collection add interesting perspectives to the existing literature on the history
and politics of gender within development institutions. Much of this literature looks at the adoption of gender mainstreaming within the UN bodies
and the Bretton Woods Institutions, although particular NGOs and bilateral
donors such as OXFAM, DFID and Sida have also been covered, as well as

processes of gender mainstreaming within state bureaucracies.[3] The glimpse that our chapters offer of the world of development bureaucracy provides a powerful case for the argument that it is almost a necessary condition for institutionalization for ideas to be blunted and reduced to slogans and ideals — they need to be domesticated to fit the exigencies of agency procedures and priorities. This has been an argument long and powerfully made by critics of gender mainstreaming, of which Standing (2004) and Woodford-Berger (2004) more recently explore troubling nuances.

This is not only a matter of the extent to which ideas are changed as they are taken up, but also of the techniques used to institutionalize and 'sensitize', such as gender training. Establishing frameworks, activities and protocols for gender training was a major site of innovation in gender and development. All the major development institutions undertook gender training during the 1990s. Although many of these training programmes were tailor-made, they drew their major content and approach from three or four main models. After the initial flurry when the models were first developed, in the early 1990s, there has been little substantive innovation for close on a decade in the tools that are commonly used for gender training. The ways in which the essentially political — and at the same time, deeply personal — issues of gender get rendered within such training frameworks and within bureaucracies more generally is discussed at length in Cornwall et al. (2004). Papers there describe how the political project of gender and development has been reduced to a technical fix so that gender 'becomes something that is ahistorical, apolitical and decontextualised' (Mukhopadhyay, 2004: 95). They also illustrate the tendency, described by Goetz (1994) for bureaucracies to incorporate information on their own terms, privileging that which fits in with their own views of the world and the shared analytical framework of those within such organizations.

Denying Dissidence

The institutional context of large development bureaucracies not only leads to the simplification of gender and development ideas, it also transforms them. This is very powerfully argued in the contribution by de la Rocha. Her chapter is particularly interesting because she revisits her own earlier 1980s' work on the urban poverty of Guadalajara, Mexico, which covered a period of economic crisis when the already low-waged urban poor suffered a dramatic fall in purchasing power. This path-breaking work expanded understandings and definitions of poverty and poor people's strategies for survival. Poor urban households responded in essentially private ways with resourceful strategies that included working harder, turning to the informal sector,

---

3. For example, in the works of Geisler et al. (1999); Goetz (1995); Jahan (1995); Macdonald et al. (1997); Porter et al. (1999); Razavi and Miller (1995).

self-provisioning, restructuring households and using social networks. De la Rocha argues that this and other studies led to the creation of the 'myth of survival' — the idea that the poor have an infinite capacity to withstand shocks and crisis through these multiple strategies. She draws attention to new approaches to poverty emphasizing the agency of the poor, and to the World Bank's emphasis on assets as part of this thinking.

Later research, however, brought into question the 'myth of survival'. In 1994, Mexico suffered a financial crisis which led to a loss of permanent male employment. De la Rocha found severe limitations on the capacity of poor households to adapt to the new adverse economic conditions. In particular, they were unable to intensify the use of their labour force to achieve survival and reproduction. De la Rocha argues that her work has been selectively used: her earlier study in which poor households did have options to survive falling incomes from formal employment was picked up, but her later work, which shows the severe limitations of these strategies, was ignored.

De la Rocha's account implies various ways in which the institutional context in which research is discussed influences its content. In its transition from the context of the work of independent scholars, to interpretation within the World Bank, her work came to be selectively inserted within a particular institutional agenda. She forcefully makes the point that it is the World Bank's commitment to liberalization, which included policies that were responsible for Mexico's crisis in the 1990s, that is behind the adoption of the myth of survival. The substantive current World Bank agenda — the post Washington consensus and the new architecture of aid based on economic liberalization — underlies its continued use of particular approaches to poverty which incorporate the myth of survival. As Gita Sen has noted, 'powerful institutions understand the importance of controlling discourse only too well' (Sen, 2005: 13).

However, the passion behind de la Rocha's contribution derives from another feature of the encounter she outlines. This is the banal but overwhelming point that there are enormous power differentials between Latin American researchers on poverty and World Bank poverty specialists. With its economic resources and the manifold political relations that constitute part of the net of global geopolitical relations, the World Bank is able to make organizational, discursive and strategic choices and decisions which have profound effects on poor people. These global inequalities are reflected on the much smaller stage of inequalities in relations with the research community.

Many of the authors represented here have experiences, often aired privately, of their work being taken up by powerful development players such as the World Bank. First brought on board because of their innovations in areas that come to be deemed relevant to World Bank thinking, researchers often find that critical, reflective and, indeed, honest accounts do not find favour. Findings have to be endlessly rewritten and reshaped to be published or adopted, or reports are received and quietly dropped, never to be referred to again. Initially and individually, gender specialists have berated themselves for their naiveté and have often acquiesced to charges that they are 'too academic' and unable to translate their work into appropriate policy language. In some cases such self-criticism is justified. But in many cases the rules of the game that we are apparently unable to learn are less about presentation, or accessible and policy-focused writing, and more about conflicts over, and indeed suppressions of, substance. The tolerance level for differing views and for challenge and critique seems to be getting lower, as major international players experience ever more intense pressure to show no doubts and admit no uncertainty (Goetz, personal communication, 2005).

The chapters in this collection also speak to ways in which the power relations of development transform discourse in another sense. The development of the policy agenda often depends on the big players achieving maximum cooperation amongst themselves in order to produce a globally agreed agenda. The arenas in which the fiercest contestations over language and objective occur are those that bind governments and other bodies to particular kinds of action. Protocols that imply subsequent legislation and end-of-summit agreed statements (such as the Platforms for Action of the UN Women's Conferences) are fought over word by word and clause by clause.

While the need for these globally binding agreements may be responsible for some of the homogenization and universalism apparent in UN policy, this is of course not the case for the Bretton Woods institutions. They are also noted for the universalism of policy analysis and policy directions that generally fail to take into account national specificities. Here the drivers are much less about getting global agreement and much more about establishing hegemony and promoting economic liberalization. It is remarkable that a central criticism frequently made of structural adjustment policies and of Poverty Assessments — that they adopt a 'one size fits all' approach — can still be made for the Poverty Reduction Strategy Papers, which have avowed country ownership and responsiveness to national 'voices' (Whitehead, 2003).

Encoding Essentialisms

This tendency towards universalism may be one reason why gender myth making in mainstream development contexts so often turns on using ideas about gender that rely on essentialized images of women. Leach looks at this in the field of eco-feminism, El Bushra in the field of women's peace activism and Goetz in relation to a myth in the making — the idea that women are less corrupt than men.

El Bushra's contribution to this collection examines the pervasive myth that women are inherently more peaceful than men — the peace-makers who smooth ruffled feathers and mediate conflict — and that women are passive victims rather than in any way actively engaged in violent conflict. She argues that there are different kinds of essentialisms in some discourses about men, women, violence, conflict and peace, but that over-generalization fails those affected by war and conflict. Working from essentialisms, it is impossible to meet the highly specific needs that particular groups of women have or to harness peace-building potentials. It also fails to distinguish amongst these groups. This chapter discusses post-conflict interventions that refuse these myths and take a more nuanced approach.

Goetz is sceptical of the way in which gender has been included in the growing anti-corruption agenda. Empirical observations that women less frequently take bribes and are less often involved in shady political deals, or that greater numbers of women in parliament lead to lower levels of corruption in politics (Dollar et al., 2001) are explained by recourse to the idea that women are more moral than men, either because of their dominant social roles, or because of their implied intrinsic qualities. As Goetz points out (this volume, p. 90): 'This idea of linking notions of womanly virtue with uncorruptability is not new. It is based upon essentialist notions of women's higher moral nature and their propensity to bring their finer moral sensibilities to bear on public life, and particularly on the conduct of politics — an argument which was much used by suffragettes a century ago'. This kind of explanation is based on 'assumptions about the way in which gender shapes people's *reactions* to corruption' (this volume. p. 95), but it is important to also consider the ways in which gender relations also condition the *opportunities* for corrupt behaviour. Goetz goes on to develop an argument that widespread gender inequalities in access in bureaucracies, low levels of institutionalization and weak democracies in many political systems, including those of South Asia, mean that women only gain very limited access to the domains of political opportunity. In so far as women are excluded from male-dominated patronage and power, they thus lack the opportunities for corrupt behaviour. Goetz's chapter is one of several in this special issue that argue that gender myths arise when commentators ignore the context-specific nature of gender relations. These chapters provide many insights into the drive towards global generalizations and universalism.

The centrality of the discipline of economics to development is singled out by several contributors, who make a number of detailed criticisms of economic analysis and methodologies. In her account of the importance of nuanced and context-specific understandings of how households embody both separate and shared interests, and both conflict and co-operation, Jackson argues that 'these intersections are absolutely critical to the workings of gender' (this volume, p. 109). However, they remain largely silenced in the research of IFPRI and the World Bank drawing on micro-economists' research on households. Why is this? For Jackson, part of the explanation is concerned with the dominance within these organizations of economists, 'for whom gender disaggregation and comparison is methodologically more tractable than researching the relational significance of gender' (ibid.).

In her analysis of how women come to be represented as more risk averse than men in rural sub-Saharan Africa, Jackson argues that this is based on two generalizations. The first is that women are committed to food crops rather than more risky cash crops. The second is that women, unlike men, use incomes to the best advantage of all household members, particularly on household nutrition and education. As she points out, such generalizations have been repeatedly criticized by feminists arguing that where these associations are found, they are highly context specific. What her chapter examines to great effect is the gulf that becomes apparent between 'received wisdom' and empirical evidence from feminist research on the gendered nature of economic behaviour in rural Africa. She goes on to look at the rich detail of specific case studies which show that women take risks in relation to farming and rural livelihoods and that marriage needs to be seen as a source of security and entitlements for women, rather than simply as a site of subordination.

Representations of gendered economic behaviour and intrahousehold relations in rural Africa are also the subject of Bridget O'Laughlin's contribution. She addresses arguments made by the World Bank that a significant way to reduce poverty is to redress gender imbalance in assets controlled by poor households. She looks in detail at two repeatedly cited studies to support an argument that gender inequality constrains agricultural productivity in Africa. O'Laughlin places the particular empirical findings about gendered patterns of fertilizer use, labour use and willingness to work on particular crops into a much wider context. She identifies a whole range of other forms of gendered economic behaviour that occur in the market and in households, but fall outside the frame of these studies. She also explores the historical processes of commoditization, individualization and immiseration that were occurring in the specific regions of Burkina Faso and Cameroon where the studies were undertaken. The argument that intrahousehold gender relations produce 'allocative inefficiency' — that is they allocate factors of production in ways that do not produce maximum output — is shown to be a narrow and constrained perspective which does not reflect the actual historical processes of impoverishment, or how these implicate gender relations and gender resistances. None of this, her account confirms, allows meaningful conceptualization of the relation between poverty and gender in Africa.

Implicitly, O'Laughlin recognizes that such criticisms are hard ones, given that much of this work comes from the gender-sensitive wing of economics — a minority in a discipline where most 'remain unconvinced of the importance of gender issues in economic development, though political correctness impedes them from saying so explicitly, at least in writing' (O'Laughlin, citing Kanbur, 2002). There is, however, little comment from gender sensitive economists on the ways in which their work has been mobilized within the World Bank for the particular approach to poverty reduction identified by O'Laughlin. Nor is there much evidence that the attempts by feminist economists to model gender power relations (as, for example, in contributions to the journal *Feminist Economics*) are being recognized for their importance to these debates.

Such criticisms do not seek to detract from the important analytical contributions that have come from feminist and micro-economists' work on

modelling the household. But the major public face of this work — its incorporation as evidence to support policies of 'pro-poor' growth — appears to
be a further example of the frequent and often repeated criticism of the way
in which gender issues are taken up within dominant agendas, namely that of
instrumentalism. And this occurs despite the fact that the welding of gender
equality concerns to these influential policy agendas may well have been the
work of ardent gender champions within key multilaterals. Instrumentalism
may have its place as a tactical manoeuvre, even if its consequences may lead
to tactics being subsumed into strategies shaped by other agendas. Our criticisms, however, go beyond those of instrumentalism. There are elements here
of familiar dynamics within development, within which a failure to deal with
complexity, context specificity, and the dynamics of power relations, is intrinsic to the relative weight that different disciplinary perspectives carry. What
remains salient to our argument here is the politics of the perspectives that
come to be shaped by these disciplinary dispositions, and what they occlude.

MYTH MAKING AND FABLE SPINNING WITHIN FEMINISM

So far our discussion has focused on relatively 'easy' targets by exploring
development institutions and development actors as a source of myth making. However, this collection makes an important additional contribution in
the form of reflexive accounts of how and why feminists make myths and
spin fables as they push for policy change in development. These essays tell
significant, but far from simple, stories about the pressures feminists experience in their encounters with development: pressures to simplify, sloganize
and create narratives with the 'power to move' that come to depend on gender
myths and give rise to feminist fables.

The Politics of Influence

The workshop out of which the contributions to this special issue emerged
brought together feminist gender advocates who had been instrumental in
developing new approaches and new languages for gender analysis and
gender politics in development. All of them had moved from initial simple
oppositional politics to becoming engaged, in some form or other, with
development policy making. The imperatives of making place for new ideas
and objectives within development organizations of various kinds require
alliances to be made, and call upon diverse linguistic, narrative and presentational strategies.

Working to influence economists may require evidence and analysis in the
form of 'stylized facts'.[4] Influencing high-powered international luminaries

---

4. This is a phrase used by Diane Elson (workshop transcript).

may require 'sound bites' — short, punchy messages preferably accompanied by seductive statistics, like the much-quoted factoid which placed women as the majority of the world's poor. These pragmatic presentational strategies are driven by the conviction that it is better to make concessions than to see no action at all. Above all, after the initial push to get gender on the agenda, the work of shaping policy requires building support with constituencies that have other priorities. The politics of influence requires not only simplification and memorable slogans, but also strategic choices and strategic languages for crossing many kinds of divide.

This point emerges very clearly from Goetz's chapter. She explains how, while her own interventions in policy are motivated by her conviction of the need for gender justice, such convictions and the arguments that might convey them are not going to be very persuasive to those designing political and bureaucratic reforms. Instrumental arguments, presenting a case that having more women in politics is good for political systems, for example, or that without them a singular perspective is missing, hold much more sway. As Goetz reflects, 'many feminist students of politics, including myself, have combined the justice argument with either the expectation that women can transform politics, or with the insistence that women are needed to represent women's interests', thus actively contributing 'to the myth of women's special contribution to politics' (this volume, p. 92). She points to some positive effects of this way of presenting the issues, noting how the idea that women's presence in the politics and public sphere may reduce corruption has led to a greater interest on the part of development agencies in promoting women in public life.

Leach's chapter, analysing why a specific representation of Southern women's relationship to the environment became so prevalent and powerful for a period of time, is also about instrumentalism. As she describes it, a women, environment and development (WED) discourse was clearly in the ascendant during the 1980s, but became much less influential after it had been subject to systematic and vocal criticism from other feminists. However, critical changes had also taken place in environmentalism more broadly. Leach describes how WED became heavily linked to ecofeminism in the 1980s, when ecofeminism was particularly politically and discursively powerful within radical environmentalism. Taking the notion that women are especially 'close to nature', ecofeminists suggested that 'women and nature have been subjected to a shared history of oppression by patriarchal institutions and dominant western culture' (this volume, p. 70).

Based on the feminist fable that women have a special relationship with the environment, which was coupled with other feminist fables about women's caring roles and natures, these arguments have served to inspire a large range of social and environmental movements, ranging from localized grassroots movements to large Northern networks. Leach argues that when taken up by development agencies under pressure to address environmental issues, WED and ecofeminism became shorn of their radicalism. This resulted in projects that called on women's labour and knowledge for environmental conservation or were aimed at women only. Her account highlights significant different feminist strands within environmentalism. There have been vocal contestations between them and occasional strategic commonalities of interests, leading to the discursive and practical dominance of some of these strands for a period of time.

Disappointments, Dreams and Desires

Feminisms' own myths and fables should help us to transcend the present, to push for progressive change, to reach out to others, but in so doing how do they deal with the differences that divide us? It is in these imaginaries, where our dreams and desires should reside, that some of our bitterest disappointments may come.

Criticism of the unreflective use of the term 'women' as if it described a pre-determined interest group with shared concerns began almost as soon as second wave feminism got off the ground. Our libraries are full of conceptual and empirical work on difference. Less thick on the ground are studies that show that women may not be as nice, peaceful, harmonious and caring as gender myths and feminist fables would have us believe. Cornwall suggests that personal, as well as political, attachment to the idealized generalizations about women encoded in feminisms' own gender myths has made it difficult for feminists to confront their implications. Her account focuses on her own fractured attachment to myths of female solidarity and female autonomy which, she argues, are 'two of the key supportive elements in feminist fables of women's liberation from male oppression' (this issue, p. 150).

Cornwall reflects on the southwestern Nigerian setting to which she had been drawn because of feminist fables about women's autonomy and solidarity. She confesses to finding it difficult initially to countenance aspects of the everyday realities of women's relationships with men and with each other that disrupted ideals about women that she held dear. Women's ability to command independent incomes appeared not to be the magic ingredient imagined by discourses on empowerment. Husbands were more often cast as 'useless' in fulfilling their provisioning responsibilities than as powerful oppressors; it was, in many women's accounts, other *women* who caused them the most grief. Questioning the restricted frame that notions of 'gender' in development offer for understanding gendered power relations, Cornwall cites Molara Ogundipe-Leslie's observation that western feminists have over-privileged 'coital and conjugal sites' (Ogundipe-Leslie, 1994: 251) at the cost of understanding the complexity of African women's identities, identifications and relationships. Yet, Cornwall reflects, what price would feminists pay if they were to open up the Pandora's box of relationships between women; and what do feminists have to gain by observing Sorel's injunction not to confuse a myth to live by with the messy realities of actual human relationships?

Reflection on the spectre of divisions between women raises a broader dilemma for development: that of how 'women' come to be represented, and by whom. No constituency can have a monopoly on claiming to be working for women's advantage. Some of the fiercest battles have been between conservatives and neoconservatives and other women, all taking place in the name of women. The literature of disappointment includes accounts of how apparently easy it is for the right to co-opt women to non-progressive political projects, using the language of women and/or gender. Batliwala and Dhanraj (2004) describe self-help groups in India, favoured for their association with 'empowerment', and suggest that they may not only have deepened the immiseration of poorer women, but deflected their energies away from other forms of engagement, not least the political. As they caution, it is precisely where right wing organizations are seizing political space that has been conceded to them by the absorption of women in self-help and small-scale enterprise activities, that we need urgently to re-examine the articulation of feminism and development.

An international example of a similar politics is provided by the fierce debates around the diametrically opposed political meanings that can be assigned to 'women' and to 'gender', as described in the 1995 Beijing Women's Conference by Baden and Goetz (1998). In these debates the role of the Vatican was particularly hotly contested, including by women's groups from within the Catholic Church (Sjorup, 1995). More generally, Sen (2005) reflects on the advances made at the various major global conferences during the 1990s (Vienna 1993, Cairo 1994 and Copenhagen 1995, as well as Beijing), arguing that these advances in positions on gender justice, reproductive rights and so on, were in the face of strong opposition from social and religious conservatives. These conferences now look like the high points in getting progressive feminism onto the development agenda. What some, such as George Weigel (cited in Haynes, 2001), refer to as the un-secularization of modern society and others more pointedly as the rise of organized neoconservative religious constituencies, has gathered strength on the international stage with alarming speed since 2001. The decision not to hold an International Women's Conference in 2005 for fear of losing gains that had been made up to 1995 is testimony to the sense of insecurity felt by feminist gender and development advocates in the face of the current global political climate.

CONCLUSION

[C]hanges in international development discourse and policy are largely a reflection of changes that are occurring in the balance of social forces. Accordingly what is needed for world development is not so much a 'rearrangement of knowledge' [as] a realignment of power. (Nederveen Pieterse, 2005, cited in Utting, 2006: 3)

This collection is centrally concerned with the relationship between knowledge production and power relations when feminist knowledge has encountered development. Those power relations within development ensure that feminist thought remains thoroughly marginal. It is seen as perfectly respectable to be an expert on poverty without having read any feminist work on poverty and to regard it as the responsibility of gender experts to convince the mainstream of its relevance. This old fashioned exclusion through particular forms of intellectual gate-keeping is today largely undiscussed. For all the feminist facts and analysis that might be marshalled, then, to make a more subtle argument about any of the topics addressed in this collection, it is other kinds of evidence that continue to hold sway and other kinds of author that are referred to back and forth in the self-referential processes of establishing intellectual legitimacy.

The institutional and organizational forms of international development, as bureaucracies with their own politics of agenda setting and requiring co-operation and alliances in global fora, produce pressures for simplification, sloganizing and lowest common denominator consensus. When development actors seize upon feminist ideas they want them in a form that is useful to their own frameworks, analyses and overall policy objectives. Feminists within these organizations work hard to keep the language and form of gender analysis close to the lived complexity of how gender and development are intertwined, but must necessarily work to these organizational and institutional pressures and rules of the game. Feminist gender advocates working in other kinds of institutions also make strategic choices, including which linguistic and presentational forms will best get particular gender issues addressed, prioritized and resourced.

The chapters in the collection also look at the nature of feminism itself as a source of myths and fables and explore ways in which debates within feminism offer up competing accounts which can be seized upon by many different political currents. But some of these debates occur precisely out of varied reactions to the re-interpretation, fudging and plain old distortion that occurs when gender ideas have been taken up in development. They have, for example, added to the various misgivings that have been raised about the language of gender itself. Plural feminisms conceive of the concept of gender in radically different ways. Its explanatory power and political salience have come under steady critique in recent years, further fragmenting the possibility of mounting coherent positions in its defence. Our chapters also raise acutely the question of whether there is something in the lack of a consistent and coherent version of what 'gender' is actually all about that serves to undermine the political potency of feminist positions. But these doubts have also served to further weaken the possibilities for its use within the development arena as a meaningful tool for sharpening political awareness and mobilizing action.

The contributions which follow give myriad examples of just how significant discursive contestation is in the context of gender and development, but, in all of them, at the heart of the account are profound concerns with the ways in which discourses are linked to particular policies, including some of the major hegemonic policy prescriptions of contemporary development practice. The struggles for interpretive power are not struggles to get the language and representations right for their own sake, but because they are a critical part in the determination of policy. As Sen's (2005) account of global feminists arrayed against conservative and neoconservative forces in various international meetings in the last two decades makes clear, these power struggles, which have discursive dimensions, are struggles over policy content which has profound implications for women's lives worldwide.

No-one can be in any doubt that local and global struggles of women's movements and gender activists against the multifaceted and highly resourced attack from neoconservatives is of utmost seriousness for the welfare and rights of women worldwide. It will be a growing factor within international and national policy making, and global feminism will have to work harder to overcome divisions of diversity and difference and to make alliances to face this challenge. Paradoxically, as Sen (2005) points out, alliances between feminists across geopolitical and other divides may be easier in the face of this kind of threat. We can expect new twists and turns in the language of gender and new ways in which myths and fables will speak to a new global politics. What this collection shows most powerfully is that such myths are not something 'out there', but are also closely connected to ideals we like to live by. Understanding this is essential if we are to get to grips with the full complexity of the reasons why gender and development interventions are inadequate to match the complexity of gender relations and of women's and men's lives.

REFERENCES

Apthorpe, R. (1996) 'Reading Development Policy and Policy Analysis: On Framing, Naming, Numbering and Coding', in R. Apthorpe and D. Gasper (eds) *Arguing Development Policy: Frames and Discourses*, pp. 16–35. London: Frank Cass.

Arce, A. (2003) 'Creating or Regulating Development: Representing Modernities Through Language and Discourse', in A. Arce and N. Long (eds) *Anthropology, Development and Modernities: Exploring Discourses, Counter-Tendencies and Violence*, pp. 32–51. London and New York: Routledge.

Baden, S. and A. Goetz (1998) '"Who Needs (Sex) When You Can Have (Gender)?": Conflicting Discourses on Gender at Beijing', in C. Jackson and R. Pearson (eds) *Feminist Visions of Development: Gender Analysis and Policy*, pp. 19–38. London and New York: Routledge.

Batliwala, Srilatha and Deepa Dhanraj (2004) 'Gender Myths that Instrumentalise Women: A View from the Indian Frontline', *IDS Bulletin* (special issue *Repositioning Feminisms in Gender and Development*) 35(4): 11–18.

Cassirer, E. (1946) *The Myth of the State*. New Haven, CT: Yale University Press.

Cornwall, A., E. Harrison and A. Whitehead (2004) 'Introduction: Repositioning Feminisms in Development', *IDS Bulletin* (special issue *Repositioning Feminisms in Gender and Development*) 35(4): 1–10.

Crewe, E. and E. Harrison (1998) *Whose Development: An Ethnography of Aid*. London: Zed Books.

Doezema, J. (2004) 'Sex Slaves and Discourse Masters: The Historical Construction of Trafficking in Women'. DPhil Thesis, IDS, University of Sussex, Brighton.

Dollar, D., R. Fisman and R. Gatti (2001) 'Are Women Really the "Fairer" Sex? Corruption and Women in Government', *Journal of Economic Behavior and Organization* 26(4): 423–9.

Escobar, A. (1995) *Encountering Development: The Making and Unmaking of the Third World*. Princeton, NJ: Princeton University Press.

Ferguson, J. (1990) *The Anti Politics Machine: 'Development', Depoliticisation and Bureaucratic Power in Lesotho*. Cambridge: Cambridge University Press.

Geisler, G., B. Keller and A. L. Norman (1999) 'WID/Gender Units and the Experience of Gender Mainstreaming in Multilateral Organizations: Knights on White Horses?'. A Report Submitted to the Norwegian Ministry of Foreign Affairs. Oslo: Chr. Michelson Institute.

Goetz, A. M. (1994) 'From Feminist Knowledge to Data for Development: The Bureaucratic Management of Information on Women in Development', *IDS Bulletin* 25(2): 27–36.

Goetz, A. M. (1995) 'The Politics of Integrating Gender to State Development Processes: Trends, Opportunities and Constraints in Bangladesh, Chile, Jamaica, Mali, Morocco and Uganda'. Occasional Paper. Geneva: United Nations Research Institute for Social Development/United Nations Development Programme.

Grillo, R. and R. Stirrat (eds) (1997) *Discourses of Development: Anthropological Perspectives*. Oxford and New York: Berg.

Hajer, M. (1995) *The Politics of Environmental Discourse: Ecological Modernization and the Policy Process*. Oxford: Clarendon Press.

Haynes, J. (2001) 'Transnational Religious Actors and International Politics', *Third World Quarterly* 22(2): 143–58.

Hirschmann, A. (1967) *Development Projects Observed*. Washington, DC: Brookings Institution.

Jackson, Cecile and Ruth Pearson (1998) *Feminist Visions of Development: Gender Analysis and Policy*. London: Routledge.

Jahan, R. (1995) *The Elusive Agenda: Mainstreaming Women in Development*. London: Zed Books.

Kabeer, N. (1994) *Reversed Realities: Gender Hierarchies in Development Thought*. London: Verso.

Kanbur, R. (2002) 'Education, Empowerment and Gender Inequalities'. Ithaca, NY: Cornell University. Available online: http://www.arts.cornell.edu/poverty/kanbur/ABCDE.pdf (accessed 1 April 2004).

King, K. and S. McGrath (2004) *Knowledge for Development: Comparing British, Japanese, Swedish and World Bank Aid*. London: Zed Books.

Laclau, E. (1996) 'The Death and Resurrection of the Theory of Ideology', *Journal of Political Ideologies* 1(3): 201–20.

Latour, B. (2005) *Reassembling the Social: An Introduction to Actor-Network-Theory*. Oxford: Oxford University Press.

Macdonald, M., E. Sprenger and I. Dubel (1997) *Gender and Organizational Change: Bridging the Gap between Policy and Practice*. Amsterdam: Royal Tropical Institute.

Marchand, M. and J. Parpart (eds) (1995) *Feminism/Postmodernism/Development*. London: Routledge.

McIlwaine, C. and K. Datta (2003) 'From Feminising to Engendering Development', *Gender, Place and Culture* 10(4): 369–82.

Miller, C. and S. Razavi (1998) *Missionaries and Mandarins: Feminist Engagements with Development Institutions*. London: Intermediate Technology Publications.

Mosse, D. (2003) 'The Making and Marketing of Participatory Development', in P. Quarles van Ufford and A. K. Giri (eds) *A Moral Critique of Development: In Search of Global Responsibilities*, pp. 43–75. London and New York: Routledge.

Mosse, D. (2005) *Cultivating Development: An Ethnography of Aid Policy and Practice*. London: Pluto Press.

Mukhopadhyay, Maitrayee (2004) 'Mainstreaming Gender or "Streaming" Gender Away: Feminists Marooned in the Development Business', *IDS Bulletin* (special issue *Repositioning Feminisms in Gender and Development*) 35(4): 95–103.

Nederveen Pieterse, J. (2005) 'Knowledge, Power and Development', *Courier de la Planète* (special issue *Knowledge and Power*) 74: 6–11.

Ogundipe-Leslie, Molara (1994) *Re-creating Ourselves: African Women and Critical Transformation*. Trenton, NJ: Africa World Press.

Porter, F., I. Smyth and C. Sweetman (eds) (1999) *Gender Works: Oxfam Experience in Policy and Practice*. Oxford: Oxfam GB.

Razavi, S. and C. Miller (1995) 'Gender Mainstreaming: A Study of Efforts by the UNDP, World Bank and the ILO to Institutionalize Gender Issues'. UNRISD Occasional Paper No 4, Fourth World Conference on Women. Geneva: United Nations Research Institute for Social Development.

Roe, E. (1991) 'Development Narratives, Or Making the Best of Blueprint Development', *World Development* 19(4): 287–300.

Sen, G. (2005) *Neolibs, Neocons and Gender Justice: Lessons from Global Negotiations*. Geneva: United Nations Research Institute for Social Development.

Sjorup, L. (1995) 'Negotiating Ethics: The Holy See, its Allies and Contesting Actors in Beijing'. CDR Working Papers No 96.1. Copenhagen: Centre for Development Research.

Sorel, G. (1908/1941) *Reflections on Violence*. New York: Peter Smith.

Standing, H. (2004) 'Gender, Myth and Fable: The Perils of Mainstreaming in Sector Bureaucracies', *IDS Bulletin* 35(4): 82–8.

Utting, P. (2006) 'Introduction: Reclaiming Development Agendas', in Peter Utting (ed.) *Reclaiming Development Agendas: Knowledge, Power and International Policy Making*, pp. 1–20. Basingstoke: Palgrave/Macmillan.

Whitehead, A. (2003) 'Failing Women, Sustaining Poverty: Gender in Poverty Reduction Strategy Papers'. Report for the UK Gender and Development Network. London: Christian Aid.

Woodford-Berger, P. (2004) 'Gender Mainstreaming: What is it (About) and Should We Continue Doing it?', *IDS Bulletin* 35(4): 65–72.

2

A Bigger Piece of a Very Small Pie: Intrahousehold Resource Allocation and Poverty Reduction in Africa

Bridget O'Laughlin

THE MYTH: PROMOTING GENDER EQUALITY TO REDUCE RURAL POVERTY IN AFRICA?

This chapter is concerned with the making of a myth about the relation between gender inequality and poverty in Africa. The myth claims that if the allocation of productive resources were not skewed against women, rural African households would be able to work more efficiently and thus to produce more. So if a greater share of credit, inputs, land and labour were to be controlled by women, overall poverty could be reduced. The myth provides an economic rationale for policy measures such as targeting women in microcredit schemes or giving women individual legal right to plots of their own.

From a feminist point of view, there is much that is appealing in the proposition that gender inequality in rural Africa is inefficient. It celebrates the skill and industry of women farmers. It is backed by abundant literature showing that women have resisted injustice by withdrawing labour from development projects that did not take their interests into account. It is grounded in a point long made in feminist research but still poorly absorbed in poverty policy circles or in mainstream economics — that the unitary household is a fiction. If gender inequality compromises economic growth, there is a reason for bureaucrats and development donors to put gender concerns higher up on their agendas. The quest for proof that gender inequality is inefficient has attracted analytical attention from neoclassical modellers using game theory, bestowing new disciplinary legitimacy on feminist economics. Nonetheless, this contribution argues, it is important both for feminist emancipatory agendas and our understanding of poverty in Africa to recognize that the inevitable inefficiency of gender inequality is mythical.

Theory and myth have some common properties. They both set out premises that frame certain aspects of reality and omit others. Both seek to generalize. Theories about social life, like myths, often employ narratives, using vignettes, anecdotes and imagery to invoke a more subtle understanding than skeletal propositions can convey. Both often employ symbolic or esoteric language to enhance the power of their arguments.

I would like to thank Naila Kabeer, Duncan Foley, Ruth Castel-Branco and particularly Ann Whitehead for very helpful comments on an earlier draft of this contribution.

In the telling of this myth, two narratives, both based in research done in the 1980s, have acquired timeless iconic status. The first is Christine Jones's account of how households in an irrigated rice scheme in northern Cameroon failed to optimize their production when men did not give women fair compensation for their work (Jones, 1983, 1996). The second is Christopher Udry's demonstration that the unequal distribution of inputs across women's and men's plots in Burkina Faso did not maximize yields (Udry, 1996). Each is repeatedly retold in the literature on gender and rural poverty in Africa, often in slightly different versions. Both deftly employ the language of neoclassical economics, fully accessible only to the initiated, and both provide the necessary magical incantation — a precise numerical estimate of the cost of gender bias.

It is one thing to disagree with a particular line of theoretical argumentation and another to call it a myth, suggesting both that its power to convince does not depend on its evidence or analytical strength and that it misrepresents or misleads. These two studies are rigorous works of scholarship, clear in their assumptions, logically argued and based in evidence. Yet a close reading shows that both have been open to mythical appropriation. The lessons drawn go far beyond the scope of the authors' findings. The myth presents a technicist rationale for reducing gender inequality that simplifies its political complexities — since co-operation within inequality can be (and often is) economically efficient. Finally, the way each study is analytically framed, tearing gender inequality out of its specific historical context of capitalist development in colonial and post-colonial Africa, leads to misrecognition of the causes of poverty.

SPINNING THE MYTH

Myths are spun through repeated retelling by powerful voices. In this case the voices are those of major development agencies, particularly the World Bank. Two World Bank reports have been influential in the promotion of the myth. The first is Blackden and Bhanu's (1999) 'Gender, Growth, and Poverty Reduction', a World Bank technical paper. The idea that targeting productive resources to women will promote significant poverty reduction with growth has been emphasized for sub-Saharan Africa because African women do so much agricultural work. Much of the evidence and argumentation put forward by Blackden and Bhanu for rural Africa has, however, been universalized in the World Bank's *Engendering Development through Gender Equality in Rights, Resources and Voice* (IBRD/The World Bank, 2001), a general mandate for reducing poverty by channelling more resources to women. Many poverty reduction strategy papers (PRSPs), the web-sites and working papers of the World Bank and the International Food Policy Research Institute (IFPRI) and major bilateral donors have endorsed the importance of promoting gender justice to foster economic growth and thus reduce poverty.[1]

The inefficiency of gender inequality belongs to a family of arguments presented in these reports to convince development practitioners that improving the relative position of women will reduce poverty. Both reports contend that when women control household expenditure, it results in better nutrition and health for the household as a whole, and particularly for children. They also argue that when women are better educated and have more access to formal employment, they have lower fertility, important if one considers high fertility to be an important constraint on growth in sub-Saharan Africa.

Although this chapter focuses on the inefficiency claim, the entire set is contestable from a feminist point of view. The idea that those who have caring roles in households (usually women) use their resources to assure better care for their children than those who do not (usually men) is common-sensical but also slippery; one would hardly want to link arguments for greater gender equality to maintaining the exclusive right to the caretaker role. Linking better access to education for women to fertility reduction makes it dependent on one of the more contested ventures in the social sciences, the attempt to establish a direct causal relation between fertility and growth (see Eloundou-Enyegue, 1999). More broadly, claims to gender justice should not depend on proving instrumental links to poverty reduction or economic growth (Jackson, 1996). Gender equality should be valued for itself, not simply because it increases output.

Blackden and Bhanu (1999) and IBRD/The World Bank (2001) do not dabble in high theory. They are practical policy-oriented documents aimed at a broad readership. They do, however, present evidence — often snippets framed in side-bars or boxes[2] — drawn from substantive research to develop their arguments. Particular attention is given to studies by neoclassical economists who have managed to model gender relations within households (intrahousehold resource allocation) and to produce statistically significant quantitative findings. The studies cited are limited in focus and time-period, but their results are generalized to a geographically unspecified and timeless rural Africa. As theory has become myth, the findings of these studies are selectively retold as empirical fact. This 'fact' is that agricultural productivity would be greater if women had individual control over productive resources — land, inputs and labour.

The myth provides different possible explanations of why gender inequality leads to inefficiency. The first, drawing on Jones's (1983, 1986) work, is that

---

1. See http://www.ifpri.org/ and http://www.worldbank.org/gender/. IFPRI's 1994–2003 Project, 'Strengthening Food Policy through Intrahousehold Analysis', has been particularly influential, both for its scholarly publications (Quisumbing, 2003; Quisumbing and McClafferty, 2006) and its web-based outreach. Titles on the IFPRI web-page include: 'Agricultural productivity increases dramatically when women get the same amount of inputs men get' and 'Gender differences in property rights hinder natural resource management'.
2. Myths should be attractive if not necessarily fully comprehensible.

women withdraw their labour when they are not adequately rewarded for it, putting it into less productive activities. This is how IBRD/The World Bank (2001: 86) presents Jones's findings:

> Losses in output also result from inefficiencies in the allocation of productive resources between men and women within households. In Cameroon, as a result of gender asymmetries in the control of income from different crops, female farmers prefer to work on their sorghum plots, for which they control the proceeds, than on rice, for which they don't (Jones, 1986). Reallocating female labour from sorghum to rice could increase household incomes by 6 per cent.

The second explanation of the inefficiency of gender inequality is that male household heads do not pool resources but instead allocate them disproportionately to their own fields. To show how this leads to measurable inefficiency, the same World Bank report draws on Christopher Udry's (1996) study of gender and agricultural productivity in Burkina Faso:

> Households do not necessarily pool resources for production, and the resulting inefficiencies can have important implications for household income and welfare. In Burkina Faso too little labor and fertilizer are used on plots controlled by female farmers, while too much is allocated to plots controlled by men within the same households ... these inefficiencies impose high costs on household production and income. Total household production could be increased by as much as 20% if some of the production inputs used on men's plots were reallocated to women's plots. (IBRD/The World Bank, 2001: 162)

The reports claim that the absence of pooling also has a direct negative impact on the ways women organize production.[3] When women have few resources they are averse to risk and thus do not make good entrepreneurs. Compared with men, women are disadvantaged in their access to and control of a wide range of resources. With fewer resources and more precarious claims to resources, women are more risk-averse, more vulnerable, have a weaker bargaining position within the household, and consequently are less able to respond to economic opportunities (Blackden and Bhanu, 1999: 40).

Having established that gender inequality is inefficient, IBRD/The World Bank (2001: 163) moves on to draw the following policy implications: 'The evidence on determinants of intrahousehold resource allocation and investments make a strong case for targeting interventions by gender — to promote gender equality and more effective development'. Although 'targeting' by gender could mean simply attending to the gendered impact of interventions, the conventional meaning is channelling benefits to women.

Successful myth-making has spawned variant retellings of the tale, often giving it wider scope. As noted, the process began in the World Bank with the transformation of generalizing arguments about Africa in Blackden and Bhanu (1999) into universal truths in IRBD/The World Bank (2001).

---

3. Here the reports refer to the work of Doss (1996) on risk in rainfed farming in Ghana. This study is not so often cited as those of Udry and Jones and thus is not discussed here.

Deininger's 2003 World Bank report on land illustrates the continuing importance of Udry's study in policy discourse on gendered land rights:

> Where the husband controls the proceeds from cultivation, this reduces women's incentives to exert efforts, and thus lowers agricultural productivity. This is particularly relevant in African countries, where women are the main agricultural cultivators, and in many Latin America and Asian countries, where men migrate or women are traditionally heavily discriminated against (Agarwal, 1994; Deere and Leon, 2001). In Burkina Faso the reallocation of factors of production from plots controlled by men to plots controlled by women within the same household could increase output by 6 percent (Udry, 1996). (Deininger, 2003: 58)[4]

Quisumbing and McClafferty (2006: 27) recently claimed that Udry's analysis showed that 'that the output of women's plots, and therefore total household output, could be increased by between 10 and 20 per cent by reallocating actually used factors of production between plots controlled by men and women in the same household'. Each new version makes slightly different and sometimes more dramatic claims. One account of Jones's (1986) study argued that gender inequality was a major reason for the failure of the rice-growing scheme that Jones studied: 'In an irrigated rice project in Cameroon, SEMRY 1, lack of incentives on part of the women farmers is considered to be a major factor in the failure of the project although lack of markets also contributed to it' (Mukhopadhyay and Pieri, 1999: 14). Others have argued that the SEMRY experience shows that women would make more long-term investments if they had security of land tenure, presumably through their own entitlement to project plots (Kabutha, 1999:15).

This is the stuff of myth in development discourse — the telling and retelling of the tales of the improvident Burkinabe husbandman and the provident Cameroonian woman contract farmer in one consultancy report after another on gender and poverty in Africa. The truth they spin becomes a common-place, only tenuously connected to the original texts and unfixed in any particular place or time: African women are more efficient farmers than are African men, so if we target women in land-titling or micro-credit schemes more will be produced and poverty will decline.

As this myth is spun, the assumptions underlying it remain unchallenged, that is, beneath the story lies another myth, an account of the causes of poverty in rural Africa, more powerful for being implicit. If rural poverty can be substantially reduced by reallocating productive resources from men to women, then the organization of rural households is an important cause of poverty. Blackden and Bhanu (1999: ix) accept that gender inequality is not the only cause of poverty in Africa, but the other causes are drawn from the current consensus of the international financial institutions: the ill-advised policy options of post-colonial regimes that inhibited growth through lack of openness to the world market, regulation of domestic markets, bad governance and so on.

---

4. Note that Deininger has reduced the estimate of increased output to be gained from giving men's plots to women from 20 to 6 per cent.

In this account, long-term structural patterns of market development rooted in colonial histories have no relevance for present patterns of poverty and inequality. There is no attempt to see how relations of gender inequality are intertwined with global relations between capital and labour or with processes that make some households prosperous and others poor. Where there is inequality it is assumed to be the expression of market imperfections, not an outcome of the ways markets work. Poverty is assumed to be the lack of commodities, bracketing the processes of intensification and prolonging of work, particularly for women, that have accompanied the expansion of commodity production. If addressing gender inequality requires that women hold individual title to productive resources, then both gender justice and the reduction of poverty depend on the individualization of collectively held resources and greater sway for market signals.

The rest of this chapter seeks to demystify this hegemonic account by returning to the original studies done by Jones and Udry, placing them in their post-colonial contexts, locating their assumptions, interrogating their methodologies and determining what can and cannot be learned from each case about the relation between gender and poverty in rural Africa.

JONES'S STUDY OF SEMRY: INDEPENDENT WOMEN AS THE STANDARD OF EFFICIENCY?

SEMRY is a large contract-farming scheme, producing irrigated rice, situated along the floodplain of the Logone on the border between northern Cameroon and Chad.[5] It began in 1954 as a colonial forced-cropping scheme. A drainage and irrigation system was constructed and rice was introduced as an obligatory crop for the Massa ethnic group living in the area.

The Massa were renowned for their lack of commitment to the French *mise-en-valeur* — cash-cropping. Neither of the principal forced crops in northern Cameroon (cotton and groundnuts) did well in the floodplain. The area was also deficient in the principal staple, red sorghums, and was vulnerable to drought. The Massa had, however, alternative ways of earning money to pay taxes and buy cereals: fishing, tobacco-growing and livestock sales. Only Massa in outlying areas of the floodplain had adopted the late transplanted varieties of sorghum grown by neighbouring groups. These demand work during the rainy season, a time the Massa preferred to use for house maintenance, artisanal work, young men's fishing expeditions, funerary celebrations, women's visits to their parents and men's prestige-conferring milk-gorging rituals. There were nonetheless inter-household differences in capacity to withstand the period of rainy season hunger when labour demands from cultivation were high and some granaries empty.

---

5. The following account of the SEMRY project is drawn principally from Arditi (1985, 1998); Claude (1989); de Garine (1978); van de Walle (1989).

The Massa pattern of residence was based on dispersed compounds inhabited by a senior compound head, his younger brothers and their wives and children. The principal fields were those heavily manured plots that surrounded the compound. These were farmed collectively with red sorghum in association with other food crops. Individual plots were opened in fallow bush land, particularly by women and also by some of the junior men. This mode of land use depended on a gradual hiving-off of junior brothers to form their own compounds. By the 1960s, however, this pattern was no longer possible in all areas, increasing individual claims on collective compound holdings and leading to a decline in reliance on the collective field as the basis for subsistence.

Cattle were herded collectively by neighbourhoods, with compounds taking their turn in providing herders. Livestock could be individually owned, including by women, but most of the cattle were controlled by elders who received them in bridewealth exchanges or in cattle-loans from other compound heads. There were also frequent labour exchanges between compounds within the same neighbourhood.

The rice scheme was built in the floodplain, thus in land that had been used for pasture and for some individual plots such as tobacco. Plots were assigned to each conjugal household, not to the compound head. Rice was sold back to the colonial authorities at fixed prices. Women worked these plots with their husbands, but the income went to men. Chiefs were responsible for enforcing rice production and were allowed to exact tribute in labour. In the 1960s, they and their sons were the only people making much money from cash cropping.

Major expenditures and control over resources thus remained under the control of the compound head, with considerable open tension between the compound head and his junior brothers and sons over the timing of marriage. We would also expect considerable tension over use of time both between men in the compound and between men and women in conjugal households. Although major expenditures were made by household heads, everyday household budgets (de Garine, 1964:112–18) show that most monetary transactions were carried out by women, including daughters as well as wives. They bought food — meat, dried fish, milk, sorghum flour, gumbo, salt, oil — and a small number of consumer goods such as soap and cloth. They sold these same things, but also sorghum brew and small amounts of fodder, wood and tobacco.

The stagnating irrigated rice scheme was reorganized and modernized in the 1970s with assistance from donors, particularly the World Bank. SEMRY became a parastatal enterprise, charged with developing the land, ploughing the rice-fields, managing the nurseries, organizing the pumping and distribution of water, maintaining the irrigation network and infrastructure, supplying fertilizer, and training and supervising the producers. Plots of one-half hectare were given to heads of conjugal households, who were expected to enlist family labour. In practice, from the outset, a large number of plots were given to established commercial producers and, in the areas close to town, to civil servants and traders who hired labour to work their plots. Producers were expected to finish levelling the ground, to make embankments, to transplant the rice, to weed, to apply fertilizer, to keep the land irrigated and to harvest the rice. Producers were allowed to keep 10 per cent of their production (sometimes as much as 17 per cent in fact), but the rest had to be sold to SEMRY, which discounted fees to cover its expenses before paying the residual to the producer. If peasants failed to fulfil their obligations, they were expelled from the project.

The SEMRY project led to major shifts in the organization of Massa livelihoods. The first change was the lengthening of the agricultural year and the intensification of agricultural work, particularly for weeding and transplanting. Weeding of red sorghums took place at the same time as the transplanting of rice, and the second cycle of rice was cultivated during the dry season. The late transplanted sorghums were rapidly adopted in the 1970s, providing some buffer against lower production of red sorghum. Young men's dry season fishing expeditions conflicted with the second rice cycle.

The land base needed to maintain the diversified livelihoods organization of the Massa was reduced, particularly in communities close to the Logone. After a number of destructive incursions, cattle were barred from the land of the project, ultimately leading to a reduction in herd size and thus the loss of both milk and manure for house land. Average cattle herds were higher outside the project boundaries than within. The availability of fallow for individual bush fields and irrigated tobacco plots declined.

Co-operation within the compound and lineage segment diminished relative to that of conjugal households. The rice plots were treated like the individual bush-plots of men. Since plots were assigned to individual conjugal households, earnings were controlled by the household head rather than the compound head, and tasks were carried out mainly by members of conjugal households. The collective compound field became less important both in application of labour time and in its contribution to subsistence.

Differences among households sharpened, based not as in the past on the availability of labour within the household and compound, but on the recruitment of wage-labour and on the quality of land. Although the project led to a sharp rise in monetary income in the region, this income was not evenly distributed. Those achieving high yields found it relatively easy to pay SEMRY fees, but others did not. Arditi (1998) calculated that about one quarter of the producers obtained 4 tonnes per hectare, and 25 per cent more than 6 tonnes per hectare. Those who achieved good yields often used wage-labour, particularly for transplanting rice, and double-cropped. Wage-labour use was initiated in the project by civil servants, traders, and political leaders who were either part-time farmers or had accumulated several plots, but some compound heads also resolved labour conflicts by hiring migrant workers. When SEMRY was expanded into neighbouring areas, this migrant labour force dried up and was replaced by local women. These women, sometimes working in associations, were hired as casual day-labourers. They came both from households that themselves had plots within the project and from households without plots. The rapid emergence of local wage-labour was at the cost of earlier collective labour exchanges.

By the early 1980s, certain problems in the project were evident, despite its apparent technical success. The project was unprofitable. It had very high costs, in part because of the infrastructural investment in SEMRY II and III, but also because of high recurrent costs for labour and inputs. Prices paid for paddy to peasants stagnated as fees rose, reducing earnings for producers. Rates of desertion and default began to rise as did sale of SEMRY rice on parallel markets, often across borders in Nigeria and Chad (Arditi, 1985). In 1981, about a third of the plots in SEMRY I were not in cultivation (Jones, 1986: 108).

By 1987 SEMRY had accumulated debts of 11.000 million CFA, despite government subsidies (van de Walle, 1989: 595). The World Bank pulled out when the project was restructured in 1984. The reorganization plan financed by the EU proposed to cut labour costs by forming neighbourhood producer groups that would take over tasks of training and supervision. Despite a proposal to give land-titles to producers, in the event SEMRY retained a land monopoly, and thus the authority to expel marginal producers.

A donor-funded evaluation of the project concluded that women were unwilling to participate in the project because proceeds were controlled by their husbands (Jones, 1986: 106). Jones's study was designed to test this conclusion, giving her an opportunity to demonstrate the analytical weakness of unitary household models. Jones carried out a year's field research in two different Massa communities, one close to the river and the other in an outlying area. Her argument on women's time use is based on two-day recall labour allocation surveys carried out during the rainy season cropping cycle in the village close to the project. Her sample consisted of twenty-four married women and twelve women heads of household — either widows or living with old or infirm husbands.

Jones's study does not advance the conclusion sometimes drawn from it in the telling of the myth, namely that incentive conflicts would be resolved if plots controlled by men were assigned to women. Jones observes that in one village, 20 per cent of the women were registered for their own plots, but they nonetheless handed the proceeds over to their husbands (ibid.: 118). She does, however, make the central claim drawn from her study by the authors of IBRD/The World Bank (2001): if men gave their wives greater compensation for their work in the rice-fields, women would reallocate their labour from sorghum to rice and household incomes would increase by 6 per cent (Jones, 1986: 116). If we look closely at the evidence and argumentation Jones presents to back up this reasonable sounding claim, we encounter some unstable ground.

Jones found considerable variation in how much time women put into rice cultivation. This variation in number of days worked reflected the amount of money women received from their husbands after the sale of the rice. If women received less than the going rate of compensation for their labour, they would refuse to work, instead putting more cultivation time into sorghum or even working as wage-labourer in the rice-plots of others. Here there is a gap in Jones's evidence. Her argument on the 6 per cent return to greater gender equality is not based on overall comparisons of gendered patterns of labour and income across all forms of household production. Her time study focused on women's work in agriculture. She did not do equivalent labour-allocation surveys for men, nor did she include non-farm forms of time use important for Massa livelihoods, such as fishing or livestock-raising.

Jones's study excluded from the outset the possibility of a complementary gendered division of labour across different activities and both rainy and dry seasons. She did not consider the possibility that women regard the compensation they receive from their husbands as only partial payment for their work in the rice fields, that a husband's sorghum production, both his individual plots and his contribution to the collective field, may be important to women, or that a share of his rice income may be spent on things that women would also spend it on, or that his income from fish and livestock rearing may be shared. Inequality is enmeshed *within* co-operation and some sharing may be better than no sharing.

To look at the impact of variation in women's allocation of labour time on household income, Jones compared the labour allocation of married women with that of women working on their own (Jones calls them independent women). There were twelve such women — seven widows, and five women with husbands too ill or old to cultivate rice (Jones, 1986: 114). She showed that these independent women spent 40 per cent more time transplanting rice than did married women, with a corresponding increase in area transplanted per active household worker (Jones, 1983: 1050).[6] Since paddy yields for the two groups were almost the same,[7] the larger area cultivated led to higher household income from rice. Women on their own spent less time than the married women on the second weeding of their sorghum crop, but Jones argued that any resulting difference in sorghum yield could easily be recovered by retaining a greater amount of paddy for consumption (Jones, 1983: 1051). Jones concluded that the households of such autonomous women gained 6 per cent more than average households from rice and sorghum production (Jones, 1986: 117).

Jones assumes here that women's preferences are most clearly revealed in the labour patterns of women who are not sharing management of resources with men. Within a neoclassical framework that posits the centrality of individual choice, taking widows and the wives of the infirm as prototypes

---

6. Independent women's households cultivated 0.47 ha per worker versus 0.31 ha for married women's households.
7. The households of married women produced 60 kg more per ha than households of independent women (Jones, 1986: 116).

of rational choice may make sense. Everything we know about the heterogeneity of women-headed households should lead us, however, to question whether the choices made by widows and women whose husbands are infirm in any way represent ideal preferences or allocational efficiency either for themselves or for women as a group.

Even on the basis of the evidence Jones provides, women on their own appear to be vulnerable. They put more total days into farm labour than does the average married woman. Their efficiency is thus in part a function of the extension of their labour time. Women working on their own may have specialized in rice production to cover their minimum cash requirements, but would be vulnerable to food insecurity unless they had other resources. It is quite possible that Jones's widows and women with invalid husbands worked much longer and more intensively than other women in order to ensure the minimum amount of cash income that their families needed to survive. Given the intensification of labour and the lengthening of the agricultural year that SEMRY irrigated rice production implied, and resistance to these processes, it does not seem reasonable to assume that all women would regard extra rice income controlled by themselves as necessarily superior to time for visiting their families of origin in the dry season, or caring for their children, or gossiping with friends.

One might thus conclude that independent women's greater involvement in rice production was an expression of their vulnerability rather than their optimizing behaviour. Jones addresses this objection by looking at the 15 per cent (this is now a very small sample) of married women who were 'allocatively more efficient', that is, cultivated as much rice land and spent as much time cultivating rice as the women working on their own. She found that they were indeed compensated by their husbands at a higher rate than those who spent less time on rice. 'Senior wives from polygamous households and women whose husbands still owe bridewealth seem to be overrepresented in the allocatively efficient group of married women' (Jones, 1983: 1053; see also 1986: 117). So Jones concluded that men's bargaining position is weaker *vis-à-vis* higher status senior wives or when they are still struggling to accumulate cattle for bridewealth. When women's bargaining power was relatively higher, this resulted in a more efficient pattern of production for the household as a whole.

Here the evidence is tenuous, but on ethnographic grounds the two kinds of women Jones mentions — senior wives in polygynous households and women whose bridewealth has not yet been paid — would appear to have quite different structural positions within extended family households. One would thus expect them to have very different bargaining positions. Relations of gender inequality are intertwined with forms of inequality based on seniority, reflected in tensions within Massa extended family compound groups over collective claims and duties. Senior wives in polygynous households expected to receive labour contributions from junior wives, particularly in domestic work, making it possible for them to spend more time on rice cultivation. Payment of bridewealth depended on contributions from compound heads, not just husbands. Where this contribution was not forthcoming, junior men might neglect their labour services to the collective sorghum field and dedicate more time to their own rice, a signal of intra-compound conflict and potential rupture. When their wives put more time into rice as a contribution to the payment of their own bridewealth, this could be a reflection of vulnerability rather than of a strong bargaining position. These are the sorts of generational tension over individual vs collective plots exacerbated by the organization of the SEMRY scheme.

Jones's study is silent on the ways intrahousehold tensions are linked to interhousehold differentiation. Her precise calculation of the costs of gender inequality, so highly appreciated by the makers of the myth, depends on averages. She cannot show that the reallocation of women's labour-time from sorghum to rice was equally possible and advantageous for all households because her sample is too small to probe interhousehold variation in intrahousehold inequality. If one is concerned with the implications of this case for the reduction of rural poverty, it is particularly important to recognize that the processes of household differentiation associated with the SEMRY project and reflected in the demise of the collective field undermine the usefulness of the concept of the average household.

Thus it is not clear, for example, that all households would be more food-secure if they put less time into growing sorghum and more into rice. For producers with good yields from rice, it may be that a day's income from rice was higher than that from sorghum. Both Arditi (1985) and Claude (1989) argued, however, that yields from rice production were very unequal because of differences in the quality of land within the project as well as different patterns of labour input. The latter include hiring in of wage-labour by some producers as well as women's participation in rice cultivation. Jones's work covered one cropping cycle, so she did not look at yearly fluctuations in sorghum and rice prices. In years of drought, the shortage of sorghum drove up its relative price (Arditi, 1998). Even if SEMRY relaxed its restriction on how much rice producers could keep, households at the low end of the productivity range could not easily switch from eating sorghum to eating rice as Jones suggests. Arditi (1998) noted that this group owed two-thirds of its income to SEMRY in fees for use of the irrigation system, inputs and marketing.

Nor is it clear that household income would be higher if those women who were doing wage-labour in the project plots of other men would work their husband's plots instead. Most of the fifteen married women who did wage labour worked only a few days a year as wage-workers (Jones, 1986: 111). Five women accounted for 67 per cent of the labour days worked. Each of the five indeed received less than the average rate of compensation from their husbands, but Jones does not tell us whether their husbands received the average rate of compensation or better. Her evidence does not exclude the possibility that these five women came from households that earned less than the average from rice-plots.

There is one final analytical silence in Jones's narrative that compromises its contribution to our understanding of gender inequality and poverty in rural Africa. Jones's study was grounded in the crisis of SEMRY — the low yields, the vacant plots. Asking whether women would put more work into rice if they received more compensation from their husbands can only yield a partial and deceptive account if one abstracts from relations of class. Struggles between husbands and wives over work and compensation were embedded in conflicts between SEMRY management and the occupants of the scheme over prices paid for rice, input charges, control of the crop, conditions of work and use of land.

Conflicts over property and the terms of work have continued to plague SEMRY. One general manager attributed its continuing financial crisis to 'the lack of spirit of initiative and solidarity on the part of the rice producers' (*Cameroun Tribune*, 2001). Producers still have no permanent rights to irrigated SEMRY plots, be they women or men. Security of use of land and water for central livelihood activities is diminished. Seasonal hunger remains an issue for many Massa households, increasingly subject to the fluctuations of cereal prices on local markets (Njomaha, 2000).[8]

What we can learn about the inefficiency of gender inequality from Jones's study is compromised by silences in its design: focusing exclusively on agricultural production; abstracting from the complexity of domestic groups; reducing interhousehold differentiation to the contrast between independent and married women; making the independent (or isolated) woman the normative rational actor; and bracketing the conflicts over compensation, conditions of work and land-use between SEMRY and those — men and women — who worked in the scheme.

Jones illustrates Whitehead and Kabeer's (2001) observation that bargaining approaches linking gender relations with allocational inefficiency often overlook the fact that households have joint as well as competing interests. With the insecurity of agricultural production in Africa, they observe, these joint interests are often protected through the diversification of livelihoods.

UDRY'S STUDY IN BURKINA FASO: THE SELFISHLY IMPROVIDENT MALE FARMER

Some of Jones's problems of research design are remedied in Christopher Udry's work on the impact of intrahousehold resource allocation on household income in rural Burkina Faso (Udry, 1996; Udry and Alderman, 1995).

8. As with other large dam projects, the environmental impact of the Phase II Maga dam on diversified rural livelihoods has proven to be much greater than at first estimated. Floodplain loss has meant loss of pasture land, surface water, fishing and grasses and thus results in a substantial loss of annual income in the regional economy (Loth, 2004). The incidence of malaria and of bilharzia have risen (Njomaha, 2000).

Udry took advantage of a detailed ICRISAT agricultural survey that followed 150 households through the period from 1981 to 1985.[9] The households were located in six communities in three different ecological zones in Burkina Faso. All three zones are subject to the insecurity of opportune rainfall. They depend in varying proportions on rainfed cultivation and livestock production. The ICRISAT survey was carried out in the context of the great famines of the Sahel of the 1970s and 1980s. Udry wrote in the mid-1990s when media images of the misshapen bodies of children, desiccated fields and scattered corpses of cattle had faded, but in a period of new concern with rural poverty in the post structural adjustment period.

In reading Udry, it is important to remember that historically, Burkina Faso is one of West Africa's great labour reserves (Amin, 1974: Sautter, 1980; Skinner, 1960). It was not a poor country in the nineteenth century, but its riches were not those easily appropriated by a colonial regime. Skinner (1960: 378) cites a French official writing in 1899, three years after conquest: 'If one considers Mossi country from the point of view of the resources it can offer for the subsistence of its inhabitants — millet, peanuts, and livestock — one can say that the country is rich . . . but if one considers the country from the point of view of exportable commodities, one must conclude that it leaves a great deal to be desired'.

The colonial response was a forced labour regime. Young men initially fled to the cocoa farms of Ghana to escape forced labour. In time, however, large numbers moved towards the cocoa and coffee farms of Côte d'Ivoire on a contract recruitment system that remained in place after the abolition of the forced labour regime in 1946. Migrant labour had contradictory effects on rural livelihoods. It withdrew men's labour both seasonally and on a longer-term basis, but remittances from migrants also buffered climatic insecurities and contributed to the accumulation of cattle, hiring of casual workers, purchase of inputs and the expansion of farms into new areas.

Udry's research confirmed that it makes analytical sense to disaggregate the household. To control for different possible sources of intrahousehold variation in productivity, he looked at yield variations between male and female plots planted to the same crop in the same household in the same year. His results, summarized in Table 1, show that yields are systematically higher on men's plots than on women's plots for the same crops. The difference in yields reflects differences in application of inputs. Women spend much more time working on men's plots than men spend working on women's plots; child labour, extra-familial labour and manure are used for men's plots more often than for women's plots.

On the basis of these differences, Udry concluded that the existing gendered distribution of individual plots within farming households sets up

---

9. ICRISAT is the International Crops Research Institute for the Semi-Arid Tropics. Udry drew on the 1981–3 data because it had the most agronomic detail. Other studies have looked at averages across the period, or focused on 1984–5, which was a drought period.

Table 1. Mean Yield, Area and Labour Inputs per Plot by Gender of Cultivator, Burkina Faso, 1981–83

	Women's Individual Plots	Men's Plots (individual and collective)
Crop output per ha (1000 CFA)	105.4	79.9
Area (ha)	0.10	0.74
Female labour (hours/ha)	859	248
Male labour (hours/ha)	128	593
Non-family labour (hours/ha)	46	106
Child labour (hours/ha)	53	104
Manure (kg/ha)	764	2993

Source: adapted from Udry (1996: 1019), based on data from ICRISAT.

incentive conflicts that lead to an inefficient pattern of resource allocation. Total household output could be increased by diverting some factors of production from men's to women's plots (the finding invariably cited in the myth), or alternatively by reallocating land from women to men (the version less appealing to feminists) (Udry, 1996: 1018). Udry (1996: 1040) estimates that household output of the crops cultivated by both men and women could be increased by 5.89 per cent with a reallocation of factors of production across plots. When his evidence is recounted in the telling of the myth, however, his alternative way of calculating the effect of gender difference is generally cited — he argues that the effect of a female cultivator is to reduce yields by over 30 per cent of average household yield (ibid: 1018).

Udry's study has become the most frequently told tale in the gender inequality/inefficiency myth, yet despite a larger data-set and rigorous econometric analysis, it shares some of the same analytical silences that mark Jones's work. Udry's study abstracts from the benefits that women obtain from belonging to a co-operative production group in which there is sharing, though on unequal and often conflictful terms. Ideally in Burkina Faso such groups are a patrilineage segment headed by a male compound head who manages land allocations and livestock, decides on priorities in crop cultivation and determines how the product of collectively worked plots should be used. All members of the compound group also cultivate individual plots, however, and control their output.[10]

The labour constraints and new sources of income associated with migration exacerbated tensions within such compounds, a point emphasized by French anthropologists working in West Africa in the 1960s and 1970s (Rey, 1976). Compound heads tried to oblige younger men and women to concentrate on collective plots. Young men evaded this control through voluntary migration, and women turned to petty trade. Despite these fragmenting tensions, the complex nesting of production groups was still important at

---

10. For a description of how such domestic groups normatively functioned in Mossi areas, see Skinner (1960).

the time of the ICRISAT study. In a mixed Bwa/Dyula community, Vierich (1986) found that compound heads could draw on accumulated savings and livestock, better land and more labour contributions. They obtained higher yields by doing so, but they could not easily abuse privilege without division of the compound. McMillan (1986) looked at the farming systems of Mossi households in 1979 in the context of growing land scarcity and the Volta resettlement scheme. Labour was allocated roughly in accord with alloca-tion of land: 62 per cent of household land was worked as collective fields and 59 per cent of household labour was allocated to these fields (McMillan, 1986: 264).

Yet the ICRISAT data did not allow Udry to distinguish between individual plots cultivated by compound or household heads and collectively worked plots under their control. Both are classed as men's plots. We cannot really therefore compare the yields, size and use of labour and inputs on men's and women's plots. It is possible that men's individual plots are as small and as productive as those of women and that labour and inputs are applied less frequently to them than to collective plots. From the outset, Udry's study is biased against the possibility that collective fields are favoured over individual holdings. Labour that is available for cultivating collective plots may not be available for men's individual plots.

There are various reasons for thinking that maintaining co-operation within a compound group can be advantageous though inequitable in Burkina Faso, as in northern Cameroon. Marcel Fafchamps (2001) has argued that returns to scale and experience may support centralized management of farm resources and the specialization of individuals in particular tasks. A particular gendered division of labour may be allocatively efficient even though inequitable. Udry could not control for the timing of agricultural tasks. Large compound groups are able to spread risk through staggered planting. Opportune weeding is an important determinant of yield. Whichever plots are weeded last will have lowest yields, all other things being equal. If women's plots are those last weeded, their yields will be lower than those on men's plots, but that does not mean that the household could obtain higher yields by weeding women's plots earlier than men's.

As Whitehead and Kabeer (2001) point out in their critical review of Udry's work, the maintenance of a collective reserve is particularly important given the uncertainty of harvests in Burkina Faso. Any short-term calculation of returns can underestimate the importance of joint interests, inequitable as they may be. With the diversification of rural livelihoods, co-operation can extend beyond agriculture, a possibility excluded from Udry's calculations. In the context of Burkina Faso, particularly Mossi areas, with long-term histories of oscillating male migration, it is possible that more labour is put into men's plots because men are working elsewhere — herding livestock, engaged in long-distance trade or working on plantations in Ghana and Ivory Coast.

Relying on the same ICRISAT survey used by Udry, Reardon and his co-authors show that the importance of income from crop production varies

Table 2. The Regionally Differentiated Impact of Drought on Composition of Rural Household Income, Burkina Faso, 1981–85

Income Source (in %)	Sahelian		Sudanian		Guinean	
	1981–85	1984–85	1981–85	1984–85	1981–85	1984–85
Own-crop	49	24	60	51	37	43
Livestock	14	26	6	7	20	14
Local off-farm	24	23	29	27	41	37
Migratory	10	18	2	8	1	3
Transfers	3	8	2	7	1	2

Source: adapted from Reardon et al. (1992: 281) and Reardon and Taylor (1996: 908) based on data from ICRISAT.

across regions and falls in drought years (Reardon and Taylor, 1996; Reardon, Delgado and Matlon, 1992; Reardon, Matlon and Delgado, 1988). Table 2 shows contributions to household income across the years 1981–5 and in 1984–5, a drought year. It shows that crop income is never more than 60 per cent of total income, and that the share of income derived from cattle sales and from migration rose sharply in the Sahelian zone during the period of drought.

Despite his creative use of the large ICRISAT data-set, Udry, like Jones, does not succeed in showing that gender inequality is necessarily inefficient. By abstracting from the complexities of households and off-farm work he fails to recognize the extent to which inequality within co-operation can be acceptable to women as a defence against poverty. Kevane and Gray (1999) do not dispute Udry's findings on differences in productivity, but they do challenge the interpretation. Differences may reflect the strength of a particular woman's bargaining position rather than its weakness. Some women may choose, for example, to work less on their own field to obtain a share of the harvest from their husbands' fields or because they gain more from wage-labour. Little is to be gained by fixing women's land rights *vis-à-vis* their husbands if institutionalized gendered norms on land rights, use and duties go unchallenged. Fertilizer and animal traction were concentrated on collective fields supervised by male household heads, for example, because they were the focus of most government extension programmes (McMillan, 1986: 267).

Udry's effusive estimate of the gains in productivity to be reaped by transferring labour and manure from men's to women's fields has exposed his study to mythical appropriation. He notes, but does not probe, other dimensions of variation in yield that have not achieved such celebration. Men who are household heads achieve a yield on their plots that is 18 per cent higher than that achieved by other men (mostly sons) in the household (Udry, 1996: 1027–8). This suggests that, as in the Massa case, gender and generational inequalities are intertwined.

Udry also notes that the yields achieved by different households simultaneously farming the same crop vary more widely than differences within a household (Udry, 1996: 1021–2). Although all the households in the ICRISAT survey may indeed have been poor (ibid.: 1016), there was also interhousehold differentiation, a pattern worth exploring for those interested in the causes of poverty. In the ICRISAT data for 1983–4, gini coefficients for total income flows varied between 0.32 and 0.34 for the three different regions, but with much higher incidences of inequality for income from live-stock, migration, off-farm labour and transfers than from crops (Reardon and Taylor, 1996: 905). Vierich (1986), working in one of the six villages in ICRISAT study, also found great variation in yields in cereal production (from 30 to 902 kg per worker), which she related to differential access to good land and use of animal traction.

The poor rely heavily on crop income in Burkina Faso, but the conditions that make it possible to increase crop income are access to arable land, access to animal traction and cash to hire labour and inputs. Depending on crop income, particularly in a period of drought, is a condition of the poor, while having a good source of off-farm income — from livestock or local trade or migrant labour — is what makes one better-off (Reardon and Taylor, 1996: 911).

Confronting the relation between gender and poverty in Burkina Faso means considering the long-term structural processes that made men's mo-bility and off-farm activities an important part of rural livelihoods and forged permeable boundaries between ethnic groups, regions and nations. Land re-settlement schemes in the 1980s have not resolved the problems of com-petition for arable land in Burkina Faso. Sex ratios calculated from recent Demographic and Health surveys show that men of productive age are still migrating out of rural areas (see Table 3). Shifting coffee prices and political tensions around migrant identity in Côte d'Ivoire shape the vulnerability of rural households in Burkina Faso.

WHERE THEORY MEETS MYTH: MARKET UTOPIANISM

Both Jones and Udry provide a strong rationale for suspending the assump-tion of a unitary household, and evidence that it is possible to do so using the methodological apparatus of neoclassical economics.[11] For most femi-nists, however, the theoretical dismantling of the unitary household model is now superfluous outside rational choice theory and neoclassical micro-economics. By the 1980s, most social science literature accepted that domestic groups in Africa, as elsewhere, were complex and overlapping and constructed through contradictory relations of gender and seniority. The issue remains important for neoclassical economics because it must define a unit of maximizing decision making. For those who think that social processes

---

11. Although, as Hart (1995) has pointed out, this is not such a difficult step to take within a framework of methodological individualism.

Table 3. Sex Ratios: Men per 100 Women, Burkina Faso, 1992–3 and 1998–9 (by age group)

| | Male/Female Ratios by Age Group | | | | | | | | | | | | | |
	15–19	20–24	25–29	30–34	35–39	40–44	45–49	50–54	55–59	60–64	65–69	70–74	75–79	80 +
1992–3														
Urban	111	125	103	110	105	111	147	70	112	79	81	70	105	70
Rural	119	75	68	60	65	89	99	53	71	108	142	131	138	104
1998–9														
Urban	94	102	108	112	98	108	124	83	96	105	96	84	160	41
Rural	98	65	60	65	65	77	79	59	70	115	167	125	153	165

Source: Calculated from data for Demographic and Health Surveys (DHS) for Burkina Faso, 1992–3 and 1998–9 (Measure DHS, 2003).

live out relations of power, hierarchy and exploitation and are concerned with the elision between individual and collective agency, no such specification of an individual unit of choice is required or even advisable.

The current importance of the canned accounts of Jones's and Udry's work in the spinning of the myth does not stem, however, from their theoretical assault on unitary household models. What matters more is the link they provide between gender justice and poverty reduction in rural Africa. A close reading of these two studies produces little solid evidence for the proposition that reducing gender inequality in the distribution of productive resources in rural African households would lead to an overall increase in efficiency and thus to a reduction in poverty. They provide scant grounds for the myth's exact calculation of just how much production could be increased by transferring resources from men to women in a Cameroonian community and Burkinabe survey population in the 1980s, and even less for the ahistorical extension of their results to a mythically uniform terrain — all of sub-Saharan Africa.

In a number of respects, both studies are framed in ways that misrepresent the relation between gender and poverty in rural Africa, that is, they are vulnerable to mythical appropriation. Both Jones and Udry focused on agricultural production instead of looking at the gendered division of labour across the range of activities in which household members participate. These relations are often hierarchical and conflictful but also co-operative (Sen, 1990); some sharing may be better than none. In both areas studied, women have rights, though unequal rights, to the product of collective fields and the proceeds of men's non-farm labour. Jones and Udry treat the productive resources controlled by male household heads as men's individual property, abstracting from the ways in which their rights over collective property are constrained by convention and contestation. The feminist mandate is not trading oppression for isolation, providing women with resources so they can make it on their own, but redressing inequality within co-operative gender relations through reconstruction of the division of labour. This can only be a disruptive and broad political process that cuts across households and communities.

Both authors abstract from the ways that differences between households shape the options open to men and women within them, options that reflect differences in vulnerability to impoverishment. Jones classes widows, women with infirm husbands and senior wives in polygynous households together and finds that all put more labour into cash-crops than do other women. Yet their reasons for doing so are surely different, not simple reflections of what women do when they do not depend on men. Udry observes that yields achieved by different households vary more widely than yields within households, but does not explore how gendered patterns of migration and off-farm labour might lead to differences between households in agricultural practices and the distribution of productive resources.

Finally, neither author has anything to say about how gendered poverty relates to broad structural and contested processes of individualization and commodification of productive resources in rural Africa. The colonial forced labour systems in both Burkina Faso and northern Cameroon initiated processes of change in rural livelihoods that underlie gendered diversification today. Women's decisions about the organization of their labour have come to be shaped not only by relations with husbands, sons, in-laws, kin and friends but also by the terms of negotiation between migrants workers and employers or by the struggle over terms of labour and price between producers and management in the SEMRY scheme.

The ahistorical tone of the studies by Jones and Udry reflects their fluency in neoclassical economics, one of the aspects of their work that makes it particularly attractive to authoritative voices within the World Bank. All modernist emancipatory projects, including many strands of feminism, have envisioned a world in which social justice is linked to a better use of resources. They differ, however, in their understanding of how social justice should be achieved. The World Bank, despite its more explicit concern with inequality in the post-structural adjustment era, remains wedded to market utopianism. Prescriptive individualization and commodification of resources will allow people everywhere to compare and choose and thus use their resources most efficiently. Poverty in Africa arises from the limited scale and sway of the market. This vision depends on diverting one's eyes from the inequality inherent in the long-term processes of market development in rural Africa.

Neither Jones nor Udry venture the kind of simplistic policy options that tellers of the myth promote, but their accounts have provided the grounds for arguing that we can reduce poverty in rural Africa by adjusting the gender distribution of resources, within a process of continuing commodification. Demanding individual land titles for women means one thing when land is already individually owned and another when it is part of a programme of prescriptive individualization and commodification of all collectively held land.

Commodification has historically implied insecurity rather than security of tenure since the consolidation of holdings is linked to the sale or seizure of indebted land. As for micro-credit, it is in itself not an asset, for it is also micro-debt. Whether or not it becomes an asset for women depends on whether they have sufficient future production for consumption smoothing, or whether they have access to sufficient labour and markets to make a profitable investment in the famously risky world of micro-enterprises. These conditions may be met by women from more prosperous rural households (often those that have dependable off-farm sources of income), but are unrealistic for the very poor.

Poor households in rural Africa command very few productive resources indeed. To suggest that assuring poor women a larger piece of this very small pie will lead to a significant reduction in poverty, misrepresents the political processes needed to efface the gaps between rich and poor and to achieve gender justice. The improvident male farmer and the entrepreneurial woman on her own have become stock figures of mythical narratives — simple but dramatic stories, told in somewhat esoteric language, recited repeatedly by people with powerful voices — and deeply misleading. Words such as class, colonialism and imperialism have been edited out of these narratives, yet one cannot understand the relation between gender and poverty in rural Africa without them. Inequality is difficult to conceptualize within the neoclassical language of prescriptive commodification and individual choice.

REFERENCES

Agarwal, B. (1994) *A Field of One's Own: Gender and Land Rights in South Asia.* Cambridge: Cambridge University Press.
Amin, S. (1974) 'Modern Migrations in Western Africa', in S. Amin (ed.) *Modern Migrations in Western Africa*, pp. 65–124. London: Oxford University Press.
Arditi, C. (1985) 'Quelques Réflexions Socio-économiques sur la Riziculture Irriguée dans le Nord-Cameroun (SEMRY I et SEMRY II)', *Journal des Anthropologues* 20: 59–82.
Arditi, C. (1998) 'Pourquoi les Massa préfèrent-ils le sorgho? Heurs et malheurs de la riziculture irriguée au Nord Cameroun', *Journal des Anthropologues* 74: 117–31.
Blackden, C. M. and C. Bhanu (1999) 'Gender, Growth, and Poverty Reduction, Special Program of Assistance for Africa: 1998 Status Report on Poverty in Sub-Saharan Africa'. Washington, DC: The World Bank.
Cameroun Tribune (2001) 16 October. Available online: http://www.cameroon-tribune.cm (accessed 18 February 2003).
Claude, D. (1989) 'Production and Commercialisation of Rice in Cameroon: The Semry Project', in B. Campbell and J. Loxley (eds) *Structural Adjustment in Africa*, pp. 202–33. Basingstoke: Macmillan.
Deere, C. D. and M. Leon (2001) *Empowering Women: Land and Property Rights in Latin America.* Pittsburgh, PA: Pittsburgh University Press.
Deininger, K. (2003) *Land Policies for Growth and Development: A World Bank Policy Report.* Washington, DC: IBRD/The World Bank.
Doss, C. (1996) 'Intrahousehold Resource Allocation in an Uncertain Environment', *American Journal of Agricultural Economics* 78(5): 1335–9.
Eloundou-Enyegue, P. M. (1999) 'Fertility and Education: What Do We Now Know?', in C. Bledsoe, J. B. Casterline, J. Johnson-Kuhn and J. G. Haaga (eds) *Critical Perspectives on Schooling and Fertility in the Developing World*, pp. 287–305. Washington, DC: National Academy Press.
Fafchamps, M. (2001) 'Intrahousehold Access to Land and Source of Inefficiency: Theory and Concepts', in A. de Janvry, G. Gordillo, J.-P. Platteau and E. Sadoulet (eds) *Access to Land, Rural Poverty and Public Action*, pp. 68–96. Oxford: Oxford University Press.
de Garine, I. (1964) *Les Massa du Cameroun, Vie Économique et Sociale.* Paris: Presses Universitaires de France.
de Garine, I. (1978) 'Population, Production and Culture in the Plains Societies of Northern Cameroon and Chad: The Anthropologist in Development Projects', *Current Anthropology* 19(1): 42–57.
Hart, G. (1995) 'Gender and Household Dynamics: Recent Theories and their Implications', in M. G. Quiriba (ed.) *Critical Issues in Asian Development Theories Experiences and Policies*, pp. 39–74. Hong Kong: Oxford University Press for the Asian Development Bank:
IBRD/The World Bank (2001) *Engendering Development through Gender Equality in Rights, Resources and Voice.* Washington, DC: The World Bank; New York: Oxford University Press.
Jackson, C. (1996) 'Rescuing Gender from the Poverty Trap', *World Development* 24(3): 489–504.

Jones, C. W. (1983) 'The Mobilization of Women's Labor for Cash Crop Production: A Game Theoretic Approach', *American Journal of Agricultural Economics* 65(5): 1049–54.

Jones, C. W. (1986) 'Intra-household Bargaining in Response to the Introduction of New Crops: A Case Study from North Cameroon', in J. L. Moock (ed.) *Understanding Africa's Rural Households and Farming Systems*, pp. 105–23. Boulder, CO: Westview Press.

Kabutha, C. (1999) 'The Importance of Gender in Agricultural Policies, Resource Access and Human Nutrition'. Paper presented at the Seminar on Agricultural Policy, Resource Access and Nutritional Outcomes, Addis Ababa (3–5 November).

Kevane, M. and L. C. Gray (1999) 'A Woman's Field is Made at Night: Gendered Land Rights and Norms in Burkina Faso', *Feminist Economics* 5(3): 1–26.

Loth, P. (2004) *The Return of the Water: Restoring the Waza Logone Floodplain in Cameroon.* Gland, Switzerland and Cambridge, U.K., International Union for the Conservation of Nature and Natural Resources (IUCN).

McMillan, D. E. (1986) 'Distribution of Resources and Products in Mossi Households', in A. Hansen and D. E. McMillan (eds) *Food in Sub-Saharan Africa*, pp. 260–73. Boulder, CO: Lynne Rienner.

Measure DHS (2003) 'Statcompiler: DHS+ Surveys for Burkina Faso, 1992–3 and 1998–9'. Calverton, MD: Measure DHS. Available online: http://www.statcompiler.com (accessed 2 February 2003).

Mukhopadhyay, M. and C. Pieri (1999) 'Integration of Women in Sustainable Land and Crop Management in Sub-Saharan Africa, Vol 2003'. Collaborative effort between Gender in Rural Development (GENRD) team and Sustainable Land and Crop Management SLCM) Thematic Team. Available online: http://lnweb18.worldbank.org/ESSD/essdext.nsf/22DocByUnid/7F232B0EE14EF46A85256B880079D688/$FILE/IntegrationofWomeninSustainableLand&CropManagementinSSA.pdf (accessed 15 April 2003).

Njomaha C. (2000) 'Impact sanitaire et nutritionnel du barrage rizicole de Maga dans le Nord Cameroun', *Cahiers d'études et de recherches francophones / Agricultures* 9(5): 54.

Quisumbing, A. R. (ed.) (2003) *Household Decisions, Gender, and Development: A Synthesis of Recent Research.* Washington, DC: International Food Research Institute; Baltimore, MD: Johns Hopkins University Press.

Quisumbing, A. R. and B. McClafferty (2006) *Food Security in Practice: Using Gender Research in Development.* Washington, DC: International Food Research Institute.

Reardon, T., C. Delgado and P. Matlon (1992) 'Determinants and Effects of Income Diversification amongst Farm Households in Burkina Faso', *Journal of Development Studies* 28(1): 264–96.

Reardon, T., P. Matlon and C. Delgado (1988) 'Coping with Household-level Food Insecurity in Drought-Affected Areas of Burkina Faso', *World Development* 16(9): 1065–74.

Reardon, T. and J. E. Taylor (1996) 'Agroclimatic Shocks, Income Inequality, and Poverty: Evidence from Burkina Faso', *World Development* 24(4): 901–14.

Rey, P.-P. (1976) *Capitalisme négrier, la Marche des Paysans vers le Prolétariat.* Paris: Maspero.

Sautter, G. (1980) 'Migrations, Société et Développement en pays Mossi', *Cahiers d'études africaines* 20(79 Cahier 3): 215–53.

Sen, A. K. (1990) 'Gender and Cooperative Conflicts', in I. Tinker (ed.) *Persistent Inequalities: Women and World Development*, pp. 123–49. New York and Oxford: Oxford University Press.

Skinner, E. P. (1960) 'Labour Migration and its Relationship to Sociocultural Change in Mossi Society', *Africa* 30(4): 375–401.

Udry, C. (1996) 'Gender, Agricultural Production and the Theory of the Household', *Journal of Political Economy* 104(5): 1010–46.

Udry, C. and H. Alderman (1995) 'Gender Differentials in Farm Productivity: Implications for Household Efficiency and Agricultural Policy', *Food Policy* 20(2): 407–23.

van de Walle, N. (1989) 'Rice Politics in Cameroon: State Commitment, Capability, and Urban Bias', *Journal of Modern African Studies* 27(4): 579–99.

Vierich, H. (1986) 'Agricultural Production, Social Status and Intra-Compound Relationships',
    in J. L. Moock (ed.) *Understanding Africa's Rural Households and Farming Systems*,
    pp. 155–65. Boulder, CO: Westview Press.
Whitehead, A. and N. Kabeer (2001) 'Living with Uncertainty: Gender, Livelihoods and Pro-
    poor Growth in Rural Sub-Saharan Africa'. IDS Working Paper 134. Brighton: University of
    Sussex, Institute of Development Studies.

3

The Construction of the Myth of Survival

Mercedes González de la Rocha

INTRODUCTION

Household-focused research has made crucial contributions to the ways in which scholars understand the survival and reproduction of the urban poor. However, ideas coming from research on the social and economic bases of survival have been mythologized and have become development orthodoxy. This chapter discusses the main elements of a powerful myth that has spread throughout international development agencies: that poor households are able to survive in spite of macroeconomic policies that foster unemployment, increase poverty and decrease the amount of resources in the hands of the poor.

A crucial function of myths is to provide justifications or to legitimize social oppositions and tensions. The main actor in the construction of the myth of survival is the World Bank, a global institution that has nurtured itself with scholarly ideas which have been taken out of their contexts, making them its own. Its views of survival under poverty conditions and of social capital overemphasize the resourcefulness of the poor, while it promotes economic policies that deeply — and negatively — affect the access of the poor to resources: 'The poor almost never talk about income, but they do frequently refer to assets they consider important. The set of assets they handle is diverse: physical, human, social, and ecological. These assets comprise a wide range of tangible and intangible resources, both material and social, that individuals, households, and communities use during moments of crisis' (Narayan et al., 2000: 49). And again: 'The data provide grounded demonstration that monetary incomes are, for many of the world's poor, only a parcel of a much wider set of possible assets' (ibid.: 65).[1]

The World Bank, together with other development agencies and scholars who study poverty in different regions, form an eclectic and heterogeneous, but solid, international constellation of powerful institutions and groups that support the concept of the resourcefulness of poor populations. As we know, myths are acted out and reproduced in rituals. In this case, fora where members of academic institutions, governments and international agencies meet to discuss social policy and poverty issues have become spaces in which the myth of the availability of resources for the poor household is repeatedly aired, to mitigate or redeem guilt. It becomes a useful thing to say. But the

---

1. Translated from Spanish by the author of this chapter.

question arises: if the poor have so many types of assets and resources, why do we bother making money and jobs available to them?

In this contribution, I draw on my own long-term research on shifting dynamics of household organization to re-examine the fable of the good survivor and to question the myth of survival. Mexican and cross-country evidence shows the need to debunk this myth if we want to understand the way in which the lives of women and men have been remodelled by economic and social change.

THE MYTH OF SURVIVAL

The myth of survival has been constructed together with a fable (or a fairy-tale?), which emphasizes adaptation, solidarity and reciprocity as the major tools for surviving in conditions of poverty. It has two main ingredients. The first is the resourcefulness of the poor — that the poor manage to implement survival strategies that are based on their endless capacity to work, to consume less and to be part of mutual help networks. The second is that resources in the hands of the poor are plentiful: they are both tangible and intangible and comprise a wide range of types, including material, human and social resources. Mutual help and support systems are inherent elements of society and, therefore, they can be considered natural components of safety nets to overcome poverty or, at least, to achieve survival. It does not matter how aggressive and violent economic shocks are: the poor will keep on working, reciprocating and relying on their own safety nets (Chiarello, 1994; Durston, 2003; Gershuny, 1994; Narayan et al., 2000).

Before they were converted into a sacred narrative, the principal elements of the myth of survival were crafted by social science researchers in Latin America and other parts of the world, and they have gained considerable general support. Research conducted by anthropologists and sociologists in the past devoted a great deal of attention to networks and support systems (González de la Rocha, 1984, 1986; Lomnitz, 1977; Stack, 1974). Women's work — both remunerated and in the production of goods and services for family consumption — was seen as an integral part of survival strategies, as were reciprocal relationships based on trust and social exchange.

As these findings were repeated again and again, without being confronted with new or different realities, observations about social networks and social exchange were converted into the solution to the problem of scarcity (Durston, 2003), a cushion against the impact of economic change, and an asset that the poor can always turn to in case of need (a core ingredient of a 'survival kit'). But the increasing pressure and reliance on kinship ties and neighbour support in social and economic contexts characterized by increasing poverty and lack of employment is leading — in Mexico and Argentina, in Latvia, Bulgaria, Angola and many other countries — to the erosion of relationships of mutual help, solidarity and social exchange (Amado, 1994;

Auyero, 2000; Bazán, 1998, 1999; Estrada, 1999; González de la Rocha, 1999, 2000; Trapenciere et al., 2000). Increasing economic and social pressures on households are leading to premature separation of their members, decreasing solidarity and co-operation within the family, increasing gender conflicts and domestic violence (often over scarce resources), higher incidence of suicide among men, and social isolation.

The myth of survival became a useful tool for policy makers in their design of more aggressive economic policies. Many scholars seemed to be comfortable with the dissemination of the idea that, when a new economic crisis hits, the poor work harder, help each other, and eat less in order to make ends meet. In my view, reproducing the idea that the poor manage to have access to a diverse pool of resources, while monetary incomes are only a morsel within such a broad pool, hides the very real problem of survival which poor people experience nowadays. The myth of survival diverts our attention from the real nature of survival and its mounting constraints. By overemphasizing the existence of resources in the hands of the poor, the myth ignores the process of cumulative disadvantages that the lack of work (from employment and even self-employment) is producing in other dimensions of people's lives. In fact, social support systems can break down and self-provisioning activities are clearly finite in situations where labour cannot be mobilized and regular wages stop flowing.

Survival notions became a dogma within development orthodoxy as a result of uncritical and naive repetitions of fashionable and suggestive ideas, without paying attention to contextual economic and social changes and to new constraints to survival and reproduction of the poor household. Contradicting these ideas, or revising them in a critical way, was virtually unthinkable. My exposition on the erosion of the survival model in the late 1990s received a hostile response from scholars, activists and professionals working in development agencies. How dare I argue that reciprocity, solidarity among the poor, and mutual help could reach limits? My critics made me feel not just that I was wrong, but that I was being almost blasphemous. The paper in which I developed the shift from the 'resources of poverty' to the 'poverty of resources' was rejected by different periodicals, in spite of various positive, independent reviews.[2] However, the myth of survival is not only untrue, but also perilous.

The Scholarly Origins of the Myth: The Survival Strategy Approach

The survival strategy approach predates crisis-focused empirical research. The concept of family or household strategies was adopted as a way to move beyond orthodox structural views that denied agency to individuals,

---

2. It was finally published in 2001 by *Latin American Perspectives* (González de la Rocha, 2001).

households and communities (Anderson, 1980; Roberts, 1995; Schmink, 1984; Tilly, 1987). Empirical analyses of the survival strategies of Latin America's urban poor flourished during the 1980s; my own longitudinal research shows some of the main elements that were present in our research agendas and fed into development orthodoxy. It also shows that the current situation can no longer be explained by popular dogmas.

Researching how the urban poor cope with poverty and economic crises led me to recognize their agency without ignoring intra-household conflict, unequal relations, and gender/generation differences within households (González de la Rocha, 1994). The following discussion outlines the main components of the analytical model that I constructed in the past — in the light of the survival strategy approach — in order to understand survival and reproduction of poor urban households in Guadalajara, Mexico, during the 1980s. My aim is to describe the structural conditions that are necessary for this survival model to work and the main changes experienced over the last decade. The 'resources of poverty' model of survival has been eroded, and the lives of the poor are better described today by the reverse formulation: the poverty of resources.

The Resources of Poverty

The resources of poverty model alludes both to the diversity of income sources and to the social organization of households or the social base that makes survival possible. It was developed on the basis of research carried out in Guadalajara during 1981 and 1982, immediately before the economic crisis (González de la Rocha, 1986, 1994). Although it was meant to describe and to explain the survival of the urban poor in a particular Mexican city, research conducted by scholars in other Mexican cities and in other urban Latin American contexts revealed many similarities (see, for example, Barrig, 1993; Chant, 1991; Feijoó, 1991; Pastore et al., 1983). This research describes how the household acted as the social unit in charge of the reproduction of the labour force and of the survival of its members in spite of low wages. It showed how household members managed to cope with scarcity through social mechanisms that included the participation of more than one household member and the combination of diverse income sources and remunerated occupations.[3]

---

3. My 1981–82 research was carried out in Guadalajara, Mexico, and comprised 100 in-depth case studies of households whose members were participating in different types of occupations, both in the formal and in the informal sector. The selection of the cases was guided by an analytical sample, constructed in order to include a wide variety of household types (in terms of household structure, stage of the domestic cycle, and types of occupations). Research outcomes from studies carried out by other scholars around the same period in other Mexican cities were similar to those of my study (Benería and Roldán, 1987; Chant, 1991; García et al., 1982; Selby et al., 1990).

Thus, what emerged from this body of work were survival strategies of urban poor households, characterized by diverse income sources and multiple income earners, and based on the following four structural conditions for household capability:[4] the possibility to earn wages; labour invested in petty commodity production and petty trade; labour invested in the production of goods and services for consumption; and income from social exchange (or the cost of social isolation). We will examine each of these in turn.

■ *The possibility of earning wages*: low wages have always been a great obstacle for survival, especially of households with only one worker. My research on poor urban households found that whilst men were usually the main wage earners, women also often acted as important generators of incomes, both coming from wage-earning and non-remunerated occupations. Women's participation in the labour market depended on the social and household structure and the stage of the domestic cycle. Extended households with several adult women were more conducive to female participation in the labour market than nuclear households (see also Chant, 1991). The traditional division of labour (wage-earning men, and women devoted to the reproduction role) was common, particularly among young households, but women became engaged in wage activities when the household economy demanded more incomes (in order to cope with extra expenses), and/or when the main provider failed to act as such, due to sickness or other causes.

Most households in later stages of the domestic cycle (when children had grown up) had at least two members fully participating in the labour market. While it was not uncommon to find young housewives working for a wage during emergencies (which are frequent and sometimes lengthy), other women — often in extended and/or older households — worked on a more regular basis. Wages coming from the labour market and employment opportunities for household members were thus a crucial element in household survival, but they were not the sole element. The main basis for household support remained a multiplicity of income sources, where employment (wages) co-existed with other activities and incomes.

■ *Labour invested in petty commodity production and petty trade*: apart from wages, the urban household economies of my study relied heavily on other income sources such as the product of petty commodity production and petty trade (González de la Rocha, 1984). The role of

---

4. Sen's concept of capabilities (Sen, 1993) is appropriate for alluding to alternative combinations of characters and functions that households may have at different points of time or under different social situations. This concept allows one to analyse wider or narrower alternative combinations and, therefore, more or less opportunities to act and perform certain functions.

women was especially important in this type of income source. Women who would bake, cook or sew in order to sell the product of their labours were found in almost all households. Men also participated in petty production, in such areas as carpentry, bricklaying and plumbing. Children often helped their mothers in the process of assisting their families to produce extra incomes by, for example, offering homemade products for sale along the streets.

■ *Labour invested in the production of goods and services for consumption*: household production of goods and services for household consumption was an almost invisible but nonetheless important component, as documented by different studies conducted during the early 1980s (Benería and Roldán, 1987; Chant, 1991; González de la Rocha, 1984). This work was, and continues to be, mainly performed by women. It included daily activities such as cooking, laundry and ironing, house cleaning, as well as sewing, child care, and participating in housing construction. Women's working days were long, especially when working for a wage, since that did not free them from domestic chores. Daughters, but also sons, frequently helped in these tasks, particularly when adult women were also engaged in waged work.

■ *Income from social exchange, or the cost of social isolation*: income coming from social exchange, through networks and support systems, proved to be a crucial asset for urban working poor households. Networking includes both men and women, but 'social territories' could be traced as following men's and women's networks, according to their main activities and the social arenas in which they spent their working and social time. Social exchange, or the flow of goods and services within networks of friends, neighbours, workmates and relatives, was highly relevant for low-income households (Lomnitz, 1977). The importance of networks could be observed not only when social exchange and its benefits were present, but also when they were not, in which cases a poorer condition was evident. The poorest of the poor were socially isolated, but they were seen as 'deviant cases' (González de la Rocha, 1984), while the majority of households enhanced their economic base through the benefits of social exchange.

The possible combinations of these four structural conditions for survival strategies meant that households were not homogeneous in occupational terms. It was common to find different types of workers within particular households. A single worker might participate in different occupational niches of the labour market, not just over the course of a lifetime, but even during a workday. Occupational heterogeneity — household members being engaged in diverse types of occupations — was conceived as a coping mechanism against temporary unemployment of some members.[5] Formal workers co-existed with street vendors, informal labourers, artisans, domestic employees and the self-employed. Households acted as melting pots, where labour market segmentation vanished without producing social differences within the working class.

The participation in survival strategies of household members who were not considered the primary bread-winners, such as women, youth and older people, was a crucial element for the success of the strategy. It is important to stress that women's participation in income-generating household strategies paralleled men's, and there was no reason to think about a 'feminization' of household economies.[6] It could be argued that the combination of income sources and the co-existence of different types of workers within households was the forced product of low wages and the outcome of the need to include several (and different) incomes to accomplish survival — a forced by-product of poverty. Before and even during the economic crisis of the 1980s, job availability and alternative opportunities for work (although poorly remunerated) existed. The model of survival which I called 'the resources of poverty' depended on the availability of jobs and was the outcome of the relationship between the labour market (with more or less open opportunities) and the workings of the household.

THE TRANSITION: RESTRUCTURING THE HOUSEHOLD

The 1980s were difficult years for the Mexican economy and society. While real wages experienced a dramatic drop, currency devaluation, capital flight and fiscal austerity conspired to create a very insecure and fragile panorama. The crisis triggered a series of changes in the structure and organization of households. Research carried out during the 1980s and early 1990s showed the way households were experimenting with what was called a 'privatization of the crisis' (Benería, 1992; González de la Rocha, 1988, 1991). One of the most interesting developments in the field of household research has been the study of household transformations in the context of economic change. Structural adjustment has produced deep social restructuring at various levels of society and certainly at the household level. Indeed, the linkages between change at the macro level of national economic policy and changes at the

---

5. Occupational heterogeneity and the high rates of labour mobility led us to argue that the urban working class in Guadalajara was not socially differentiated in spite of the strong segmentation of the labour market (Escobar, 1986; González de la Rocha, 1986). Households encompassed a wide variety of job types and workers, and social differentiation vanished at the household level since the household 'melted' the differences found in the labour market.
6. Except in the case of some female-headed households.

micro level of household organization highlight the usefulness of a political economic approach.[7]

Empirical analyses of the survival strategies of Latin America's urban poor conducted during the 1980s provided a critical reaction to prevailing theories concerning the poor, and a means to assess the way ordinary people lived with the great economic adversity of those years. Research showed that urban households in Mexico, as in many other Latin American countries, went through a process of restructuring and adjustment as the larger economy experienced structural changes (Benería, 1992; Cravey, 1997; Chant, 1991, 1996; Escobar and González de la Rocha, 1995; González de la Rocha, 1994; García and Oliveira, 1994). It was apparent from these studies that the survival and reproduction of the working poor could not be guaranteed on an individual basis either before or during the economic crisis, because of low wages and a dramatic fall in real wages between 1982 and 1986. It became evident that household organization and restructuring was a key element for survival (González de la Rocha, 1994; Roberts, 1995). This included the increased participation of household members in the labour market, especially adult women who worked mainly in precarious activities in the informal sector. It also included increasing domestic work, as households became extended and crowded, as well as restrictive consumption practices (see González de la Rocha, 1988, 1991).

Household responses to the crisis of the 1980s meant the intensification of the elements that made up the resources of poverty model, particularly the use of labour and help from equals. Households' flexibility and capacity to adapt to the new economic conditions kept household income from falling as rapidly as individual wages. Household total income in Guadalajara fell only 11 per cent from 1982 to 1985, while individual wages fell 35 per cent.[8] The notion of the resourcefulness of the poor was indeed useful to understand the private responses to the crisis in Mexico and other Latin American countries (Barrig, 1993; Cravey, 1997).

The four structural conditions for the success of the survival model were still present, but there were many more problems. My own longitudinal research conducted in the early and mid 1980s[9] shows how the crisis of that decade affected the four conditions. Regarding wages and the

---

7. There is a considerable literature on this. See, for example, Barrig (1993); Benería and Feldman (1992); Escobar Latapí and González de la Rocha (1995); Feijoó (1991); González de la Rocha (1994); González de la Rocha and Escobar Latapí (1991); Moser (1989, 1996); Selby et al. (1990).

8. Data from other countries show the same trend: household income in Venezuela fell 22 per cent, while individual incomes fell 34 per cent. The figures for Costa Rica were 14 per cent and 22 per cent respectively (CEPAL, 1991: 23).

9. A follow-up of the same households studied in 1981–82 was conducted in 1985–86, within the framework of a different research project, in order to find out the impact of the economic crisis on the social organization (division of labour, distribution of resources, etc.) and the livelihoods of the previously studied households.

possibilities to obtain them, research conducted in Mexico showed a rising number of women in the labour market as a result of increased household needs. The importance of women as income producers rose in a context of falling contributions from male heads to the household economy.[10] Apart from adult women, young males also increased their participation in the labour market. The intensification strategy implied the increasing and more permanent participation of women, and the earlier entrance of male sons, in the labour market. As formal employment was losing ground, many workers went into informal occupations.[11] In contrast to the previous situation, where informal employment co-existed with formal jobs, now informality proliferated while formal employment fell: increasing the number of income generators was mainly achieved through informal activities and self-employment, as formal employment decreased significantly. A process of intensification in the use of available labour was clearly among the main assets in coping with the crisis (González de la Rocha, 1988, 1991).

Urban households, apart from increasing the number of wage-earners, widened their income sources in order to counterbalance the 'fragile' wage source. Household income structure changed in such a way that the wages proportion of household total incomes diminished, while the share of income from independent work (mainly self-employment and self-provisioning) grew (CEPAL, 1991). Self-employment increased as the relative attraction of independent work grew with the decline in formal wages. The number of women working in family businesses without a wage is difficult to measure, but some calculations suggest that among Guadalajara employed women, unpaid family workers comprised only 2.7 per cent in 1978, in comparison to 8 per cent in 1987 (Escobar, 1996). Data from case studies in Guadalajara showed that households increased the use of labour devoted to independent work (González de la Rocha, 1991).

Domestic chores also increased as the size of households grew to include more members and as many households stopped buying goods and services which could be substituted by 'home-made' equivalents — recycling objects, repairing domestic appliances, sewing clothes, eating homemade meals instead of restaurant food, and so on (González de la Rocha, 1988, 1991; Selby et al., 1990). This translated into an increased burden on women, since the overall household transformation did not include a redistribution of tasks within the household.

---

10. García and Oliveira (1994) demonstrate how the factors that shape and determine women's work changed during this process. Instead of single, young and relatively educated women, the Mexican labour market absorbed massive amounts of married, non-educated women with child-bearing responsibilities. According to CEPAL (1991), the contribution of male heads of households dropped to represent no more than 60 per cent of households' incomes in most Latin American countries.

11. Between 1980 and 1987, informal employment grew by 80 per cent in absolute terms (CEPAL, 1992a) and rose from 24 per cent to 33 per cent as a proportion of the economically active population (Escobar, 1996; Roberts, 1995).

The importance of being part of social exchange networks increased. Collaboration, mutual help, exchange of favours and daily flow of goods and services among relatives, neighbours and friends became fundamental ingredients for the protection of well-being. Women's networks became a crucial factor in daily life during the difficult years of the 1980s. The exchange of favours and help on a daily basis were of great relevance for these women who needed support for child care and household chores, and crucial information about sources of income (Gershuny, 1994; González de la Rocha, 1994; González de la Rocha et al., 1990; Selby et al., 1990).

Implications for the Model

Household survival and reproduction were achieved in this context through a combination of elements of which the collaboration of the collective unit was an important ingredient, with significant and sometimes crucial participation by members other than primary breadwinners. Important as it was, women's participation in income-generating activities was at best equal to men's, and except in the case of some female-headed households there was no concept of the feminization of household economies.

Recognizing the importance of collective collaboration does not, however, mean overlooking inequality and skewed relationships, uneven distribution of resources, and conflict between individual interests and collective ones. As I have argued elsewhere (González de la Rocha, 1994; González de la Rocha et al., 1990), the household is a highly contradictory social unit characterized by the co-existence of solidarity and conflicts (between individual and collective interests, differing gender and age interests), and violence. Households are social settings in which daily confrontations and negotiations are developed in a context of internal inequality and differential distribution of burdens and rewards. In this way, poverty affects women, men, children and adults in different ways.

Observing households' internal differences and dynamics was necessary for detecting the poorest of the poor within households. Similarly, household restructuring did not weigh equally upon all household members. The accumulated evidence suggests that women endured a heavy share of the social cost of restructuring and change (cf. Benería, 1992). Women had to work harder both as waged workers in the labour market and as producers of goods and services within the household. The case of female-headed households is particularly interesting. Contrary to the common notion that these households are characterized by greater poverty and vulnerability, studies conducted in Mexico and elsewhere showed that female-headed households are spread over all income strata and are in fact relatively more frequent among the non-poor (González de la Rocha, 1999; see also CEPAL, 1997, for Latin America as a whole). My findings showed that female-headed households were better equipped to protect their patterns of consumption than male-headed households. They demonstrated less dramatic changes in their diets, less violence and a more equal distribution of responsibilities during the crisis years (González de la Rocha, 1991, 1999; see also Chant, 1997, 1999, 2004). The fact that women had greater control over household income seemed to be an important tool for protecting priority consumption areas (food and health).

The impact of the crisis was differential: different household structures and stages of the domestic cycle were more vulnerable to poverty than others. The better-off among the working-class households were usually larger and more extended, and in the 'mature' (consolidation or equilibrium) stage of the domestic cycle. In contrast, the worse-off households were frequently nuclear, smaller and either younger (in the expansion stage), or composed mostly of elderly people, with limited capacity to defend their incomes (by intensifying work) and consumption patterns. The role of providers changed with each stage, as did the nature of the household economy. The more comfortable situation enjoyed by households in the consolidation or equilibrium stage was achieved mainly through the contributions of grown-up children.

Although nuclear households continued to comprise the majority of all households, the proportion of extended households increased. The extension of households was achieved mainly through the incorporation of additional adult members. This was interpreted both as a savings mechanism (shared housing costs) and as a way to increase the number of available members for income-generating activities. Extended households, although less numerous than nuclear households, gave shelter to a greater number of people during those years (CEPAL, 1992a). Staying in the household of origin after marriage became a more common practice (González de la Rocha, 1988, 1991, 1995). The extended household appeared to be an efficient structure for protecting members from falling real wages and increasing insecurity.

Life was not easy, particularly for women and young children, in this period. Women bore a heavy burden when the household lacked sufficient members for income-generating activities, or when the main provider(s) failed to act as such. In the context of poor or non-existent water, sewage and other services, domestic chores were time- and energy-consuming. The important distinction with the later period, however, was the availability of jobs. Men and women could — albeit with varying degrees of difficulty — find jobs. Grown-up children (from around fifteen years old) were also expected to start working, and although their early entrance into the labour market meant an end to their education, their contributions to the household economies were highly valued by their parents and siblings. Unemployment was very low: in my research I did not hear anyone saying, as people commonly do nowadays, that there were no jobs. Individuals could opt for informal and formal employment. Labour market specialists argued that informal activities were an attractive option, and wages coming from this sector were not necessarily lower than those obtained in formal occupations (see, for example, Escobar 1986).

It was evident that economic change in Mexico produced a rapid deterioration of living conditions for the majority of urban households, and household members paid a high price for the protection of their household income.[12] Nevertheless, my research emphasized the relative success of household responses to the crisis, their adaptability, flexibility and capacity to rely on social exchange.

THE POVERTY OF RESOURCES: RETHINKING THE MYTH OF SURVIVAL

According to Escobar (1996), the 1994 financial crisis signalled a watershed for Mexican labour markets because, for the first time since 1982, the population did not respond with a general intensification of work and informal employment. Instead, unemployment soared. While women's participation rates continued to rise, the rates for men fell for the first time since the 1982 crisis.[13] Unemployment among male youth reached unprecedented levels in 1995, touching almost 30 per cent in the main metropolitan areas during that year. Escobar suggests that the abatement of these levels after 1995 may have been due to withdrawal from the job search rather than successfully finding work, since male employment continued to fall.

Escobar and González de la Rocha (1995) argue that informal employment and informal incomes were stagnating at the end of the Salinas period (the early 1990s). This stagnation resulted from the saturation and economic marginalization of the sector, since Mexican labour-intensive industries (which relied most heavily on subcontracting and informal work) were drastically affected by the opening of external trade and the influx of low-priced Asian products. The opening of doors to both imports and exports had a dramatic impact on Mexican firms, especially small and medium-sized manufacturing enterprises, which found the competition with commodities produced abroad was a challenge too difficult to sustain (ibid.).

The implications of current economic conditions for the social organization and economies of urban poor households are to be found in the impact of labour exclusion and precarious employment. These conditions are not conducive to strengthening the social organization of the urban poor households that has served as the social base of survival. On the contrary, they reduce the capacity of poor households to respond in a traditional (resources of poverty) way by gathering and creating resources and intensifying the use of their labour to achieve survival and reproduction. As economic

---

12. They had to work more for lower wages under worse conditions. Households depended more on informal activities as formal ones became scarce and even exceptional. Households' occupational heterogeneity diminished and was replaced by more homogeneously informal and precarious work arrangements. And people had to eat less, and spend less on education and health care, and entertainment/leisure activities.
13. Escobar (1996) shows that 700,000 women entered the labour force between 1993 and 1995, compared to only 300,000 men.

restructuring and a neoliberal ethos make extreme hardship a defining condition of the poor's existence, the resources of poverty model is no longer empirically or theoretically viable. Rather, it is 'poverty of resources' that characterizes the stage we are in today. This poverty of resources is the outcome of labour exclusion and poverty intensification, and it signals the erosion of the social and economic conditions for survival. It is worth looking again at the four structural conditions for survival strategies in the context of this new trend of labour exclusion.

- *The possibility of earning wages*: if we maintain that labour is the most important resource for the urban poor (González de la Rocha, 1994; Moser, 1996), then labour market trends towards exclusion will have inevitable implications for the survival and reproduction of the poor. Male unemployment is a feature of many households today. Case studies carried out in Guadalajara show the problems faced by households during long periods of unemployment of their members. More women working for less income seems to be the predominant situation for many households in Guadalajara today. Unemployment means, first and foremost, the loss of a regular wage; but it also means losing a whole series of experiences and social links which are crucial for the individual's well-being and social identity — physical activity, social contact, collective purpose, time structure, and social status (Jahoda, quoted by Gershuny and Miles, 1985).

  The ongoing difficulty of finding a job primarily affects young males. This is having a major impact on the household's capacity to supplement the income of male and female heads through the participation of young members in the labour market. As noted above, young people are important income-generators during the stage of the domestic cycle when the heads face declining incomes. The 'consolidation' stage of the domestic cycle, when children are able to fully participate in the world of work, is the time when households experience higher incomes. Historically, this has been the time when the youngest members could take advantage of their siblings' contribution to the household economy to continue their education to levels impossible to achieve in other circumstances.

  One of the newest responses to the lack of employment observed at individual and household levels is the increasing emigration of young urban men and women to the USA (see Safa, 1995, for a similar finding in Dominican Republic). The difficulties of finding a job and remaining employed in the Mexican cities, together with the low pay which most jobs offer to young workers, are behind the decisions to emigrate and to become part of transnational communities of labourers. While international migration used to be a phenomenon of poor rural areas of Mexico, it now increasingly affects the urban population. Young males are the main actors of this exodus. Illegal activities, such as petty theft and drug exchange, are among the alternatives for young urban poor men who stay behind.

- *Labour invested in petty commodity production and petty trade*: lack of employment has also eroded other income sources such as petty commodity production and petty trade, activities that need money to be 'invested' in materials, transportation and other tasks that are part of the production and trade process. It is important to clarify that precarious employment was present in the previous situation, but it co-existed with formal employment and 'autonomous' income sources. The current situation combines unemployment and precarious employment for the majority of workers; permanent employment has become rare and only available for a reduced number of workers. A new type of segregation seems to be emerging, not along the 'formal' and 'informal' lines, but between a very privileged group of workers who are permanently employed, and the vast majority who struggle to survive with very scarce resources amidst precarious employment and unemployment. Lacking regular incomes from at least one household member makes it even more difficult to start or to continue autonomous activities.

- *Labour invested in the production of goods and services for consumption*: labour exclusion diminishes the capacity of individuals to participate in household petty production and in self-provisioning. My research in the late 1990s in Guadalajara (González de la Rocha, 2001) shows that people without regular incomes (obtained in the labour market) face enormous difficulties: there is simply no money to invest in self-provisioning activities which require at least a minimum quantity of cash to pay for materials and transportation. This questions the 'autonomous' nature of self-provisioning, and leads us to formulate a different hypothesis: self-provisioning activities and household production of goods and services for household consumption are dependent on regular wages coming from the labour market. In contexts where there is at least one regular wage, individuals within households have a wider margin to devote time and other resources (including some money) to self-provisioning and household production. Where wages are sporadic, casual or non-existent, individuals have very little margin or real possibilities for self-provisioning. Labour exclusion thus leads to other types of exclusion, in a shrinking of options process, or what I call cumulative disadvantages.

- *Income coming from social exchange, or the cost of social isolation*: households need regular wages in order to obtain survival resources from other income sources. Even income from social exchange networks depends, to a certain extent, on regular wages coming into the household. Networks are the outcome of the actors' participation in

establishing those links and keeping them active: they are social constructions which require, as in the case of self-provisioning activities,
some resources to be invested. To participate in a specific network has
'costs'; reciprocity demands a flow of goods and services. Many women
and men interviewed talk about social isolation related to their increased
poverty condition. What were formerly seen as 'deviant cases' are more
frequent.

Cumulative Disadvantages and the Erosion of Survival

Although with great difficulty, the resources of poverty model operated as
long as there were opportunities to work, either in waged activities, formal
and informal, or in self-employed occupations. Work was associated with
low wages, but households still had the option of sending their members
to the labour market. A good deal of household income had sources other
than wages (such as social exchange, domestic production of goods and
services), but households depended primarily on the availability of jobs for
the necessary monetary income. Furthermore, they depended on wages from
relatively stable work to allow them to pursue other sources of income, such
as petty commodity production, petty trade and social exchange.

Urban poor households face significantly different conditions today. The
current situation, characterized by new forms of exclusion and increasing
precariousness, is unfavourable to the operation of traditional household
mechanisms of work intensification. This erosion of social systems of support
and self-help is due not to any inherent incapacity of the poor to survive or
to escape from poverty but to the increasing deterioration of labour markets.
Moser (1996) argues persuasively that persistent economic crises (having to
'adapt' to a new crisis after the previous one) have undermined the urban
poor's strategies and resourcefulness to the point where they are insufficient
to offset the erosion of their asset base. Additionally, I would argue that it
is not only the social capital assets of the poor that are being eroded but
their capacity to participate in alternative occupations and self-provisioning
activities in what amounts to a process of cumulative disadvantage.

The general lack of employment has had a profound impact on household
economies and forms of organization. Low, irregular wages and lack of work
opportunities also threaten urban poor households' internal resources for
survival: the capacity of adult men to act as providers has been undermined;
the role that sons used to play within the household organization has been
disrupted through emigration or unemployment. Female labour is one of the
very few resources that is available for many households' survival. As the
role of men as breadwinners continues to decline, women work for wages
which have become crucial for daily household maintenance (Safa, 1995).
Rather than generating 'additional' incomes, women — young and adult,
married and single, with or without formal education — are today among

the main providers in many urban poor households, although their wages remain very low or have even decreased. Labour exclusion also diminishes the capacity of individuals to participate in self-provisioning, self-employment, and household petty production. The idea that people would increasingly turn to these types of activities in the spare time made available by unemployment is flawed, as people without regular incomes face enormous difficulties in self-provisioning. Therefore, unemployment and, more generally, labour exclusion implies lack of access to a whole range of other income-generating options.

More generally, we could argue that households need regular wages in order to obtain survival resources from other income sources. Even social exchange networks depend to a certain extent on regular wages: individuals with the resources to be part of a relationship of reciprocity will be in a position to maintain that link, while those who lack resources to exchange will not. The relevance of wages (in urban settings and increasingly also in rural contexts) for subsistence and reproduction cannot be ignored. Sources of household income other than wages seem to depend on the capacity of the household to generate monetary income and, in this sense, wages play a crucial role in their capacity to produce other resources. The better-off households used to be those which maintained multiple strategies to generate incomes from diverse sources, with grown-up sons and daughters playing an important role. As emigration or unemployment increase, these roles are disappearing, and the comparative advantages enjoyed by those households are vanishing.

The poor do not have endless resources. Sources of income other than wages can complement but cannot substitute for wages in urban capitalist societies. Household flexibility and the capacity to adapt to new economic changes by juggling their scarce resources do not represent infinite possibilities. On the contrary, there are signs that the capacity to adapt to ever-harder economic conditions has being eroded as household resources have been depleted. The emphasis on the 'multiplicity' of income sources which formed part of the resources of poverty argument, as evidenced by households' responses to the crises of the 1980s, helped to build the idea that the poor survive even when employment options are lacking. I believe that this view is wrong. Our past analyses did not put sufficient emphasis on the importance of wages coming from the market as the trigger for other activities and, therefore, as the motor of reproduction, and thus it could not predict the erosion of other sources of income when wages are absent from the scene.

Households are dynamic and diverse social units which evolve and change both as a response to external forces and according to their internal dynamics. There is evidence of this process of change and some indicators of the crisis of the nuclear family model. Some types of households have been better suited to cope with external social and economic changes, such as extended households and those in the consolidation stage of the cycle, since they have a larger pool of labour to draw from. However, current economic conditions are erasing the comparative advantages of consolidated households who face many difficulties in putting their labour to work.

Occupational heterogeneity, inherent to the resources of poverty model, led us to argue that the Mexican working class was a socially homogeneous group, and that households acted as melting pots, mixing the segmentation trends of the labour market. It was hard to classify a household as belonging to a particular occupational category, since each household combined many different workers, with those different types of workers sharing the household setting, arrangements and organization. Working class homogeneity was the outcome of the relationship between a productive structure and a labour market which offered different options, and a household organization which was based on the multiple insertion of its members in such a structure. The second half of the 1990s, however, marked by scarcity of job options for the majority, has seen a process of real deterioration of income and survival sources. A huge gap is opening up between the very privileged, who can access permanent employment, and the excluded. New forms of segmentation are emerging and this time households seem to be less able to counterbalance them. The 'melting pot' does not have as many ingredients for the soup.

Asserting that poor individuals, households and communities have responded to economic change with innovative strategies and resourcefulness is an accurate portrayal. The survival of the poor has been mostly supported by 'private' initiatives. However, it is crucial to acknowledge that households are very sensitive to economic and social change. Households' social organization is intimately affected by trends in the labour market, and economic policies that bear upon the dynamics of the wage labour market are thus a major determinant of household well-being. The decline of wage employment and growing difficulties for poor households to mobilize labour as an asset have major implications for the economy and social organization of these households, affecting their patterns of division of labour and their income-generating strategies. Traditional household responses to economic misfortune have included strategies of work intensification; household members worked longer hours and harder, often in precarious and low-paid jobs; women, children, the elderly and the youth were incorporated into the workforce as well as engaging in a range of cash and subsistence activities. As a result, the relative weight of informal work in the household economy rose, and so did the share of goods produced and consumed at home. Nevertheless, unemployment, the 'saturation' of informal labour markets, and the depletion of people's capacity to engage in self-employment and self-provisioning activities impose severe limitations on these traditional responses. When mobilizing additional household labour fails to protect family well-being or forestall vulnerability, shifting consumption and reducing total household expenditures take place. Shifting and cutting consumption are a clear sign of vulnerability since reducing food is a last-resort measure when no other options are available.

CONCLUSION

This chapter has sought to show that the notion of the resourcefulness of the poor is increasingly problematic in the context of diminishing labour options and choices for poor individuals and households. The continued use of such a notion has led to the construction of a myth that is not only false but also hazardous. It can be used to legitimize economic policies that further damage the living conditions of the poor without seriously taking their already eroded asset base into account. Reproducing the myth is also perilous in the sense that it may distort the actual impact of social policy programmes; social and economic policies should be designed and implemented with a view to strengthening the resources of the poor, instead of taking them for granted.

The much-heralded resilience of the poor has its limits. We have to question analytical models based on the assumption that the poor can always adapt to changing conditions and still survive. Emphasis on the agency of the poor should not make us oblivious to the fact that actions to secure a livelihood take place in a context of structural constraints, and under certain circumstances these constraints can be overwhelming. When economic conditions reach the point where ordinary people lose the ability to earn adequate incomes, this has a profound impact on every aspect of their lives. Although they try to turn to subsistence production, self-provisioning, independent work and petty-commodity production for sale as alternative income sources, wages obtained in labour markets cannot be substituted. Households are thus forced to make costly 'private adjustments', with potentially serious implications for their well-being and sustainable reproduction.

The household and the immediate family constitute an essential mechanism for the survival and reproduction of the poor. Yet, current economic and social conditions are not conducive to strengthening the social organization of poor households that has provided the social basis for their livelihood. Falling incomes and rising poverty are also eroding the capacity of poor people to be part of social networks of support, leaving them unable to engage in and maintain social exchange. By cutting people off from vital sources of support, social isolation — a critical but often neglected outcome of poverty — makes them even more vulnerable to adverse shocks and crises. Thus, a process of cumulative disadvantages sets in, which could further impinge on the ability of the poor to recover and climb out of their plight.

While critical household-focused research concentrated on the analysis of survival strategies employed by the urban poor and the working class, the limits of such models were not explored. Rather, the idea that the poor simply work harder in order to make ends meet persisted as the received wisdom. Earlier analyses failed to understand the full significance of wages coming from the market as the trigger for other activities (resources and income sources) and, therefore, also failed to predict the erosion of other sources of income when wages were absent. In so doing, we left the door open for the construction of the powerful myth of survival amidst the reproduction of the signs of global deprivation.

REFERENCES

Amado, F. (1994) *As condições de sobrevivencia da população pobre em Angola.* Luanda: Africa Databank, The World Bank Group.

Anderson, M. (ed.) (1980) *Sociology of the Family.* Harmondsworth: Penguin.

Anderson, M., F. Bechhofer and J. Gershuny (1994) 'Introduction', in Michael Anderson, Frank Bechhofer and Jonathan Gershuny (eds) *The Social and Political Economy of the Household,* pp. 1–16. New York: Oxford University Press.

Auyero, J. (2000) 'The Hyper-shantytown. Neo-liberal Violence(s) in the Argentine Slum', *Ethnography* 1(1): 93–116.

Barrig, M. (1993) *Seis familias en la crisis.* Lima: ADEC-ATC/Asociación Laboral para el Desarrollo.

Bazán, L. (1998) 'El último recurso: las relaciones familiares como alternativas frenta a la crisis'. Paper presented at the International Congress of the Latin American Studies Association, Chicago (24–26 September).

Bazán, L. (1999) *Cuando una puerta se cierra cientos se abren. Casa y familia: los recursos de los desempleados de la refinería 18 de Marzo.* Mexico City: Centro de Investigaciones y Estudios Superiores en Antropología Social.

Benería, L. (1992) 'The Mexican Debt Crisis: Restructuring the Economy and the Household', in Lourdes Benería and Shelley Feldman (eds) *Unequal Burden: Economic Crises, Persistent Poverty, and Women's Work,* pp. 83–104. Boulder, CO: Westview Press.

Benería, L. and S. Feldman (eds) (1992) *Unequal Burden: Economic Crises, Persistent Poverty, and Women's Work.* Boulder, CO: Westview Press.

Benería, L. and M. Roldán (1987) *The Crossroads of Class and Gender: Industrial Homework, Subcontracting and Household Dynamics in Mexico City.* Chicago, IL: University of Chicago Press.

CEPAL (1991) 'La equidad en el panorama social de América Latina durante los años ochenta'. LC/G.1686. Santiago, Chile: Comisión Económica para América Latina

CEPAL (1992a) 'El perfil de la pobreza en América Latina a comienzos de los años 90'. LC/L.716 (Conf.82/6). Santiago, Chile: Comisión Económica para América Latina

CEPAL (1992b) 'Hacia un perfil de la familia actual en Latinoamérica y el Caribe'. LC/R.1208. Santiago, Chile: Comisión Económica para América Latina

CEPAL (1997) *Panorama social de América Latina 1996.* Santiago, Chile: Comisión Económica para América Latina.

Chant, S. (1991) *Women and Survival in Mexican Cities: Perspectives on Gender, Labour Markets and Low Income Households.* Manchester: Manchester University Press.

Chant, S. (1996) *Gender, Urban Development, and Housing,* Vol 2. United Nations Development Programme Publication Series for Habitat. New York: UNDP.

Chant, S. (1997) *Women-Headed Households: Diversity and Dynamics in the Developing World.* London: Macmillan.

Chant, S. (1999) 'Las unidades domésticas encabezadas por mujeres en México y Costa Rica: perspectivas populares y globales sobre el tema de las mujeres solas', in Mercedes González de la Rocha (ed.) *Divergencias del modelo tradicional: Hogares de jefatura femenina en América Latina,* pp. 97–124. Mexico City: Centro de Investigaciones y Estudios Superiores en Antropología Social and Plaza y Valdés Editores.

Chant, S. (2004) 'Dangerous Equations? How Female-headed Households Became the Poorest of the Poor: Causes, Consequences and Cautions', *IDS Bulletin* 35(4): 19–26.

Chiarello, F. (1994) 'Economía informal, familia y redes socials', in René Millán (ed.) *Solidaridad y producción informal de recursos,* pp. 179–221. Mexico City: Universidad Nacional Autónoma de México.

Cravey, A. J. (1997) 'The Politics of Reproduction: Households in the Mexican Industrial Transition', *Economic Geography* 73(2): 166–86.

Durston, J. (2003) 'Capital social: parte del problema, parte de la solución, su papel en la persistencia y en la superación de la pobreza en América Latina y el Caribe', in Raúl Atria and Marcelo Siles (eds) *Capital social y reducción de la pobreza en América Latina y el Caribe: en busca de un nuevo paradigma*, pp. 147–202. Santiago de Chile: CEPAL; East Lansing, MI: Michigan State University.

Escobar Latapí, A. (1986) *Con el sudor de tu frente. Mercado de trabajo y clase obrera en Guadalajara.* Guadalajara: El Colegio de Jalisco.

Escobar Latapí, A. (1996) 'The Mexican Labor Market, 1976–1995'. Unpublished manuscript.

Escobar Latapí, A. and M. González de la Rocha (1995) 'Crisis, Restructuring and Urban Poverty in Mexico', *Environment and Urbanization* 7(1): 57–76.

Estrada, M. (1999) *1995: Familias en la crisis.* Mexico City: Centro de Investigaciones y Estudios Superiores en Antropología Social.

Feijoó, M. del C. (1991) *Alquimistas en la crisis. Experiencias de mujeres en el Gran Buenos Aires.* Buenos Aires: UNICEF.

García, B. and O. de Oliveira (1994) *Trabajo femenino y vida familiar en México.* Mexico City: El Colegio de México.

García, B., H. Muñoz and O. de Oliveira (1982) *Hogares y Trabajadores en la Ciudad de México.* Mexico City: El Colegio de México/Instituto de Investigaciones Sociales, Universidad Nacional Autónoma de México.

Gershuny, J. (1994) 'La economía informal: su papel en la sociedad postindustrial', in René Millán (ed.) *Solidaridad y producción informal de recursos*, pp. 107–28. Mexico City: Universidad Nacional Autónoma de México.

Gershuny, J. and I. D. Miles (1985) 'Towards a New Social Economics', in Bryan Roberts, Ruth Finnegan and Duncan Gallie (eds) *New Approaches to Economic Life: Economic Restructuring, Unemployment, and the Social Division of Labour*, pp. 24–47. Manchester: Manchester University Press.

González de la Rocha, M. (1984) 'The Social Organisation and Reproduction of Low Income Households: The Case of Guadalajara, Mexico'. PhD Thesis, Manchester University.

González de la Rocha, M. (1986) *Los recursos de la pobreza. Familias de bajos ingresos de Guadalajara.* Guadalajara: El Colegio de Jalisco, CIESAS, SPP.

González de la Rocha, M. (1988) 'Economic Crisis, Domestic Reorganisation and Women's Work in Guadalajara, Mexico', *Bulletin of Latin American Research* 7(2): 207–23.

González de la Rocha, M. (1991) 'Family, Well-being, Food Consumption, and Survival Strategies during Mexico's Economic Crisis', in Mercedes González de la Rocha and Agustín Escobar (eds) *Social Responses to Mexico's Economic Crisis of the 1980s*, pp. 115–27. La Jolla, CA: University of California, San Diego, Center for US–Mexican Studies.

González de la Rocha, M. (1994) *The Resources of Poverty: Women and Survival in a Mexican City.* Oxford: Blackwell.

González de la Rocha, M. (1995) 'The Urban Family and Poverty in Latin America', *Latin American Perspectives* 22(2): 12–32.

González de la Rocha, M. (1999) 'Hogares de jefatura en México: patrones y formas de vida', in Mercedes González de la Rocha (ed.) *Divergencias del modelo tradicional: Hogares de jefatura femenina en América Latina*, pp. 125–53. Mexico City: Centro de Investigaciones y Estudios Superiores en Antropología Social and Plaza y Valdés Editores.

González de la Rocha, M. (2000) 'Private Adjustments: Household Responses to the Erosion of Work'. New York: UNDP.

González de la Rocha, M. (2001) 'From the Resources of Poverty to the Poverty of Resources? The Erosion of a Survival Model', *Latin American Perspectives* 28(4): 72–100.

González de la Rocha, M. and A. Escobar Latapí (eds) (1991) *Social Responses to Mexico's Economic Crisis of the 1980s.* La Jolla, CA: University of California, San Diego, Center for US–Mexican Studies.

González de la Rocha, M., A. Escobar and M. de la O Martínez (1990) 'Estrategias vs. conflicto: reflexiones para el estudio del grupo doméstico en época de crisis,' in Guillermo de la Peña, Juan Manuel Durán, Agustín Escobar and Javier García de Alba (eds) *Crisis, conflicto y sobrevivencia. Estudios sobre la sociedad urbana en México*, pp. 351–67. Guadalajara: Universidad de Guadalajara and Centro de Investigaciones y Estudios Superiores en Antropología Social.

Lomnitz, L. (1977) *Networks and Marginality: Life in a Mexican Shantytown*. New York: Academic Press.

Moser, C. (1989) 'The Impact of Recession and Adjustment Policies at the Micro-level: Low-income Women and their Households in Guayaquil, Ecuador', in UNICEF *The Invisible Adjustment: Poor Women and the Economic Crisis*, pp. 137–66. Santiago de Chile: UNICEF.

Moser, C. (1996) *Confronting Crisis: A Comparative Study of Household Responses to Poverty and Vulnerability in Four Poor Urban Communities*. World Bank Environmentally Sustainable Development Studies and Monographs Series no 8. Washington, DC: The World Bank.

Narayan, D. with R. Patel, K. Schafft, A. Rademacher and S. Koch-Schulte (2000) *La Voz de los Pobres. Hay alguien que nos escuche?* Madrid, Barcelona, México, DF: Ediciones Mundi-Prensa, for the World Bank.

Pastore, J., H. Zlberstajn and C. Silvia Pagotto (1983) *Mudanca social e pobreza no Brasil: 1970-1980 (O que ocurreu com a familia brasileira?)*. Sao Paulo: Fundacao Instituto de Pesquisas Económicas/Livraria Pionera Editora.

Roberts, R. B. (1995) *The Making of Citizens: Cities of Peasants Revisited*. London: Arnold.

Safa, H. I. (1995) *The Myth of the Male Breadwinner: Women and Industrialization in the Caribbean*. Boulder, CO: Westview Press.

Schmink, M. (1984) 'Household Economic Strategies: Review and Research Agenda', *Latin American Research Review* 19(3): 87–101.

Selby, H., A. Murphy and S. Lorenzen (1990) *The Mexican Urban Household: Organizing for Self-Defense*. Austin, TX: University of Texas Press.

Sen, A. (1993) 'Capability and Well-being', in Martha Nussbaum and Amartya Sen (eds) *The Quality of Life*, pp. 30–53. New York: Oxford University Press; Oxford: Clarendon Press.

Stack, C. B. (1974) *All our Kin: Strategies for Survival in a Black Community*. New York: Harper & Row.

Tilly, L. A. (1987) 'Beyond Family Strategies, What?', *Historical Methods, A Journal of Quantitative and Interdisciplinary History* 20(3): 123–5.

Trapenciere, I., R. Rungule, M. Pranka, T. Lace and N. Dudwick (2000) *Listening to the Poor: A Social Assessment of Poverty in Latvia*. Riga: Ministry of Welfare and United Nations Development Programme.

4

Earth Mother Myths and Other Ecofeminist Fables: How a Strategic Notion Rose and Fell

Melissa Leach

INTRODUCTION

The woman carrying firewood on her head across a barren landscape has become an environment and development icon. Reproduced in policy reports, NGO glossies and academic books alike, her image encapsulates powerful and appealing messages. For a time in the 1980s, the message was that women have a special relationship with the environment. They are deeply reliant on land and trees in their day-to-day work; they are so purely as 'women' (the image is uncomplicated by men, kin, differences or relationships); this is a timeless, perhaps even natural role; subsistence, domesticity and environment are entwined as a female domain; women are victims of environmental degradation (walking ever further for that wood) but also environmental carers, and key fixers of environmental problems.

Such images became extremely powerful in certain development and activist circles from the 1980s. This, it seems, is because they offered a materialist discourse about women's environmental roles which suited donor and NGO preoccupations at the time. These material dimensions were bolstered by fables about women's natural, cultural or ideological closeness to nature; varieties of 'earth mother' myths which could be, and were, used to justify women's roles, as well as to give cultural and political appeal to the notion of global environmental sisterhoods. In the first part of this chapter, I briefly trace the rise of this women and environment discourse, and its key assumptions. Poorly conceptualized and inherently fragile as it was, I suggest that the idea of women's inherent closeness to nature could only be sustained because of the strategic interests it served.

In the early to mid-1990s, a thoroughgoing critique of this notion of women as natural environmental carers was articulated by several vocal academics. From a range of theoretical perspectives, but with a shared emphasis on gender relations and on particular contexts, women and environment assumptions were debunked, images reinterpreted and contextualized and alternative implications for policy and practice put forward. As one of those involved, I reflect in the second section of the chapter on why these critiques seemed so important at the time, whom they engaged, and the arguments presented.

The third part of the chapter brings us up to date. To what extent are images of nature-caring women still deployed, where and why? A brief review of some key donor and NGO documents from recent years suggests — tentatively — that such images are far less prominent than a decade ago. Statements which were then commonplace are now hard to find, and would seem slightly ridiculous. Reflecting on this observation, which initially surprised me, I conclude not that we were spectacularly successful as debunkers, but that the discourse was doomed, and only ever temporary. A flawed argument served a time-bound purpose which has diminished as broader environment and development concerns have altered. Older concerns with women and environment have now been recast in terms of property rights, resource access and control. While welcome in some respects, however, there is a danger that the baby has been thrown out with the bathwater; gender-blind environment and development work seems to be on the rise, and there is rather little evidence of a more politicized, relational perspective on gender and environment taking root.

WOMEN AND ENVIRONMENT: NATURAL CONNECTIONS?

Although building strongly on earlier concerns, and underpinned by an array of factors, the 1980s saw an unprecedented rise in global environmental concern. Amidst rising scientific and popular concern with global environmental change, many development agencies embraced concerns with environmental protection and sustainable development. In particular, this was the era of major, media-prominent droughts and famines in Africa; land and soil degradation ('desertification') and deforestation especially became key issues for policy, and on which development agencies were expected to act.

It was in this context that the notion that women have a special relationship with the environment first began to be highlighted in development circles. A series of documents and publications in the 1980s by NGOs, donor agencies and scholars writing in relatively popular presses put forward the view that women were the primary users and managers of the environment at the local level (for example, Dankelman and Davidson, 1988; Rodda, 1991). It was argued that women's work — especially in reproductive and subsistence-focused activities — involves them closely with the environment and its resources, as hewers of wood, haulers of water and cultivators of food. Women were seen to have responsibilities which make them closely dependent on and give them distinct interests in natural resources, especially as sources of food and fuel. This in turn was deemed to give women deep and extensive environmental knowledge and experiential expertise. While in the early 1980s there was much emphasis on women as victims of environmental degradation — the fuel wood gatherer walking ever-further to fulfil her roles in a deforesting landscape — by the end of the decade the positive image of women as efficient environmental managers and conservers of resources was far more prominent.

The assumptions underlying these arguments had much in common with Women in Development (WID) perspectives, which had of course been around for considerably longer. Indeed what came to be termed the Women, Environment and Development (WED) approach could, scholars later argued, be seen as a translation of WID perspectives into the environmental domain — a rather late one, given that WID was already coming under critique in other domains. Like WID, the starting point for WED was the gender division of labour, and a somewhat static conception of women's roles. As with WID, the focus was almost exclusively on women's activities, with men barely appearing in the picture. And as with WID, there was a tendency to portray women as a homogeneous group. As a result, an image of women and men operating in parallel worlds appeared, with any connections men might have with the environment invisibilized. Conceptual connections with other prevalent feminist fables can also be seen: the image of women caring for the environment as an extension of their caring roles for their families linked with ideas of maternal altruism, while (at least in Africa) arguments about women's special relationship with the environment drew heavily on stereotypes concerning female farming systems.

While those advocating WED perspectives did not necessarily believe, or state, that these women–environment connections were natural and universal, their generalized styles of writing, and the static, roles-based and women-only emphases of WED arguments often gave the impression that they were. However, it was through the alliances that developed between WED and ecofeminist arguments that the idea of natural connections became more strongly forged. Ecofeminism is based on the notion that women are especially 'close to nature' in a spiritual or conceptual sense. As a multi-stranded set of approaches, developed largely amongst northern academics, it is riven with theoretical differences and debates. Most stark, perhaps is the distinction between those taking an essentialist position, attributing the connection between women and nature to biological roots, and those who see it as a social or ideological construct. However, even the latter theorists have tended to portray it as a universal connection, or at least one spanning such wide cultural sweeps as to be universal. As Maria Mies put it: '[women] conceived of their own bodies as being productive and creative in the same way as they conceived of external nature as being productive and creative. . . They co-operate with their bodies and with the earth in order to "let grow and make grow"' (Mies, 1986: 56).

Ecofeminists argue that (connected) women and nature have been subjected to a shared history of oppression by patriarchal institutions and dominant western culture. Thus the scientific revolution, spanning the sixteenth and seventeenth centuries, is seen as having replaced organismic theory in which the earth (viewed as a nurturing female) lay at the centre of a cosmology in which nature and society were dynamically interconnected, with a mechanistic view of nature which upheld competition and domination as necessary to the pursuit of progress (Merchant, 1982; Plumwood, 1986; Warren, 1987). It is also argued that such western post-enlightenment images have been imposed on 'indigenous' societies in Asia and Africa through scientific and development processes. Thus Mies and Shiva (1993) reasonably portray imperialism and colonialism as bearers of a particular western, mechanistic science and rationality, but characterize this as patriarchal or 'masculinist', so 'doing violence' to women and nature. Such rationality, it is argued, undermined pre-existing conceptions which were very different, viewing people and 'nature' as interdependent and grounded in a feminine principle. In the ecofeminist view, hope for environmentally sustainable and egalitarian development lies in the recovery of this feminine principle.

While predominantly originating in the north, ecofeminism acquired a vocal international presence in the 1980s. The work of Vandana Shiva was particularly influential. Not just through widely published and accessible writings but also through presentations at international meetings, her work generalized from her particular interpretations of women's experiences and the feminine principle in Hindu cosmology to construct a notion of all third world women as still connected with the remnants of a not quite extinct feminine principle, which could be recovered.

Grounded in radical criticism of mainstream development approaches, ecofeminism has been seen as the basis for socially and politically transformative struggles and practices. Indeed, it is more strongly grounded in radical environmentalism than in mainstream sustainable development theory. In this respect, ecofeminist arguments have served to inspire a large range of social and environmental movements, from specific forms of grassroots activism around the environment, to large networks such as the Women's Environmental Network which has since the 1980s promoted green consumerism and other issues in Britain. The very vagueness and generality with which 'nature' is defined in most ecofeminist accounts, and their tendency to generalize from specific situations to posit very general connections between women and nature, seem to have facilitated the flexible deployment of ecofeminist precepts, implicitly as well as explicitly, by a vast array of movements pursuing different causes. It is perhaps this generality, too, which has allowed ecofeminist fables to draw together and unite groups and movements which might otherwise have contrasting political and material stances and aims. Thus echoes of ecofeminist discourse strongly coloured the Miami declaration adopted by a large international conference of women activists prior to the United Nations Conference on Environment and Development (UNCED) conference in Rio, 1992. It equally coloured the preamble to Women's Action Agenda 21 discussed at Rio, which linked the highly specific experiences of diverse groups of women in localized environmental protection with a broad critique of mainstream economic and military processes.

However, ecofeminist fables also came to be deployed in far less critical and politicized ways. They came to be major props to the women, environment and development approaches being developed by mainstream development agencies, largely because strong overlaps between ecofeminism and WED allowed them to be mutually supportive. One overlap lies in the lack of reference to men: Shiva's (1988) work, for example, subsumed any reference to men into 'peasants' or 'tribes'. Thus as in WED, it appears to be only women who have any environmental connection. Another is in the shared emphasis on women's environment-related 'sustenance' or 'survival' activities, and on the non-monetized reproductive sphere in general. In ecofeminism these come to be described not just as the foci of women's environmental inter-actions, but as repositories of spiritual and cultural value, and the central planks of a sustainable society. Perhaps one should also acknowledge that earth mother myths may have borne cultural resonance for certain (western) development experts, helping them to feel that their WED prescriptions were logical and right.

In this context, it is not surprising that echoes of ecofeminist discourse crept into the statements of donors and NGOs associated with much less rad-ical visions. Together, ecofeminism and WED supported a view that agencies should identify women as allies — or even the prime movers — in resource conservation projects. Coming at a time when agencies were under interna-tional pressure both to address environmental concerns, and to acknowledge gender differences, this was an attractive proposition. It came to be drawn on and elaborated by a wide variety of agencies. At one extreme, the World Bank developed a synergistic or 'win–win' approach to environment and gender, arguing for a general identity of interest between women and environmen-tal resources and thus for treating women as the best agents for ensuring resource conservation (see Jackson, 1993 for a fuller discussion). At the other, WED/ecofeminist assumptions were assimilated into the community-level 'primary environmental care' approach advocated by several NGOs (see Davidson and Myers, 1992). Women were conceptualized as the central agents of primary environmental care, which linked caring for the envi-ronment, meeting basic needs and community empowerment. Community approaches such as these were central to the broader Agenda 21 emerging out of UNCED, and 'women' and 'community' were often interchangeable terms in the documents of this period.

When translated into development practice, these women–environment links tended to come to mean one of two things: acknowledging women's en-vironmental roles so that they could be brought into broader project activities such as tree planting, soil conservation and so on, mobilizing the extra re-sources of women's labour, skill and knowledge; or justifying environmental interventions which targeted women exclusively, usually through women's groups. Many, many examples of both were spawned in the late 1980s and early 1990s. To take just one example, donor agencies in The Gambia relied principally on women's labour to promote fruit tree agroforestry for envi-ronmental stabilization. In justifying this, a UNDP official commented that 'women are the sole conservators of the land ... the willingness of women to participate in natural resource management is greater than that of men. Women are always willing to work in groups and these groups can be formed for conservation purposes'. The promotional literature of an NGO involved in tree planting echoed this perspective: 'In the Gambia, our primary focus

has been on women ... In the implementation of an environmental programme in the country, they could be deemed our most precious and vital
local resource' (both cited in Schroeder, 1999: 109).

Such projects and programme approaches have had a variety of effects. As
those who went on to question the assumptions have pointed out (see Green
et al., 1998; Jackson, 1993; Leach, 1994), in practice, many have proved
counterproductive for women or have failed to conserve the environment,
or sometimes both. Project 'success' has often been secured at women's ex-
pense, by appropriating women's labour, unremunerated, in activities which
prove not to meet their needs or whose benefits they do not control. New
environment chores have sometimes been added to women's already long list
of caring roles. At the same time, the focus on women's groups — as if all
women had homogeneous interests — has often marginalized the interests
and concerns of certain women not well represented in such organizations.
Fundamentally, it came to be argued, the assumption of women's natural link
with the environment obscured any issues concerning property and power.
This meant that programmes ran the risk of giving women responsibility for
'saving the environment' without addressing whether they actually had the
resources and capacity to do so.

Interventions cast in these terms have, in many cases, been actively struggled over or resisted. Thus in the Gambian garden-orchards cited above,
women struggled — sometimes successfully — to regain labour control
into their own horticultural activities and to sabotage the agro forestry trees
whose fruit commodities their husbands would control (Schroeder, 1999).
When women apparently took up such conservation tasks willingly, their
motivations for doing so often proved contradictory: thus Rocheleau (1988)
describes how women's groups in Kenya digging soil conservation terraces
did so to secure the patron–client relations which might bring them famine
relief food from the agencies concerned, not because (as those agencies stated
at the time) they felt close to nature or even had much interest in conservation.
However, it is worth noting that in both these cases women's participation
remained open to interpretation by others as evidence of their closeness to
nature, their special relationship with the environment. Re-contextualizing
these actions would require a different conceptual lens, which pushes the
images into new light. In a similar way, the woman head-loading fuelwood
in a barren landscape, deployed as an iconic image of women's natural connections, is open to quite other interpretations through different theoretical
lenses. It is to the debunking of ecofeminist/WED assumptions that I now
turn.

CRITIQUING NATURAL CONNECTIONS

From the early 1990s, a number of thoroughgoing critiques of these WED
and ecofeminist perspectives began to appear. These were largely the work

of academics, notably in India (Agarwal), the UK (Jackson, Leach, Joekes), the USA (Rocheleau, Fortmann), and the Netherlands (Wieringa), although usually in the context of particular relationships with development agencies, environmentalist groups and women and men in developing countries. As one of these academics, I can recall how imperative it seemed at the time to promulgate such critiques. For while appreciating the attempt by environmental agencies to address gender, it seemed appalling and dangerous that this was occurring through an approach with glaring flaws influenced by dubious ecofeminist work. I was shocked by the jarring mismatch between WED images and my understanding of gender and environment relations from my fieldwork in West Africa's forests, and concerned that feminist insights which had proved helpful in understanding those relations — insights around intra-household dynamics, resource access, and agrarian property and power, for instance — were being so overlooked in the rush to construct women as saviours of a vaguely-defined nature.

Others may have had other motivations, but the result was a series of lectures and presentations, published articles, books and reports, which put forward a range of alternative perspectives. These carried new labels, such as feminist environmentalism (Agarwal, 1992), feminist political ecology (Rocheleau et al., 1996), and gender, environment and development, or GED (Braidotti et al., 1994; Green et al., 1998; Leach, 1994). They had particular emphases, reflecting the other literatures and preoccupations which these debunkers brought to the debate. Thus feminist environmentalism emphasized the material aspects of gender–environment relations, and their interplay with particular ideological conceptions. Drawing from the broader school of political ecology, feminist political ecology drew particular attention to the nature of gendered knowledge, questions of resource access and control, and the engagement between local struggles and more global issues. GED, on the other hand, applied the perspectives of gender analysis as developed much earlier in other domains, such as around agriculture and economy, in the environmental domain. Nevertheless they shared a number of core ideas, centring around a conceptualization of gender–environment relations as embedded in dynamic social and political relations, and an emphasis on particular contexts rather than universalisms and essentialisms. And they presented some common challenges to WED perspectives and their ecofeminist fables.

These critiques cast women's (and men's) relationships with the environment as emerging from the social context of dynamic gender relations, and thus challenged any notion that women *a priori* have a special relationship with the environment, let alone a natural and unchanging one. The critiques ran alongside (and sometimes, though not by any means always, connected with) critiques of 'nature', which emphasized the dynamism of ecologies and the social construction of resources and environmental 'problems' (for example, Leach and Mearns, 1996). Thus, if women in any particular setting appeared to be closely involved with natural resources or ecological processes, this needed to be explained. It might be explicable in terms of unequal power relations, or lack of access to alternatives: for instance if women gather wild foods, this might reflect their lack of access to income from trees on private holdings (cf. Agarwal, 1992; Rocheleau, 1988); and the fuelwood headloader might have failed to negotiate with her husband to purchase fuels as others in her village might be doing. Stemming from these critiques, then, was a challenge to the notion that women's environmental interests are synonymous, or synergistic. Women may be locked into natural resource dependence through particular relationships and feel that their interests lie in moving into other livelihood activities, as they see men do.

This body of work also unpacked 'women' as a category, pointing out the very different interactions with land, trees, water, and so on, associated with women of different ages, backgrounds, wealth and kinship positions — differences which apply to men too. Thus mothers may be able to devolve much 'environmental care' onto daughters or daughters-in-law; women with access to trading capital may reduce their dependence on natural resources, and so on. That some women become involved in environmental action does not mean that this represents all women's interest and agency (Jackson, 1993). Recognizing differences and social relations amongst women clearly undermines any notion of groups formed through homogeneity of position and interest, and forces new questions to be asked about the hierarchies and distributional issues that operate when women do form groups for environmental purposes.

In shifting the focus from roles to relationships, these critiques emphasized how relations of tenure and property, and control over labour, resources, products and decisions, shape people's environmental interests and opportunities, and how environmentally-related rights and responsibilities are almost always contingent on kin and household arrangements and the negotiations these entail. They pointed out how gender boundaries with respect to environmentally-related activities can shift with changing economic and social circumstances, whether due to changes in global market conditions or shifts in the policy context. Property relations were a particular focus of feminist environmentalism and political ecology, including an emphasis on the layers of contingent rights, and the informal practices, which underlie formal arrangements (see, for example, Agarwal, 1995; Mackenzie, 1991), and the need for policy makers to acknowledge these.

Following on from this concern with access to and control over resources, and with household arrangements, gender analyses of environmental relations pointed out the fallacy of assuming that women's participation in environmental projects is coterminous with benefit. Social institutions and negotiations can clearly deny women control over products which their own labour has produced, while diversion of women's labour without remuneration may reduce their access to own-account income. And they suggest the possibility of conflicts between environmental and women's gender interests; for example, allocating women responsibility for saving the environment could increase their workloads or reinforce regressive gender roles, rather than representing progressive change or enhanced gender equity (Jackson, 1993; Leach, 1992).

While these aspects of critique focused particularly on the material and policy aspects of WED discourse — aspects which proved remarkably easy to challenge — scholars also critiqued the ecofeminist arguments which supported them. Vandana Shiva's work came under fire in this respect. Thus, for example, Agarwal (1992) accused Shiva (1988) of unwarranted extension of principles she associates with Hinduism when she suggests that all pre-colonial societies 'were based on an ontology of the feminine as the living principle' (Shiva, 1988: 41). Agarwal (1992) argues that the imagery of Prakriti varies in its connotations and relevance even among Hindu groups in India, and is of comparatively little importance among non-Hindu people. Scholars have also reinterpreted the Chipko movement — which Shiva draws upon as an iconic feminine environmental movement — in other terms: not as evidence of women's closeness to nature but as a struggle for material resources in the context of gender-ascribed natural resource dependence, and women's limited opportunities to out-migrate as compared with men (Jain, 1984; Peritore, 1992). The movement can be alternatively interpreted not as feminist, but as a peasant movement which emerged at a particular historical juncture (Guha, 1989), in which men were also involved, and in which women's participation was actually conservative of their subordinate position (Jain, 1984).

Other lines of critique exposed the problems in dualisms that linked women with nature — or indeed in the assumption, in some versions of ecofeminism, that non-western societies lack such dualisms. Scholars such as Leach (1994) and Jackson (1992, 2001) referred to anthropological studies showing wide cross-cultural and historical variability in the meanings attributed to 'female' and 'male', and the ways they are linked with concepts relevant to environment (MacCormack and Strathern, 1980; Moore, 1988). At a meeting in Oxford in 1996, a group of academics assembled specifically to compare the relations between gender and spirituality in different societies, resoundingly contested the view that women are everywhere viewed as sacred custodians of the earth (Low and Tremayne, 2001). A woman's procreative roles are by no means necessarily seen to place her closer to a universally-conceived nature, and to exclude men from this relationship. As a generalized category, 'nature' certainly fails to capture complex ideas about the physical and non-physical attributes of different micro-environments and ecological processes (cf. Croll and Parkin, 1992; Fairhead and Leach, 1996).

Related lines of critique challenged the assumption that pre-colonial, or-ganic, sacralized views of nature went hand-in-hand with harmonious en-vironmental practices and egalitarian gender relations. As Jackson (2001) elaborated, the relationships between religious beliefs and environmental practices are contingent and multiply-determined. At the same time, indige-nous organic conceptions can evidently encompass struggle and conflict between people and certain ecological processes, as well as harmony (Croll and Parkin, 1992). That certain ecological processes are socialized in local thought, and certain resources culturally valued, does not translate into an all-encompassing respect for nature (Persoon, 1989), and often speaks to local power relations (Fairhead and Leach, 1996). Indeed, as Jackson (1995) points out, there is plenty of evidence linking organic conceptions of society and ecology with oppressive social institutions: the territorial cults which managed land and fertility concerns in late nineteenth century southern Africa have, for example, been associated with the aristocratic domination and lethal taxation of commoners, as well as the subordination of women (Fairhead, 1992; Maxwell, 1994; Moore et al., 1999; Schoffeleers, 1979). Political ecology analyses of ecological knowledge and gender ideology, in contrast, locate the ways in which certain ideas are produced and debated within social and political processes, and in relation to particular groups and institutions.

Finally, critics problematized the image of western thought and colonial science as monolithically wiping out other views and knowledges (leaving perhaps a shadowy residual of the old feminized order; see Leach and Green, 1997). They pointed out how this obscures the complex content and political–economic relations of production of colonial and modern scientific discourses, and the processes through which they articulate with rural people's own. While recognizing the value of ecofeminism in drawing critical attention to the constituents of scientific epistemology and their operation through colonialism, and in raising questions about links between science and oppressive social relations, they suggested that such a critique needs to be developed through engagement with the highly diverse and contradictory theories and practices of which science is constituted (Molyneux and Steinberg, 1995: 92).

In short, these critical perspectives did not necessarily deny the events which ecofeminism interprets — the female fuel gatherer, women's involvement in some environmental movements or in conserving soil or planting trees, for instance. But they interpret these as particular to certain times, places and social relations, and interrogate the power relations which may produce them.

While it may have taken a group of vocal academics to articulate and elaborate some of these ideas, we were clearly not the only people thinking them. I vividly recall the hungry reception of my critique of WED amongst the various student, practitioner, donor and NGO audiences to which I presented these ideas in meetings in the early 1990s. It seemed that many people found the notion of women's natural environmental connections highly questionable, even ridiculous, and lapped up the critiques as speaking to their concerns. As the decade progressed, a spate of Masters and PhD studies began to appear — some but not all supervised by scholars active in the first round of debunking — which reviewed the gender and environment debate and explored field material through a gender relations, or feminist political ecology, lens (for example, Resurreccion, 1999; Schroeder, 1993).

Indeed, it seemed that by the early 1990s, even some of the donors who had promoted those images in the first place were ready to reconsider them. For example presentations by myself, Dianne Rocheleau and Louise Fortmann which eventually became the basis of published papers were first invited by Swedish SIDA, and discussed at a meeting they hosted of Scandinavian donors and conservation agencies. Many there agreed that the time was ripe for a gender perspective on environment (rather than a women-only perspective), and the workshop report reflected this emphasis (SIDA, 1992). The British government's DfID funded and attended the Oxford meeting mentioned above, which set out to challenge the image of women as sacred custodians of the earth; USAID commissioned a study from the Institute of Development Studies in Brighton to elaborate a gender perspective on environmental relations (Joekes et al., 1995); while Netherlands Development Assistance employed consultants to help their Women and Development programme, and Environment programme, to do the same (NEDA, 1997). Thus, at least to some extent, these critiques were elaborated in engagement with donor agencies, and generally found ready reception amongst them, stimulating efforts by individuals within these agencies. They were also elaborated in conjunction with certain grassroots groups. For instance, some of the contributors to Rocheleau et al. (1996) are environmental activists, or claim to represent their interests. It seems that by the mid-1990s certain activist groups, at least, were finding it more useful to present themselves in feminist political ecology terms, as engaged in struggles over rights and resources in a globalized field, than as groups of spiritually-connected earth and tree huggers.

GENDER AND ENVIRONMENT IN THE NEW MILLENNIUM

Having diverted my gaze somewhat from gender–environment issues during the last few years, I welcomed the opportunity to refocus it, and examine the kinds of messages present in development agency statements a decade on from the first round of WED critiques. I have not had time for a full review (although this might be worth doing), so these are only impressions, which I hope colleagues will add to or refute. My overriding feeling is that the kind of statement about women's special relationship with the environment, which was commonplace a decade ago, has all but disappeared. Earth mother myths may still be perpetuated through ecofeminist writings and certain strands of ecocentric environmental activism, mainly in the north. But they appear no longer to permeate, even implicitly, the environment and development policy and action statements of donor agencies, governments and NGOs. On the one hand, it seems, there are many fewer references to women, or gender, at all. On the other hand, when they do appear, their messages appear to be cast in more relational and rights-based terms. A brief array of examples illustrates these points.

The World Bank's World Development Report 2003 — *Sustainable Development in a Dynamic World* — appeared just over a decade on from the WDR in which its famous 'win–win' approach to women and environment was publicized. Yet it barely mentions women or gender except in two paragraphs under the heading 'Nurturing women's human capital', where it states that: '[women's] largely unrecorded role in agriculture explains the survival of many traditional subsistence communities on marginal lands . . . Traditional communities depend on women and girls to fetch fuel wood and water, and to produce and prepare food' (World Bank, 2003: 71). Even these WED-like statements are contextualized: 'in many places, traditions, limited mobility, and lack of voice or access to information make women the most marginal group. With the men seeking work elsewhere, women tend the fields and look after the children' (ibid.). While perhaps perpetuating other gender myths, such explanations begin to shift women's environmental connections from the natural and unquestionable, to see them emanating from a context of dynamic social relations.

DfID's strategy document for achieving the international development targets (DFID, 2000) contains, in its 56 pages of text, no mention at all of gender or women. Its discourse is couched entirely in terms of 'the poor' and 'communities'. In the one boxed case example where gender is mentioned — reporting on women's and men's differential involvement in a community-managed wells project in Mali — the focus is on inequalities in gendered labour allocation within the project and women's resistance to these. This is a far cry from any assumption that cleaning wells is a natural extension of women's caring roles.

A major report on biodiversity and livelihoods, prepared by IIED with DfID support (Koziell and Saunders, 2001), is couched in similar undifferentiated terms, concerned with 'the poor' and 'community knowledge and practices'. At the few points where social difference in people's relationships with biodiversity are acknowledged, the language used is of stakeholders, and their 'rights, responsibilities, rewards and relationships' (ibid.: 53).

ActionAid, once a contributor to WED statements, no longer has a policy or research programme devoted to environment. Their website's statements in the arenas which touch on environmental concerns — their programmes on food rights, and on emergencies — do not mention gender or women, and they have no publications with these in the title. What is clear is that their programme directions in these areas (for instance around the debate over genetically-modified crops, and vulnerability to drought and war) are driven by questions of rights, and of resource access and control.[1]

Water issues represent one arena where several agencies do have documents which contain a gender focus. These include reports produced amidst the follow-up processes for the 2002 World Summit on Sustainable Development, in which water was a central theme. For example, the Women's

---

1. From their website: http://www.actionaid.org/ourpriorities/ (accessed 2 June 2003).

Environment and Development Organization (WEDO) convened an expert consultation resulting in the report 'Untapped Connections: Gender, Water and Poverty. Key Issues, Government Commitments and Actions for Sustainable Development' (WEDO, 2003). While starting with a WED-like statement about women's roles — 'Women and girls are responsible for collecting water for cooking, cleaning, health and hygiene . . . in rural areas they walk long distances. . .' (ibid.: 3), its advocacy for 'tapping' the connections is grounded in an explicit conception of gender relations, and in concepts of gender equality in resource rights and decision-making.

A final, telling example is 'Women's Action Agenda for a Healthy and Peaceful Planet 2015', the document prepared for and discussed at the 2002 World Summit on Sustainable Development in Johannesburg (WEDO and REDEH, 2002). Formulated through regional meetings and in partnership with a diverse array of women's groups and networks worldwide, this was conceived explicitly as an updating of Women's Action Agenda 21, the 1992 Rio document that so epitomized the ecofeminist/WED discourse of that time. Its focal areas are peace and human rights; globalization; access and control of resources; environmental security and health; and governance for sustainable development. As far as I can see, there are no statements suggesting any natural connection between women and environment. While women's particular contributions to biodiversity conservation, water provisioning and so on are emphasized, this in the context of advocacy for equal property rights, inheritance rights, access to services, and for gender mainstreaming. Furthermore, and again by contrast with the 1992 document, global and international issues are much more prominent. The problems of global climate change and biodiversity loss, international militarization, and economic globalization within the neoliberal paradigm assume centre-stage, with the emphasis on how these create vulnerabilities for people, especially the poor, and the need to reinforce and reform relevant international agreements — or transform development paths more radically. While there is a notion that 'women' have specific vulnerabilities and concerns in this context, the document's language portrays women as representing, and advocating for, the more general concerns and struggles of people disenfranchised and marginalized by pernicious global processes.

What might one conclude from this brief review? If, as it suggests, images of women as natural environmental carers have receded, why might this be, and what has replaced them? First, one set of reasons may lie in broad shifts in international processes and development priorities. As concerns with war and complex emergencies, with globalization and its consequences, and with broader questions of governance have come to dominate development agendas, so environmental agendas have receded somewhat as programme priorities. At the same time, constituencies that might once have argued the 'women's case' in relation to global processes and governance, such as WEDO or DAWN (Development Alternatives with Women for a New Era), appear by necessity to be using their influence to press the more general case of the poor and disenfranchized, in a world of growing global inequality and conflict along many axes. The fuelwood head-loading woman in a barren landscape could, in these terms, become an image of the poor excluded from globalization's benefits, or of the devastation of African economies by international banks.

Second, within the environmental arena, policy priorities have, at least to some extent, moved away from the issues which first spawned the WED discourse. Fuelwood and social forestry, land degradation and soil conservation may still attract practical development attention on the ground, but have been superseded in international discussions by global climate change, biodiversity, and water — the big issues which dominated the 2002 Johannesburg meeting. Many dimensions of these involve global or transboundary processes which are seen to require international, or at least multi-levelled, approaches to governance, and new relationships with the private sector. The possible connections with women's day-to-day work and knowledge are possible to make, though far less obvious. Water is, perhaps, the exception, offering an obvious arena where gender relations shape patterns of need and provisioning at the micro-level, and it is therefore not surprising that to the extent that development discussions have pursued the gender and environment theme, it has often been in the water context.

Third, the last decade has seen a consolidation of decentralized, community-based approaches to governance and development, and a renewed focus on poverty. The environmental arena is a case in point, where a vast array of community-based and co-management approaches (to water, forests, wildlife and so on) have been launched, spawning a related social science literature reflecting on their successes and failures. In a similar vein, agencies such as DfID and UNDP (re-)discovered and pursued a debate on poverty–environment linkages. These programme approaches and the agency literature about them tend to be very gender-blind, promoting images of undifferentiated, consensual communities or 'the poor'. They have, it must be acknowledged, been influenced by discussions of resource rights, institutions and social difference emanating from other contexts, such as the sustainable livelihoods approach embraced by many donors during the last five years, and more recently, rights-based approaches to development more generally. Nevertheless, gender does not necessarily figure in these.

Fourth, just as environment and development debates have moved on, so have those about gender. The broader influence of GAD perspectives in academic, donor and practitioner circles, and the move towards gender mainstreaming, now make it difficult for statements about women's natural connections with environment (or indeed natural connections with anything else) to be made with credibility. WID was already sinking when environmental activists picked up on it to create WED in the 1980s, so perhaps it has now been fully submerged? Yet this would of course be a crass conclusion when the WID debate was, and is, multi-stranded and multi-sited. Many WID/WED assumptions, such as the idea that women's labour can be unproblematically utilized in land reclamation projects for household benefit, continue to be reproduced through practice in field-level projects. The real change may be in the rhetoric that development agencies are able to use to justify such practices.

SOME CONCLUSIONS

My conclusion, then — albeit tentative — is that the discourse of women as natural environmental carers had its day, but that day has passed. Emerging at a very particular moment, amidst the confluence of pressures to do something about environmental degradation amidst 1980s' droughts and in the lead-up to Rio 1992, and to address 'gender' in an era when this could more easily be taken as 'women', it offered both convenient practical prescriptions and powerful justifications for them. That the ecofeminist fables which crept into the discourse may have chimed with the beliefs and backgrounds of some of its proponents may have added to their conviction in portraying women as close to nature for otherwise quite instrumental ends. As environment and development discourses have moved on, so these ecofeminist fables seem largely to have retreated back into the world of academic writings and fringe environmental groups which originally spawned them.

While the debunking of WED's assumptions during the 1990s, through its particular engagements between academics and practitioners, may have played a role, it seems that it was swimming with a tide. However, a full assessment of both the rise and fall of WED discourses, and the influences on these, would require a proper analysis of the policy processes involved and their co-production with knowledge and research. I have not been able to undertake this here, and to do so, following leads in the large literature on policy processes in general and environment in particular (for example, Fairhead and Leach, 2003; Jasanoff and Wynne, 1998; Keeley and Scoones, 2003) would doubtless reveal forms of agency, dispute within organizations, and complexities of discourses and of actor-networks to which this chapter has done little justice. It would draw more detailed attention to the roles of particular political interests, funding flows, and events and meetings, and should demand attention to the interplay of research, policy and popular culture, including how mass-media influence these. Nevertheless, even the story of WED's rise and fall as I have sketched it here should alert us to the fact that what we regard as enduring myths may sometimes prove to be much more fragile, upheld less by enduring power structures than by relatively fleeting strategic interests. This is an interesting story for those who study science and policy processes, where the literature to date dwells more on the co-production of relatively enduring ideas or the gradual overturning of long-held paradigms, than on the contingent up-and-down of 'crazy' ideas. In turn, it should have implications for how feminist scholar-activists who seek to destabilize problematic gender assumptions might understand their task and go about their work.

For such a scholar-activist of a feminist environmentalist/feminist political ecology persuasion, the picture is now positive in some respects, but
depressing in others. The problematic WED discourse has waned, but there
is little evidence of a well-conceptualized gender relations perspective on environmental relations in policy literature. Issues of rights and resource access
and control are now acknowledged, but not necessarily in relation to gender,
and rarely through the relational, multi-layered lens which feminist political
ecologists and gender analysts of land have seen as important. Gender-blind
perspectives on community and the poor as actors in relation to ecological
and global political–economic processes seem to be more prominent than
ever. In academic literature, meanwhile, sophisticated studies have continued to appear which explore the intersection of gender, dynamic ecological
processes and environmental politics across multiple scales (such as Li, 2002;
Schroeder, 1996), showing the value of understanding people's current engagements with global processes in gendered terms. Perhaps it is time for a
new round of concerted engagement with the changed world of environment
and development policy which attempts to put gender back in the picture on
more politicized terms.

REFERENCES

Agarwal, B. (1992) 'The Gender and Environment Debate: Lessons from India', *Feminist Studies*
     18(1): 119–58.
Agarwal, B. (1995) *A Field of One's Own: Gender and Land Rights in South Asia*. Cambridge:
     Cambridge University Press.
Braidotti, R., E. Charkiewicz, S. Häusler and S. Wieringa (1994) *Women, the Environment and
     Sustainable Development: Towards a Theoretical Synthesis*. London: Zed Press/INSTRAW.
Croll, E. and D. Parkin (eds) (1992) *Bush Base: Forest Farm: Culture, Environment and Devel-
     opment*. London: Routledge.
Dankelman, I. and J. Davidson (1988) *Women and the Environment in the Third World: Alliance
     for the Future*. London: Earthscan Publications.
Davidson, J. and D. Myers (1992) *No Time to Waste*. Oxford: Oxfam.
DfID (2000) 'Achieving Sustainability: Poverty Elimination and the Environment'. Strategies
     for Achieving the International Development Targets document. London: Department for
     International Development.
Fairhead, J. (1992) 'Indigenous Technical Knowledge and Natural Resources Management in Sub-
     Saharan Africa: A Critical Overview'. Paper prepared for Social Science Research Council
     project on African Agriculture, Dakar (January).
Fairhead, J. and M. Leach (1996) *Misreading the African Landscape: Society and Ecology in a
     Forest-Savanna Mosaic*. Cambridge and New York: Cambridge University Press.
Fairhead, J. and M. Leach (2003) *Science, Society and Power: Environmental Knowledge and
     Policy in West Africa and the Caribbean*. Cambridge: Cambridge University Press.
Green, C., S. Joekes and M. Leach (1998) 'Questionable Links: Approaches to Gender in En-
     vironmental Research and Policy', in C. Jackson and R. Pearson (eds) *Feminist Visions of
     Development*, pp. 259–83. London and New York: Routledge.
Guha, R. (1989) *The Unquiet Woods: Ecological Change and Peasant Resistance in the Himalaya*.
     Delhi: Oxford University Press.

Jackson, C. (1992) 'Gender, Women and Environment: Harmony or Discord?'. Gender Analysis in Development Discussion Paper Series 6. Norwich: University of East Anglia, School of Development Studies.

Jackson, C. (1993) 'Women/Nature or Gender/History? A Critique of Ecofeminist "Development"', *Journal of Peasant Studies* 20(3): 389–419.

Jackson, C. (1995) 'Radical Environmental Myths: A Gender Perspective', *New Left Review* 210(March/April): 124–40.

Jackson, C. (2001) 'Gender, Nature and the Trouble with Anti-Dualisms', in A. Low and S. Tremayne (eds) *Women as Sacred Custodians of the Earth?*, pp. 25–43. New York and Oxford: Berghahn.

Jain, S. (1984) 'Women and People's Ecological Movement: A Case Study of Women's Role in the Chipko Movement in Uttar Pradesh', *Economic and Political Weekly* XIX(41): 1788–94.

Jasanoff, S. and B. Wynne (1998) 'Science and Decisionmaking', in S. Rayner and E. Malone (eds) *Human Choice and Climate Change: An International Assessment. Vol 1: The Societal Framework of Climate Change*, pp. 1–88. Battelle Press.

Joekes, S., C. Green and M. Leach (1995) 'Integrating Gender into Environmental Research and Policy'. Report of commissioned study for EPAT/MUCIA, United States Agency for International Development (USAID) (September).

Keeley, J. and I. Scoones (2003) *Understanding Environmental Policy Processes: Cases from Africa*. London: Earthscan.

Koziell, I. and J. Saunders (eds) (2001) *Living off Biodiversity*. London: IIED.

Leach, M. (1992) 'Gender and the Environment: Traps and Opportunities', *Development in Practice* 2(1): 12–22.

Leach, M. (1994) *Rainforest Relations: Gender and Resource use among the Mende of Gola, Sierra Leone*. International African Library. Edinburgh: Edinburgh University Press; Washington, DC: Smithsonian Institution.

Leach, M. and C. Green (1997) 'Gender and Environmental History: From Representations of Women and Nature to Gender Analysis of Ecology and Politics', *Environment and History* 3(3): 343–70.

Leach, M. and R. Mearns (1996) *The Lie of the Land: Challenging Received Wisdom on the African Environment*. Oxford: James Currey.

Li, T. M. (2002) 'Local Histories, Global Markets: Cocoa and Class in Upland Sulawesi', *Development and Change* 33(3): 415–37.

Low, A. and S. Tremayne (eds) (2001) *Women as Sacred Custodians of the Earth?* New York and Oxford: Berghahn.

MacCormack, C. and M. Strathern (eds) (1980) *Nature, Culture and Gender*. Cambridge: Cambridge University Press.

Mackenzie, F. (1991) 'Political Economy of the Environment, Gender and Resistance under Colonialism: Murang'a District, Kenya, 1910–1950', *Canadian Journal of African Studies* 25(2): 226–56.

Maxwell, D. (1994) 'Religion and Environmental Change in North-east Zimbabwe 1880–1990'. Paper presented at the African Studies Association of the UK Biennial Conference, University of Lancaster (5–7 September).

Merchant, C. (1982) *The Death of Nature: Women, Ecology and the Scientific Revolution*. London: Wildwood House.

Mies, M. (1986) *Patriarchy and Accumulation on a World Scale*. London: Zed Books.

Mies, M. and V. Shiva (1993) *Ecofeminism*. London: Zed Books.

Molyneux, M. and D. L. Steinberg (1995) 'Mies and Shiva's *Ecofeminism*: A New Testament?', *Feminist Review* 49: 86–107.

Moore, H. (1988) *Feminism and Anthropology*. Cambridge: Polity Press.

Moore, H., T. Sanders and B. Kaare (1999) *Those Who Play with Fire: Gender, Fertility and Transformation in East & Southern Africa*. London: Allen and Unwin.

NEDA (1997) *Gender and Environment: A Delicate Balance between Profit and Loss*. The Hague: Netherlands Development Assistance.

Peritore, N. P. (1992) 'India's Environmental Crisis and Chipko Andolan', *Asian Thought and Society* VXIII(51).

Persoon, G. (1989) 'Respect for Nature among Forest People', *BOS Newsletter* 18(8): 11–27.

Plumwood, V. (1986) 'Ecofeminism: An Overview and Discussion of Positions and Arguments', *Australian Journal of Philosophy* 64: 120–38.

Resurreccion, B. P. (1999) 'Transforming Nature, Redefining Selves: Gender and Ethnic Relations, Resource Use and Environmental Change in the Philippine Uplands'. PhD Thesis, Institute of Social Studies, The Hague, The Netherlands.

Rocheleau, D. (1988) 'Women, Trees and Tenure', in L. Fortmann and J. Bruce (eds) *Whose Trees? Proprietary Dimensions of Forestry*, pp. 254–72. Boulder, CO, and London: Westview Press.

Rocheleau, D., B. Thomas-Slayter and E. Wangari (eds) (1996) *Feminist Political Ecology: Global Issues and Local Experience*. London and New York: Routledge.

Rodda, A. (ed.) (1991) *Women and the Environment*. London: Zed Books.

Schoffeleers, J. M. (1979) 'Introduction', in J. M. Schoffeleers (ed.) *Guardians of the Land: Essays on Central African Territorial Cults*, pp. 1–46. Zimbabwe: Guelo.

Schroeder, R. (1993) 'Shady Practice: Gender and the Political Ecology of Resource Stabilization in Gambian Garden/Orchards'. PhD Thesis, University of California at Berkeley.

Schroeder, R. (1996) '"Gone to their Second Husbands": Marital Metaphors and Conjugal Contracts in The Gambia's Female Garden Sector', *Canadian Journal of African Studies* 30(1): 69–87.

Schroeder, R. (1999) *Shady Practices: Agroforestry and Gender Politics in The Gambia*. Berkeley, CA: University of California Press.

Shiva, V. (1988) *Staying Alive: Women, Ecology and Development*. London: Zed Books.

Shiva, V. (1989) 'Development, Ecology and Women', in J. Plant (ed.) *Healing the Wounds: The Promise of Ecofeminism*, pp. 80–90. London: Green Print.

SIDA (1992) 'Gender and Environment: Some Interlinkages'. Report of a SIDA Seminar. Stockholm: SIDA.

Warren, K. J. (1987) 'Feminism and Ecology: Making Connections', *Environmental Ethics* 9(3): 3–20.

WEDO (2003) 'Untapped Connections: Gender, Water and Poverty. Key Issues, Government Commitments and Actions for Sustainable Development'. New York: Women's Environment and Development Organization.

WEDO and REDEH (2002) 'Women's Action Agenda for a Healthy and Peaceful Planet 2015'. New York: Women's Environment and Development Organization.

World Bank (2003) *World Development Report 2003: Sustainable Development in a Dynamic World*. Washington, DC: World Bank.

5

Political Cleaners: Women as the New Anti-Corruption Force?

Anne Marie Goetz

INTRODUCTION

A myth in the making — that women tend to be less corrupt than men — is being widely circulated. For instance, the World Bank's most important recent policy statement on gender equality, *Engendering Development*, asserts a strong relationship between relatively high levels of female involvement in public life and low levels of government corruption. The report concludes that this finding lends 'additional support for having more women in politics and in the labor force — since they could be an effective force for good government and business trust' (World Bank, 2001: 96). Thus the challenge of increasing the numbers of women in public life, long defended by feminists as a matter of human rights and democratic justice, can now be seen to have an efficiency payoff — more women in power may have the effect of reducing corruption — although, as we shall see, the causal relationship between numbers of women in the public arena and the extent or type of corrupt activity is not very clear.

Like any instrumentalist argument, the 'women are less corrupt than men' justification for bringing women into politics and public institutions is not just vulnerable to exposure as a myth; it puts women's engagement in the public arena on the wrong foot. Women are seen as instruments to achieve a broader development goal, not welcomed to public office as a matter of their democratic and employment rights. The new stress on women's gender as a useful instrument for good governance is another example of the dangers of using the notion of 'women' as a single category in social analysis and in development policy. Critical social differences between women disappear before the presumed fact of the probity and virtues inherent to their gender. But politics is the very worst place to ignore differences between women: arrangements for the inclusion of women in politics that are insensitive to differences of race, class, and ethnicity between women will see elite women capturing public office.[1]

This chapter first explores the emergence of the myth of women's lesser propensity to engage in corrupt activity. It shows that the notion that women

---

1. This is exactly the point made by opponents of the proposed 84th Constitutional amendment in India, to reserve seats for women-only competition in the national parliament. Opponents say that this will reverse the trend to greater caste diversity in parliament by bringing more upper caste MPs — upper caste women — to office.

are less corrupt than men, more likely to behave with probity and integrity, is ironically the reverse of a myth that has kept them out of the public realm for centuries. That earlier myth justified women's exclusion from politics and public administration on the grounds that their rootedness in the world of care and family left them ill-equipped for rational public debate using principles of impartiality and universality. Next, the chapter examines the evidence for the new image of women as 'political cleaners', demonstrating that this is mainly based upon assumptions about women's inherent probity made by a range of actors, including women themselves. The chapter then argues that gender does indeed shape *opportunities* for corruption, but this is different from the new myth that women's gender determines their *reactions* to corruption.

We can understand these gendered opportunities by examining how women are recruited into and treated within key institutions that shape public life: political parties and state bureaucracies; this contribution examines cases from South Asia to illustrate this. What matters is not the 'simple access' (Jónasdóttir, 1988) of women to power and public life. What matters is the *means* of their access (have women come through the women's movement or through democratic party processes that connect them to a social base pressing for equity?) and the nature of the institutions in which they function (how do these institutions hold public actors to account? To what constituencies do public actors answer?). The chapter concludes by asking whether it is useful to analyse problems of governance — or accountability failures — from a gender perspective. This is a question about what governments can do for women, as opposed to what women can do for good governance.

THE MYTH: WOMEN AS 'POLITICAL CLEANERS'

Experiments are underway in some contexts to feminize notoriously corrupt public agencies. For instance, in 1998 Peru's President Fujimori announced that the 2,500-strong traffic police force in Lima would be completely transformed into an all-women force. In June 2003, the Mexican Customs Service announced that its new crack force of anti-corruption officers on land and sea borders would be entirely female (*The Herald Tribune*, 2003). In other contexts we can see similar assumptions about women's probity guiding the portfolios given to women new to office. In Uganda for instance, the vast majority of positions as treasurer in the new local government system are assigned to women, where it is hoped they will apply their prudence in managing domestic accounts to curb mis-spending in local public office.

These integrity experiments call upon women to use their gender as the intrinsic regulator of probity in public action. Consider the justification for selecting only women provided by Commander Pedro Montoya, when training an all-female motorcycle brigade of traffic cops in Lima: 'the women are more honest and morally firm than the men. It's undeniable'. Montoya went on to posit that women are more honest because of their role in the family. He asserted that they have an aversion to taking money from male drivers, because they feel this act would resemble prostitution.[2] Thus, while the positive motive for women's less corrupt behaviour is that women's experiences as nurturers and family managers are the basis for a more caring and honest approach to interactions with clients or colleagues in public sector jobs, Montoya also hints at a darker incentive. Engagement in nefarious acts — being seen taking money from men who are not relatives — has drastic implications for women's sexual integrity. Sexual impropriety is very rarely an implication when men engage in dirty deals, though of course politicians and officials suffer from any hint of male homosexual encounters: the mere suggestion of such was enough to blackmail male public officials in the West until very recently.

In Commander Montoya's defence of women's virtues as traffic cops, we see that two of the justifications used by politicians and philosophers in Europe for centuries for keeping women out of public life are now being used to bring them in. Women's caring roles in the private arena of the home are now seen as a positive qualification for public service, and the fear that a public life might compromise women's sexual integrity has now been dropped as the main reason for keeping them at home. Instead, it is hoped that the risk of being branded as sexually immoral will discourage women in public life from dabbling in dirty deals in dark places.

It is not just male reformers hoping to capitalize on women's supposed integrity who use these images. Women leaders do the same. Around the world, women leaders often try to deflect the mistrust and criticism with which the public regard them because of their gender with reassurances that their interest in politics is as mothers, as guardians, as carers of the nation.[3] Right-wing parties and right-wing political leaders love the rhetoric of women's inherent probity. For women leaders in fundamentalist religious or chauvinistic nationalist parties, rhetoric about women's purity, integrity, and self-sacrifice can be employed to explain away personal characteristics and behaviours that would otherwise be unacceptable and that directly contradict their conservative social policies, such as, their unmarried status or their striking militancy and calls to violence.[4]

This idea of linking notions of womanly virtue with incorruptibility is not new. It is based upon essentialist notions of women's higher moral nature and their propensity to bring their finer moral sensibilities to bear on public life, and particularly on the conduct of politics — an argument which was much used by suffragettes a century ago. Ironically, it directly contradicts another

2. Associated Press, *CNN*, 21 August 1998.
3. See Jayalalitha's public imagery machine centred on the image of 'Tamilttaay' — mother, desirable woman, and virginal goddess (Bannerjee, 2004), Indira Gandhi as Mother India, even Margaret Thatcher the tea maker for her kitchen cabinet.
4. Consider for instance the public rhetoric of Uma Bharti or Sadhvi Rithambara of the Baratiya Janata Party in India. Both are single, never-married women who flaunt rules about the conduct of unmarried women; see Basu (1995) for a discussion of how these and other women leaders in the Hindu fundamentalist party BJP 'invert' feminist discourses to justify their decidedly non-traditional activities and personal lives.

essentialist notion that has for so long denied women direct access to politics — articulated by philosophers from Plato to Rousseau — about women's inherent incapacity for abstract thought, and their unfitness to govern because of their inability to grasp basic notions of justice and ethical reasoning.[5] In Rousseau's conception, for instance, this unfitness comes from their 'natural' role as caretakers and custodians of affectivity, desire, and the body in the home. If appeals to personal connections and desires were allowed to move public debates, the principles of universality, impartiality, and justice would be subverted, as too would the convenient separation between the private and the public realms.[6]

In the twentieth century, Western psychology attempted to provide a scientific basis to these sexist assumptions about women's essential nature, starting with Freud's (1925: 257–8) insistence that women 'show less sense of justice than men, ... are less ready to submit to the great exigencies of life, ... are more often influenced in their judgments by feelings of affection or hostility'. In Kohlberg's famous experiments about resolutions of moral dilemmas, women are assumed to be able to reach only stage three in a six-stage measure of moral development. Kohlberg saw women to be deficient in moral judgement because they think of morality in interpersonal terms where goodness is equated with helping and pleasing others — a conception of goodness that may be functional in private but is inadequate to the needs of public life, where relationships must be subordinated to rules, and rules to universal principles of justice (Gilligan, 1982: 18).

The current view of women's inherent probity and hence appropriateness as leaders, bureaucrats, police officers and customs officials sees this old myth flipped around. The very traits that traditionally branded women as deficient in moral development, their concern to help and to please, are now seen as functional for good governance reforms in developing and transitional societies. Not only are women's domestic virtues seen as functional for combating corruption, but they may remedy a wider range of current political ills. According to Uganda's President Museveni, for instance, who has cultivated the female electorate as his support base: 'Women have stabilised politics in a way because they tend not to be so opportunistic ... They are not so reckless like men' (quoted in Simmons and Wright, 2000).

For the last century at least, feminist activists and scholars have contributed to this kind of expectation that women can transform power and politics, appealing selectively to essentialist ideas about women's effectiveness as conflict mediators, as moderators between extreme positions, as effective managers of the public purse. Anne Phillips (1991: 62–3) sets out the three most common justifications employed by feminists for bringing women into politics: first, the argument that women can bring to politics a different set of

---

5. Two excellent discussions of what male philosophers over the centuries have said about women to justify their confinement to the household and their incapacity for engagement in public debate and decision making can be found in Lloyd (1984) and Okin (1979).

6. For studies of Rousseau's perspectives on women, see Schwartz (1984).

values, experiences, and expertises — 'that they will enrich our political life, usually in the direction of a more caring, compassionate society'. Second is the more radical argument that because women and men are in conflict, women must be present in public life to represent women's interests as a gender. The third is that it is simply a matter of justice: 'just as it is unjust that women should be cooks but not engineers . . . so it is unjust that they should be excluded from the central activities in the political realm'.

Phillips (ibid.: 63) then demolishes the first argument on the grounds that it is based on unproven essentialist assumptions, and also that the values women bring to politics could even be undemocratic, given their lack of schooling in democratic practice. She challenges the second point on the familiar grounds that women do not constitute a single interest group. She also argues that given the way votes are assigned to seats in most electoral systems, no woman political candidate can seriously present herself as representing women alone, but has to look to the common interests of her constituency. She concludes that the only argument for women's inclusion in politics that can be defended is the one drawn from principles of justice, and this case for justice 'says nothing about what women will do if they get into politics'.

Arguments based upon fairness, however, are less persuasive to policy makers than instrumentalist ones that imply that the conduct and substance of politics will change. Thus many feminist students of politics, including myself, have combined the justice argument either with the expectation that women can transform politics, or with the insistence that women are needed to represent women's interests. There is indeed evidence from industrialized democracies that women in politics do focus more than men on passing legislation and implementing policies in areas benefiting women, such as child support programmes, family leave legislation, abortion rights, prevention of violence against women, and gender equity in education (Burrell, 1994: 151–2; Rule and Hill, 1996). The same appears to be true for developing countries in which changes to electoral rules or the reservation of local and national government seats have brought more women into politics. Uganda and South Africa — countries in which more than a quarter of the legislature is female — have seen the revision of laws on rape, domestic violence, and domestic relations (Goetz, 2003; Hassim, 2003; Meintjes, 2003). In Indian local government, where one third of seats are reserved for women, observers in Karnataka, Rajasthan, West Bengal and Maharashtra report that local spending patterns are now a little more responsive to poor women's concerns (Chattopadhyay and Duflo, 2001: 19; Datta, 1998; Kudva, 2003; Mayaram and Pal, 1996).

Assumptions about women's responsiveness to other women have also been made about women in service bureaucracies. Research in industrialized country bureaucracies has shown that bureaucrats from minority or socially excluded groups do indeed use their discretion to reduce the discrimination which minority clients have suffered (Meier et al., 1989; Selden, 1997), but there has been rather less work on this in the South, and it has produced less emphatic findings. My own work on women fieldworkers in government and NGO micro-finance programmes in Bangladesh (where they were minorities in a male-dominated work environment) established that women fieldworkers and managers did identify with some of the problems of their female clientele and acted as advocates for them within their organizations, exhibiting a form of 'local heroism' on behalf of poor women (Goetz, 2001). The work of Simmons (1996) on family planning programmes in Bangladesh finds, similarly, that women staff represented a new advocacy resource for poor women in the rural context. But work by Jewkes et al. (1998) in South Africa, and Sargent (1989) in Benin, on nurses and midwives in maternity clinics, find alarming levels of abuse of pregnant patients by women staff.

The point of this very brief review of feminist work on women politicians and public servants is to suggest that feminist scholars and advocates have contributed to the myth of women's special contribution to politics. However, few have gone so far as to suggest that women are less corrupt than men. Very little of the feminist literature on women in politics and bureaucracies has focused upon women's reaction to and engagement in corruption. The obvious reason for this is that it is extremely difficult to research. Most of the evidence on women's corruption or lack of it in politics or public services is anecdotal, and this is why a series of World Bank studies of this question, using cross-national regressions, attracted so much interest.

THE EVIDENCE

We have already noted that international development agencies are taking an interest in the relationship between proportions of women making up political assemblies, and levels of corruption. The basis for this interest comes from two studies published in 2001. The first, 'Gender and Corruption', by Anand Swamy, Steve Knack, Young Lee and Omar Azfar, was produced by the IRIS Center, University of Maryland in April 1999 (see Swamy et al., 2001). The second, 'Are Women Really the "Fairer" Sex?', by David Dollar, Raymond Fisman, and Roberta Gatti (2001) came from the World Bank's Development Research Group.

Both papers suffer from a problem afflicting any statistical analysis addressing corruption: the difficulty of finding a consistent or accurate measure of corruption. Corruption is a 'consensual crime' — both partners consent to the crime (however unwillingly) and neither reports it. Not only is it difficult to measure corruption, but it is hard to define it. Is corruption simply about the theft of public resources for private profit? What about actions that do not involve theft of money or property, such as cheating in elections? What about the systematic exercise of bias in the allocation of public services or in the treatment given to clients by public officials, be they doctors or teachers or licence-issuers?

In Dollar et al. (2001), the authors use the International Country Risk Guide's corruption index to measure corruption levels in the 100+ countries that they include in their analysis. This index is based upon other standard corruption indices, and all of these are based upon *perceived* levels of corruption as reported by business people, usually foreign investors, and sometimes by in-country bureaucrats and journalists. In other words, this measure of corruption is both relatively subjective, shaped by cultural prejudices of outsiders, and reflects the concerns of investors, and is a good illustration of the normative nature of definitions and measures of corruption. It does not capture forms of corruption that may most concern the average citizen or poor people in the country in question.

The Dollar et al. study seeks to establish a relationship between numbers of women in parliament and levels of corruption, and uses levels of GDP and levels of civil liberties as controls on its findings. It finds a very high level of raw correlation between low corruption scores and relatively high numbers of women in parliaments (0.38), and finds that a one standard deviation increase in levels of women in parliament from the average of 10.9 per cent in its sample will result in a 10 per cent decline in corruption. They also find that both variables are strongly correlated with overall development (as proxied by per capita income), and with other features of political openness such as the extent of civil liberties, average years of schooling, trade openness, and low ethnic fractionalization. Nevertheless, they find that the influence of women in parliament is large in magnitude, highly significant, and robust through a large variety of regressions. The authors conclude: 'women may have higher standards of ethical behaviour and be more concerned with the common good' (Dollar et al., 2001: 427). As Andrew Mason, one of the authors of the World Bank's 2001 *Engendering Development* report sensibly commented on these findings: 'Whether this means that women are inherently more moral beings than men, I don't know'. Rather, he added, a higher level of women's political and economic participation is likely to signify that a country is more open in general, with more transparent government and a more democratic approach.[7] Though this is unlikely to explain why numbers of women in office remain relatively low in transparent and open democracies like the US or Canada, it is probably the most sensible way to interpret very broad-brush findings such as those provided in regressions of cross-national data.[8]

---

7. See 'World Bank to Rate All Projects for Gender Impact', Women's eNews website: www.womensenews.org, 4 April 2002.
8. This is exactly the conclusion drawn by a critic of both the Dollar et al. (2001) and the Swamy et al. (2001) studies, who uses statistical analysis to show that the observed association between gender and corruption is spurious and is mainly caused by its context — liberal democracy (Sung, 2003). Sung's careful review of these two studies draws out other problems not discussed here, such as the misleading implications of proposing hypotheses about group behaviour on the basis of individual-level findings about female honesty, and the failure to impose theory-driven statistical controls to the data, resulting in a failure to pick up on the role of constitutional liberalism in both reducing corruption and promoting women's presence in public office. Like my own analysis, Sung also identifies a failure in the Dollar et al. and Swamy et al. studies to examine the *processes* that connect female participation in government to reduced corruption (Sung, 2003: 703–6).

The Swamy et al. (2001) study uses the same technique to show that in addition to large numbers of women in parliament, when women comprise a larger share of the labour force, overall levels of corruption are likely to be less severe. This study also uses micro-level data from a study of 350 firms in Georgia in 1996, where the pressure to give bribes results in serious losses — at least 9 per cent of the annual turnover. On average, women owners/managers of firms admit to giving bribes on approximately 5 per cent of the occasions that they come in contact with a government agency. The percentage is twice as large for firms owned/managed by men. The authors feel this is suggestive of a marked gender differential in the propensity to bribe.

The Swamy et al. paper also used data from World Values Surveys which, in addition to hundreds of other items, asked men and women about the acceptability of various dishonest or illegal behaviours. Aggregating over all countries in surveys from 1981 and 1991, a gender gap emerged that consistently showed greater honesty on the part of women. For all twelve items listed, a higher percentage of women than men believe that the illegal or dishonest behaviour is never justifiable. The case of greatest interest is responses to the question about 'someone accepting a bribe in the course of their duties': 72.4 per cent of men and 77.3 per cent of women agree that this is 'never justified'. The paper goes on to test this result against all manner of other variables and finds that gender consistently overrides other variables in producing a more ethical stance on probity in public life. The authors conclude from this and the results of behavioural studies that women are more trustworthy and public-spirited than men. A policy inference is drawn: 'increasing women's presence in public life can reduce levels of corruption' (Swamy et al., 2001: 36).

What is notable about the evidence in these studies is that it is based upon women's and men's reports and assumptions about the way gender shapes people's *reactions* to corruption, to the demand to give a bribe or the opportunity to take one. But it might well be that these studies are missing something. Perhaps gender relations condition the *opportunities* for corrupt or opportunistic behaviour. Perhaps gender relations limit those opportunities. They would do so if, for instance, corruption functions primarily through all-male networks and in forums from which women are socially excluded. This, as much as anything, might explain apparently low levels of female corruption, or of women's low levels of positive responses to opportunities for illegal behaviour. And this might change when all-female networks are established, when workplaces become more feminized, or when women take top leadership positions that enable them to re-direct networks of illicit exchange to their own benefit.

HOW OPPORTUNITIES FOR CORRUPTION ARE SHAPED BY GENDER

Women are relative newcomers to public office. We know that their recruitment to and treatment within the arenas of politics and public administration differ from the experiences of men, but we don't know much about how this results in different opportunities for them to engage in illicit acts. Using examples from South Asia, I will show how gender mediates women's access to the public sphere, and once there, to opportunities for illicit earnings. Interacting with class, religion, family connections, and caste relations, gender greatly restricts the access of the majority of women to political parties and to public sector jobs. In politics, this produces a markedly skewed distribution of women, with a tiny number of extremely elite women at the apex of weak party structures, and with larger numbers of women involved only when needed as voters or to increase the visibility of public demonstrations. In bureaucracies, gender biases limit the numbers of women to legislated minimum levels that quickly become ceilings. In both politics and public administration, women who want to get ahead, like men, may find it hard to avoid the informal auctions for top posts; these involve bribing politicians in exchange for a job transfer or for the award of a candidacy in a desirable constituency. However, the options that women bureaucrats and politicians have for the illicit generation of funds needed to purchase choice posts are limited by gender relations that forbid interactions with non-kin men. In socially conservative societies like India or Bangladesh, it is difficult for women to become either clients or patrons in the male-dominated patronage networks through which corrupt exchanges occur, unless they do so via mediators who are male relatives. Thus anyone's access to politics or good posts in the bureaucracy can be financially corrupting (because of the need to generate campaign funds or pay for an appointment), but for women, it can also be sexually corrupting.

Given the lack of research on how gender mediates access to networks for illicit earning, let alone the lack of explicit documentation about how such networks function, I am obliged here to grasp at straws, to pick up on rumours about women politicians and bureaucrats recounted to me over years of research on gender and policy making, that I had mostly dismissed as ill-intentioned. The questions I am asking here have made me scrabble through parts of my own past research on women in politics and bureaucracies, which I now see offers clues. On the cutting-room floor of my 1987–91 doctoral thesis research into women fieldworkers on micro-finance programmes, for instance, I rediscovered interviews and case studies about women development workers who admitted to or were accused of corruption. In the next two sections I consider how the ways women are recruited to and treated within parties and public bureaucracies affect their experiences of corruption.

Political Parties

If we are hoping that women in political leadership will prove themselves less corrupt than men, we need to understand the ways parties selectively recruit and socialize women to politics, whether political competition requires the use of 'muscle' and the generation of huge sums of money for campaigns, and whether parties offer women and men different opportunities for illicit or illegal activities.

A striking feature of party politics in all four countries of South Asia is the appearance of women leaders at the apex of parties at various times. This is not a reflection of women's political strength as a group in the region. In the mid-1990s, *The Economist* asserted that promoting women into high office in South and Southeast Asia because of their relationship as daughters or widows to powerful men who have been deposed or assassinated reflects the ineptitude of the region's political parties, which it called 'rotten organizations incapable of producing a real leader' (cited by Halloram, 1998). This same weakness, which is about an absence of democratic leadershipselection systems and a reliance on dynastic systems of organizing power relations, also results in the marked absence of women in the rank and file or in office-holding positions below the top leader.

One way to understand this weakness is in terms of low levels of institutionalization. Political parties are considered to be institutionalized when they have, and respect, rules about candidate selection, identify policy concerns, have an organization that is distinct from the personal connections of their leaders, and when their elected members form a distinct and coherent group in the legislature (Moore, 2002; Randall and Svasand, 2002). Party institutionalization is considered essential for the consolidation of democracy in developing countries, for only when parties are stable and predictable in their membership and policy positions can voters make informed choices, secure in the knowledge that their votes will influence the policies of the government. South Asian countries do have parties with deep roots in society, well-evolved internal systems, disciplined members and consistent ideological positions (notably the left parties in Kerala and West Bengal, and up to the 1970s, the Indian National Congress). But the prevalence of personalized or dynastic leadership, patronage systems for delivering votes and generating campaign finance, and the growing electoral success of crude tactics of invoking exclusive ethnic or caste loyalties and inciting communal tensions has led to growing fragmentation and violence in party systems, and in some places the virtual disappearance of coherent policy platforms between which voters can select.

Under-institutionalization is a major reason for the relative exclusion of women as members and as candidates for public office (Norris, 1993) and for the relative hostility that political parties around the world exhibit to feminist policy priorities (Baer, 1999).[9] This, even if under-institutionalization

---

9. Of course, well-institutionalized parties have also been resistant to women's participation — one need only look at the numbers of office bearers and electoral candidates who are women in the Communist Party of India (Marxist) in Kerala or West Bengal to see this. As Georgina Waylen (2000: 790–1) says, it is not 'that hyper-institutionalisation is good, but rather that low levels of institutionalisation produce problems and make lasting change difficult to achieve'. In contrast: 'in an institutionalised system there is stability in the rules of competition and party organisations matter: therefore rules, for example over quotas and candidate selection, can be enforced more easily'.

can mean that a female relative of a deposed or dead leader can get the top party post because of rank and file loyalty to a family dynasty, for most other women, it is an insurmountable obstacle to participation. Engagement at any level in the party is dependent upon access to caste, family, and usually all-male networks of patron–client relationships. Not only does this make political parties extremely unlikely arenas in which ambitions for social change can be pursued, it can make the women who do try to seek advance within parties socially unattractive, and sometimes sexually suspect. Access to leadership positions within the party, to electoral candidacies, to finance for campaigns, is dependent upon relationships with powerful men. And such relationships, unless sanctified by kinship connections, can bring discredit to women.

Since women leaders have come laterally into parties, via personal connections to powerful men rather than rising up from the bottom, they often lack experience of political alliance building, debate, long-term strategizing, campaign resource generation, and policy development. A notable exception to this is Mamata Bannerjee, a long-time activist in the Indian Congress party, whose frustrations with central party controls led her to form the intermittently successful break-way faction in West Bengal, the All India Trinamul ('Grassroots') Congress.[10] For other women leaders, lateral and late entry to politics can mean that they lack a secure constituency base. This can encourage undemocratic and possibly also corrupt leadership practices.

This problem of a shallow political base and fleeting political apprenticeship may be one reason why some women leaders in South Asia have resorted to crude populism to build up social support, and to authoritarian tactics within their parties to undermine dissent and opposition. Indira Gandhi famously began the long process of the de-institutionalization of the Congress party when, after 1972, she put a halt to internal party elections and ensured that aspirants for party posts had to petition her directly. Driven from the beginning of her first ten-year period in power by the wish to break free of the patrician 'Syndicate' of established party notables and elites, she shattered many aspects of internal party organization and centralized power in her own person and in the person of the Congress president for each state (personally appointed by herself) (Jaffrelot, 2003: 133).

For the large number of women who are interested in political participation if not directly in leadership, parties limit access because of the masculinity of party cultures and the sexual dangers that this represents. That parties are often organized around masculine patronage networks is not a new observation and is as true in the UK or USA as in any developing country (Baer, 1999; Perrigo, 1996; Short, 1996). Proof of this can always be

---

10.   Unlike any of the other current heads of parties or heads of regional branches of parties —
      Sonia Gandhi, Jayalalitha, Mayawati — Mamata Bannerjee does not have a reputation for
      corruption. This is in spite of heading for a while the Union government's Railway Ministry,
      with a large budget and plenty of opportunities for making illicit earnings. She quit the BJP
      government which she was supporting over a corruption scandal implicating senior figures
      including in the Ministry of Defence (the Tehelka affair in Spring 2001).

found in the phenomenally low numbers of women members, branch managers, and executive officers in parties around the world. In India, figures on female membership of parties are difficult to obtain, but accounts from my interviews with Members of the Legislative Assembly (MLAs) suggest that no party save perhaps the CPI (M) in West Bengal have more than 10 per cent female membership, and even there, no women are to be found in the state-level central committee.[11]

One reason that parties are ill-equipped to attract women that is rarely mentioned in analyses of South Asian politics is that parties represent an arena of sexual danger for women, and political competition brings risks of physical and sexual assault. This is not a problem for the elite women, but for others, participation in branch-level politics can be sexually compromising, exposing women to the sexual attentions of male party members.[12] In Bangladesh and Pakistan, politically active women who are not protected by high-level males are sometimes threatened with sexual assault (Jahan, 1982). Perhaps this is the reason that Jayalalitha has formed all-female branches of her AIADMK — to create sexually safe arenas in which to capture women's political energies. Parties that are highly disciplined at the branch level, such as the CPI(M) or the TDP, are reported not to suffer so greatly from this problem. Likewise, parties organized on the basis of religious or ethnic chauvinism may also offer women more sexual security than do secular parties because of their traditional and therefore protective take on women's sexual integrity. Some South Asian feminist political scientists worry that this may be one of the reasons for the apparent effectiveness of religious conservative associations in attracting women, notably the family of militant Hindu chauvinist associations supporting the BJP (Basu, 1995; Sarkar and Butalia, 1995).

The point is that the ways women are recruited (or not) to the leadership and rank-and-file of political parties restrict their opportunities for engaging in corrupt activities. These restrictions have to do with women's relative exclusion from male patronage networks, and the sexual danger associated with inclusion. The policy of simply increasing the numbers of women in the political arena through reserved seats has still barely altered these patterns of exclusion in parties. There is little evidence yet that parties are responding to the increased numbers of women with political experience by recruiting or promoting them. This is because, to put it crudely, it is not women's skills or experience or talent or charisma or even hard work that matters to parties — it is mainly their gender and their family connections. Under the circumstances, if women do exhibit less corrupt reactions than men to opportunities

---

11. It is extremely difficult to obtain gender-disaggregated figures for party membership, let alone figures for aggregate membership, as parties prefer to remain vague on this point to suggest that they have a very broad, if not explicitly signed-up and fee-paying, grassroots membership.

12. These assertions are based upon interviews with and observations of women activists in political parties and in the women's movement in Bangladesh and India.

for illicit earnings, that may simply be a sign of their freshness in office, lack of familiarity with ways of subverting the rules, and an understandable eagerness to prove themselves worthy of public office — effects that can wear off with time.

The Bureaucracy

What about women public servants: how does gender shape their opportunity structure when it comes to corruption? There are obstacles to women's employment in public bureaucracies, particularly at senior levels, the world over. Quite aside from structural problems stemming from sex-typing of women in the education system and labour markets, and from the competing demands of women's private lives, the civil service in many countries has acquired an elitist culture and has institutionalized male privilege and superiority. In South Asia, the highly competitive selection process and demanding training have been noted, until recently, for their ability to instil high levels of commitment, professionalism and probity (Heginbotham, 1975; Kothari and Roy, 1969; Potter, 1986). The selection and training processes in these professional administrative services have attracted less study for their gender biases, but percentages of women to be found in these services remain low. In Bangladesh, there is a recruitment quota system in the civil service: since 1972, about 15 per cent of posts have been reserved for women. This has in practice become a maximum ceiling for women recruits, rather than a minimum threshold.

For the few women at higher levels of public bureaucracies in South Asia, and the larger numbers at lower levels, opportunities for engagement in illicit income generation can be expected to be limited in the same ways as they are for women in politics. Women bureaucrats will have less access to networks for illicit activity — for instance through links with business — than men.[13] They are likely to have limited access to other patronage networks unless they wish to risk putting their sexual propriety on the line. This will be particularly the case in countries such as Bangladesh and Pakistan that have witnessed a contemporary stiffening of Islamic mores in public life. In notes made a decade ago whilst interviewing relatively senior women in government development service bureaucracies in Bangladesh, I uncovered a number of laments made by women: they felt isolated at the workplace because there were so few other senior women and they simply could not interact with men. They felt they had been shunted into the least interesting and attractive positions, positions that were almost always gender stereotyped. They felt that their prospects for promotion or even for moving horizontally to better posts in the bureaucracy were limited because of their inability or unwillingness

---

13. For a discussion of the importance of business links in the corruption of officials, see Honour et al. (1998: 195).

to curry favour with senior men (as this could only be misconstrued), or to offer bribes to party workers or to senior bureaucrats.

The bulk of my interviewees were lower-level government staff, field-workers on the state's flagship micro-finance programme. On revisiting my fieldnotes, I was reminded of cases that I did not follow up in my search for 'local heroes'. These were rumours about fieldworkers who were bending the rules or stealing money. The types of corrupt activities involved were most commonly the siphoning-off of a 'commission' from the tiny loan given to each woman. More rarely, bigger frauds were attempted — for instance encouraging villagers to invest in some business from which the fieldworker was due to profit. Almost always, reports of this kind of activity were accompanied by scandalized accounts of sexual impropriety. Such cases were rare, and differed from the types of corrupt acts of which male fieldworkers were accused. Male fieldworkers might, for instance, make deals with local elite men whereby it was agreed that credit money could go to the wives of these elites (who were not eligible for loans because they were not poor), or they might agree with local politicians to focus loan-giving activity on that politician's constituency in exchange for a healthy commission.

Women fieldworkers tended not to engage in these kinds of deals because of the impropriety of working in this way with non-kin male strangers. But there was another type of rule-bending to which women fieldworkers admitted, and to which men did not, that was viewed with approval by women fieldworkers and women villagers alike. I found that the women fieldworkers who helped their loanees get the best returns on their money were the ones who encouraged them to engage in activities on the margins of 'straight' market engagement: speculative purchasing and hoarding of commodities like rice or firewood for re-sale at high prices in lean seasons, on-lending at high interest rates to poorer women, adulterating products by dilution or alteration (for instance, putting chili into vegetable oil and selling it as the expensive mustard-seed oil) or illegal cross-border trading in saris and other Indian goods (in a word — smuggling).

The finding that women fieldworkers tried, when they could, to bend rules to their own or their clients' advantage may suggest that opportunities for corrupt acts or illicit earning may be more open to women when these arise in a socially acceptable environment — when there are larger numbers of female staff with whom one can collude, or when there are female clients to either abuse or collude with. The studies mentioned earlier on the abuse of patients by nurses and midwives in two African countries (Jewkes et al., 1998; Sargent, 1989) likewise suggests that in a female-dominant working environment, or where women professionals are dealing with women clients or with a socially inferior class, women professionals are not averse to extorting unofficial 'payments' for services that ought to be provided as a right.

Of course, the discussion presented here is not based upon reliable evidence: much more research is needed on the interactions between women bureaucrats and clients across a range of public services to determine if indeed there are more opportunities for illicit earnings in female-dominant public environments where the sexual risk of engaging in corrupt acts is reduced. My point has been to suggest that whatever the response of women to such opportunities, we have to note that the opportunities for corruption that are open to women are themselves limited by sexual controls and their exclusion from male networks.

GENDER AND CORRUPTION: THE QUESTIONS WE OUGHT TO ASK

One question not currently asked in the myth-making around gender and corruption is whether women face different forms of abusive or corrupt behaviour from public officials than men. Are women asked for bribes less often than men because they are not seen to have as much money? Or do they tend, as home-managers, to face corruption of different types and at different levels than men working in the formal economy — 'informal' payments for public services, payments that are not measured in formal indices of corruption levels? Is the 'currency' of corruption sometimes sexual harassment or abuse? For instance, do officials extort sexual favours, rather than money, in return for services? Evidence that women managers of firms in Georgia may pay fewer bribes (Swamy et al., 2001) must be tested against the proposition that they may be asked for bribes less frequently by male officials than are male business managers. These are questions about gendered opportunity structures in corrupt exchanges.

By suggesting that corrupt practices may function differently by gender, I am suggesting that in all the excitement about the potential of exploiting supposed feminine virtues in the fight against corruption (what can women do for good governance?) we might overlook the challenge of combating corruption in ways that respond to women's concerns (what governments should be doing for women).

To expect that women's gender alone can act as a magic bullet to resolve a corruption problem that is much bigger than they are, that is systemic, is unrealistic to say the least. It reflects not just wishful but almost desperate thinking. If women do exhibit preferences for less corrupt behaviour, that may simply be because they have been excluded from opportunities for such behaviour, and that effect is bound to change over time as greater numbers of women enter public office. The state in Peru can only afford to pay women traffic cops in Lima a salary of just 200 dollars a month; not enough to keep a family alive. Men previously in these jobs had to supplement the salary by demanding bribes from motorists to let them off real or trumped-up traffic violations, or by selling them tickets for non-existent police charity barbeques. Women traffic officers have not yet stooped to this, perhaps out of pride in their work and also out of a desire to maintain the image of sexual purity, not taking money from strange men. But their families still have to be fed. I am afraid that women's exemplary performance in this area is a cousin to their performance in the micro-finance field: their success in managing on so little, and in managing with such impeccable credentials, is contingent on their exercise of a female-identified behavioural pattern — self-exploitation. Is that a good thing? Under the circumstances, when we look at the petty corruption encouraged in borrowers by female fieldworkers on micro-finances in Bangladesh in the late 1980s, should we read this not as a sign of venality, but of a type of rebellious empowerment simply not permitted to women in the disciplined and clean development world they are expected to construct?

If there is one thing of which we can be sure, it is this: women will not passively conform to the idealized notions of their finer moral nature when they have families to feed and if there is money to be made from public office. A massive cultural change is underway in the public sector the world over: more and more women are entering public sector jobs and elected public office. They are bound to bring changes of style and substance, and not all in the ways that the World Bank would like to predict. Their actions will be a response to the structural contexts in which they operate. As subalternized recent entrants, unschooled in the qualities possessed by the political and administrative establishments and therefore unable to compete directly with them, they may well experiment with patterns of leadership and management that could demonstrate impeccable integrity. Or they might do the opposite, and damage democratic accountability systems.

It is a huge exaggeration to say that women are now seen as a panacea for problems of corruption in politics and public bureaucracies by the World Bank or other major development agencies. However, now that an instrumentalist argument may be available for advancing women's presence in politics and the public service, the Bank and other development agencies are taking more interest than before in the challenges of promoting women in public life. My concern in this contribution has not been to prove or disprove assertions that women are less corrupt than men. Rather, I am concerned about the way the seductiveness of a hunch about a feminine reluctance for dirty dealing is rushed into the status of a home truth in a context where 'bad governance' is now seen as the reason why countries stay poor, and donors are all looking for a quick fix for that problem. In the meantime, insufficient attention is paid to the possible reasons why women may be exhibiting greater integrity in public dealings. It may well be that women are demonstrating less corrupt behaviour when in public office precisely because they are generally excluded from male-dominated patronage and power networks in political parties and public bureaucracies. A policy to engineer more access for women to these arenas may either produce a sub-set of public actors who are relatively isolated from the arenas in which real power is exercised, or it may mean that women make their way into these still unreformed power arenas, and join in the take. Investing in the myth of women's incorruptible nature instead of investigating the reasons for that behaviour will postpone the institutional reform necessary for a transformation of public institutions in the interests of gender and social equity.

REFERENCES

Baer, D. L. (1999) 'Political Parties: The Missing Variable in Women and Politics Research'. *Political Research Quarterly* 46(3): 547–76.

Bannerjee, M. (2004) 'Populist Leadership in West Bengal and Tamil Nadu: Mamata and Jayalaitha Compared', in R. Jenkins (ed.) *Regional Reflections. Comparing Politics Across India's States*, pp. 285–96. New Delhi: Oxford University Press.

Basu, A. (1995) 'Feminism Inverted: The Gendered Imagery and Real Women of Hindu Nationalism', in T. Sarkar and U. Butalia (eds) *Women and the Hindu Right: A Collection of Essays*, pp. 181–215. New Delhi: Kali for Women.

Burrell, B. C. (1994) *A Woman's Place is in the House*. Ann Arbor, MI: University of Michigan Press.

Chattopadhyay, R. and E. Duflo (2001) 'Women as Policy Makers: Evidence from an India-Wide Randomized Policy Experiment'. NBER Working Paper no 8615. New York: National Bureau of Economic Research.

Datta, B. (ed.) (1998) *And Who Will Make the Chapatis? A Study of All-Women Panchayats in Maharashtra*. Calcutta: Stree.

Dollar, D., R. Fisman and R. Gatti (2001) 'Are Women Really the "Fairer" Sex? Corruption and Women in Government', *Journal of Economic Behavior and Organization* 26(4): 423–9.

Freud, S. (1925) 'Some Psychical Consequences of the Anatomical Distinction Between the Sexes', in J. Strachey (ed.) *The Standard Edition of the Complete Psychological World of Sigmund Freud, Vol. XIX*, pp. 243–58. London: The Hogarth Press.

Gilligan, C. (1982) *In a Different Voice: Psychological Theory and Women's Development*. Cambridge, MA: Harvard University Press.

Goetz, A. M. (2001) *Women Development Workers Implementing Rural Credit Programmes in Bangladesh*. Dhaka: The University Press Limited.

Goetz, A. M. (2003) 'The Problem with Patronage: Constraints on Women's Political Effectiveness in Uganda', in A. M. Goetz and S. Hassim (eds) *No Shortcuts to Power: African Women in Politics and Policy-Making*, pp. 110–39. London: Zed Press.

Halloran, R. (1998) 'Asia's Women Leaders on the Outs'. *Global Beat Issue Brief* No 34 (6 May). New York: Global Reporting Network Publications. Available online: www.nyu.edu/globalbeat/pubs/ib34.html

Hassim, S. (2003) 'Representation, Participation and Democratic Effectiveness: Feminist Challenges to Representative Democracy in South Africa', in A. M. Goetz and S. Hassim (eds) *No Shortcuts to Power: African Women in Politics and Policy-Making*, pp. 81–109. London: Zed Press.

The Herald Tribune (2003) 'Mexico is Gaining on Smugglers' (7 June).

Heginbotham, S. J. (1975) *Cultures in Conflict: The Four Faces of Indian Bureaucracy*. New York: Columbia University Press.

Honour, T., J. Barry, and S. Palnitkar (1998) 'Gender and Public Service: A Case Study of Mumbai', *International Journal of Public Sector Management* 11(2/3): 88–200.

Jaffrelot, C. (2003) *India's Silent Revolution: The Rise of the Lower Castes in North India*. London: Hurst and Company.

Jahan, R. (1982) 'Purdah and Participation: Women in the Politics of Bangladesh', in H. Papanek and G. Minault (eds) *Separate Worlds: Studies of Purdah in South Asia*. Columbia, MO: South Asia Books.

Jewkes, R., N. Abrahams and Z. Mvo (1998) 'Why do Nurses Abuse Patients? Reflections from South African Obstetric Services', *Social Science and Medicine* 47(11): 1781–95.

Jónasdóttir, A. (1988) 'On the Concept of Interest, Women's Interests, and the Limitations of
Interest Theory', in K. Jones and A. Jónasdóttir *The Political Interests of Gender: Developing
Theory and Research with a Feminist Face*, pp. 33–65. London: Sage.

Kothari, S. and R. Roy (1969) *Relations Between Politicians and Administrators at the District
Level*. New Delhi: Indian Institute of Public Administration and the Centre for Applied
Politics.

Kudva, N. (2003) 'Engineering Elections: The Experiences of Women in *Panchayati Raj* in
Karnataka, India', *International Journal of Politics, Culture and Society* 16(3): 445–64.

Lloyd, G. (1984) *The Man of Reason: 'Male' and 'Female' in Western Philosophy*. Minneapolis,
MN: University of Minnesota Press.

Mayaram, S. and P. Pal (1996) 'The Politics of Women's Reservation: Women Panchayat Representatives in Rajasthan, Performance, Problems, and Potential'. Jaipur Institute of Development Studies Working Paper No 074. Jaipur: Institute of Development Studies.

Meintjes, S. (2003) 'The Politics of Engagement. Women Transforming the Policy Process:
Domestic Violence Legislation in South Africa', in A. M. Goetz and S. Hassim (eds) *No
Shortcuts to Power: African Women in Politics and Policy-Making*, pp. 140–59. London: Zed
Press.

Meier, Kenneth J., Joseph Stewart, Jr. and Robert E. England (1989) *Race, Class, and Education:
The Politics of Second-Generation Discrimination*. Madison, WI: University of Wisconsin
Press.

Moore, M. (2002) 'Elites Oppose the Development of Political Parties (Russia)', *Governance and
Development Review* (January). Available online: www.ids.ac.uk/gdr/reviews/review-01.html

Norris, P. (1993) 'Conclusions: Comparing Legislative Recruitment', in J. Lovenduski and P.
Norris (eds) Gender and Party Politics, pp. 309–30. London: Sage.

Okin, S. M. (1979) *Women in Western Political Thought*. Princeton, NJ: Princeton University
Press.

Perrigo, S. (1996) 'Women and Change in the Labour Party', in J. Lovenduski and P. Norris (eds)
Women in Politics, pp. 118–31. Oxford: Oxford University Press.

Phillips, A. (1991) *Engendering Democracy*. Cambridge: Polity Press.

Potter, D. C. (1986) *India's Political Administrators 1919–1983*. Oxford: Clarendon Press.

Randall, V. and L. Svasand (2002) 'Party Institutionalization in New Democracies', *Party Politics*
8(1): 5–29.

Rule, W. and S. Hill (1999) 'Ain't I a Voter? Voting Rights for Women'. Takoma Park,
MD: Center for Voting and Democracy. Available online: http://www.fairvote.org/women/
voting_rights.htm

Sargent, C. (1989) *Maternity, Medicine, and Power: Reproductive Decisions in Urban Benin*.
Berkeley, CA: University of California Press.

Sarkar, T. and U. Butalia (eds) (1995) *Women and the Hindu Right: A Collection of Essays*. New
Delhi: Kali for Women.

Schwartz, J. (1984) *The Sexual Politics of Jean-Jacques Rousseau*. Chicago, IL: University of
Chicago Press.

Selden, S. C. (1997) *The Promise of Representative Bureaucracy*. Armonk, NY: M. E. Sharpe.

Short, C. (1996) 'Women and the Labour Party', in J. Lovenduski and P. Norris (eds) *Women in
Politics*, pp. 17–25. Oxford: Oxford University Press.

Simmons, R. (1996) 'Women's Lives in Transition: A Qualitative Analysis of the Fertility Decline
in Bangladesh', *Studies in Family Planning* 27(5): 251–68.

Simmons, Ann M. and Robin Wright (2000) 'Gender Quotas puts Uganda in Role of Rights
Pioneer', *LA Times* 23 February.

Sung, H. (2003) 'Fairer Sex or Fairer System? Gender and Corruption Revisited', *Social Forces*
82(2): 703–23.

Swamy, A., S. Knack, Y. Lee and O. Azfar (2001) 'Gender and Corruption', *Journal of Development Economics* 64(1): 25–55.

Waylen, G. (2000) 'Gender and Democratic Politics: A Comparative Analysis of Consolidation in Argentina and Chile', *Journal of Latin American Studies* 32(3): 765–94.

World Bank (2001) *Engendering Development through Gender Equality in Rights, Resources and Voice*. Oxford: Oxford University Press.

6

Resolving Risk? Marriage and Creative Conjugality

Cecile Jackson

As a woman with both a weakness for gambling and impulse, and a knee-jerk response to essentialisms, I have always been rather sceptical about generalizations that women are more risk averse than men. Yet this is a powerful assumption made in everyday discourse and social science understandings of human behaviour. It also has a degree of support from economics and psychology; women appear to be more risk averse than men in investment behaviour (Eckel and Grossman, 2003; Olsen and Cox, 2001), experimental economics of risk behaviour (Carlsson et al., 2001), and health management (Rosen et al., 2003). However, the experimental evidence has been questioned by work showing that much depends on context, there being gender differences in abstract gambles but not in specific investment decisions. Schubert et al. (1999) find that gender differences in risk attitudes depend on differences in opportunity sets, and apparent gender differences to risk in investment decisions are actually gender differences in attitudes to ambiguity, since they depend on information which has ambiguous probability information. Women have a higher ambiguity aversion than men in investment decisions due to lower confidence in their knowledge and information (Schubert et al., 2000: 6).[1]

Alongside the idea of women as risk averse, is the concern that they also have less access to insurance mechanisms than men. After considering risk behaviour and gender relations in examples from African agrarian societies, I argue that their position is mediated by marriage in important ways, and reflect on whether women are disadvantaged in access to insurance. Certainly, this may be true of formal insurance institutions, but is it still true when the institutions of kinship and marriage are considered as insurance institutions, as they most certainly are, since they legitimate entitlements? A consideration of risk behaviour and insurance therefore requires examination of a set of deeper mother-myths about households and marriage in gender analysis, in their popular and applied forms; that women and men within domestic groups have separate and opposing interests; that disaggregating the household (an article of belief for feminist research) amounts to differentiating the interests of men and women, husbands and wives, and comparing them as gender categories; and that marriage is largely a mechanism of subordination. I argue

I would like to thank Andrea Cornwall for her incisive and helpful comments on this chapter; as usual, the weaknesses are my responsibility alone.

1. The detail of this complex experiment suggests the hypothesis that women may both perceive higher risks and also be more risk-tolerant than men (Schubert et al., 2000: 7).

that we should not lose sight of the shared interests of women and men in domestic groups, and the perceived and potential value of marriage to women.

One feature of myths is their taken-for-granted character, such that they may not necessarily be regularly articulated because they have a self-evident quality. Indeed, that which is vigorously and overtly debated clearly has a more provisional and contested position within the field, whilst that which is not, is more doxic — that is, it forms part of the unquestioned feminist habitus, the dispositions of thought which may be reproduced over generations of scholars. In naming and discussing these 'myths' (I am ambivalent about the term in this context) relating to marriage, I aim not at wholesale rejection and substitution, but simply at dredging them up from our discursive sediments and subjecting them to renewed scrutiny.

RISK AND WOMEN: QUESTIONING THE ORTHODOXY

Since the 1990s, influential publications of development institutions have emphasized that rural women are 'caretakers of household food security' (IFPRI, 2002: 153), and 'the key to food security' (as in the title of one such paper), and that they play a major role in 'ensuring food security in the developing world' (Quisumbing et al., 1995). This popular consensus suggests that women do the great majority of farm work, domestic labour and food processing and preparation, and are primarily concerned with food crop production rather than 'cash crops'; yet they own the least property, are the worst nourished and the most overworked (Price Gittinger et al., 1990: 3) and reducing gender disparities will produce better food and nutrition for all, particularly children. Finally, women are said to use their incomes to invest in children's nutrition and education to a greater extent than men do (IFPRI, 2002: 153), and thus women's incomes are especially important to household food security. This is sometimes put down to the bad behaviour of men (wine, women and song) but latterly the impact of different income flows (smaller and more frequent for women, larger and more infrequent for men) on expenditure patterns has been partly recognized. Whatever the pathway, it is argued that women can be relied upon to use incomes to the best advantage of all household members. The implications are that women take a 'safety first' approach in which food production is prioritized over cash crops, and incomes are invested in household nutrition and education.

Thus, investing in women is investing in those who are at the sharp end of maintaining food security. Food security, however, continues to be seen as primarily based on food production rather than entitlements, and women are represented as having a special (if not exclusive) commitment to less risky food crops rather than more risky cash crops. These generalizations are all debatable, of course, but what is striking about them is the extent to which such research continues to work with the idea of women as a separate category for comparative analysis alongside men as a separate category, without taking on board the idea of gender as social relations.[2] Households embody both separate and shared well-being and interests, their members both conflict and co-operate, and these intersections are absolutely critical to the workings of gender. Why are they muted? At least part of the answer must lie in the domination of these research organizations by economists, for whom gender disaggregation and comparison is methodologically more tractable than researching the relational significance of gender. The challenge of the relational and the recursive has been difficult to deliver, compared to the relative simplicity of gender category comparisons. Analysing behaviour in ways which take account of social relations is a complex matter but no less important as a consequence. One experimental study of risk aversion in northern Zambia (Wik et al., 2004) finds that women are more risk averse than men, but this result comes from including gender as simply a factor along with wealth, age and so on in experimental games, and does not consider how it works as a social relation — that is, how it may have contingent effects. To do this one needs methods which show how risk behaviour varies with particular sets of relations with men within households.

The following example, taken from a short research project (Balderrama et al., 1987) in a dry communal area, Chivi, in southern Zimbabwe in 1987,[3] suggests the need to rethink some of these assumptions. The task set for the research team was to investigate why there was a steady shift to maize cultivation in a region agro-climatically better suited to millet cultivation.[4] Maize needs more rainfall to succeed; millet can be successfully grown on much less rainfall, and therefore maize is a much riskier crop. Despite a major drought in 1982/3, when massive numbers of cattle died, and a drought in 1986/7, the data showed a shift to maize cultivation. Our research established, through analysis of seventy-four years of rainfall data, that the rainfall requirements for maize are met in only ten of these years, while those for maximum yield for millets are met in forty-four of the seventy-four years, and for good yields in sixty-one of the seventy-four years. The better storage life of millet (several years) compared to maize (ten months) also makes it better for drought-prone regions.

Yet maize has come to dominate the cropped area, accounting for about 60 per cent in 1985/6 compared to 42 per cent in 1974/5, whilst small grains fell from 33 per cent in 1974/5 to 19 per cent in 1985/6. Respondents confirmed a swing towards maize, despite the risk. Millets are of low productivity in infertile soils, and many younger people prefer the taste of maize, but most significant in explaining preference were the labour requirements. Labour

---

2. Interestingly it is the participant discussion, in IFPRI (2002: 162), which raises the criticism of the 'need to look not at women in isolation, but rather at how women and men relate to each other'.
3. Ken Wilson and Ian Scoones played an important role in stimulating the investigation of risk and cropping patterns pursued in this research project.
4. Other crops grown are sorghum, groundnuts and bambara nuts, but maize and millet are the major staple crops.

inputs per hectare for land preparation (a male task) are the same for maize and millets, but the planting and harvesting and processing demands (women's work) are much higher for millets, over four times as much. While maize is cut, dehusked, and then mechanically milled, millets by contrast, require enormous hand processing time.

The preference for maize over millet was forcefully expressed by women. As we observed:

> In Shona society women have no responsibility to provide food in times of drought. They are obliged to provide subsistence food, and before the land Husbandry Act of 1951 when they had their own farms, women would feed their families from their granaries first and then eat from the granaries of the husband. If and when this became empty he would have to sell livestock or obtain food in some other way. (Balderama et al., 1987: 46)[5]

It remains the responsibility of the husband to provide for the family in times of crisis such as drought. The conjugal contract should not be seen as a set of norms and obligations which hold in all circumstances, for clearly in normal years and in drought years these expectations are not the same. The context is one of high out-migration by men to work in urban centres, and married women, in the absence of husbands, can exercise their preferences for maize over millet and plant more of the former, to minimize the labour of processing; in the event of crop failure, the problem is the husband's. How far women are prepared to take risks with crop choices will depend upon their assessment of a husband's ability to provide insurance. Judgements about the durability of a marriage and reliability of remittances matter here and a key factor will be a husband's livelihood portfolio, for example, holding livestock or having relatively secure off-farm employment. Study data confirmed that the ratio of maize to millet is higher in better-off households.

Although the switch to maize from millet was also explained by factors other than gender relations within households, the primary explanation seemed to be that since the 1970s an increasing proportion of women managed farms, as a consequence of male migration to work; the strong preference of women for maize as a result of the very heavy processing labour demands of millets,[6] in a context where the conjugal contract puts limits on women's obligations to provide food, and where men have other important sources of income, meant that women were less risk averse than men, as revealed in their crop choices. However, it is not my intention to substitute one generalization, women are less risk averse than men, for another, women are more risk averse than men, but to show how unsatisfactory these generalizations are, since behaviour in relation to risk is dependent on gender *relations* not on gender *characteristics*.

5. This sequential use of women's crops before men's crops has been noted in many other societies, for example amongst non-secluded Hausa of Northern Nigeria; see Cooper (1997).
6. Han Seur notes that in Serenje District, Zambia, women in the 1950s were not interested in extending cultivation of millet because of the high labour demand in weeding; they preferred to extend their gardens of local maize and cassava rather than grow millet (Seur, 1992: 231)

The ways in which conjugality changes in times of crop failure need to be recognized. It may also be the case that a further shift occurs in times of real famine. In Megan Vaughan's study of the 1949 famine in Nyasaland (Malawi), she reports that as the crisis developed men went back to areas they had migrated from to seek help from their relatives:

> It was seen as a husband's duty to find food for his wife and family, and those men who did not do this were chided in the women's songs: 'What type of husband are you/Staying at home with the women?/The other men are off to Mwanza now/Why not you? You just stay here and your only "work"/Is to fondle women'. (Vaughan, 1985: 186)

However, often the men just stayed away until the famine was over, or married in other areas to which they had gone for food, and 1949 is known as the year of many divorces. One pounding song went 'We have suffered this year/Our men are divorcing us/Oh what shall we do with this hunger?' (ibid.: 189). Men who returned after the famine to attempt reconciliation were often rejected. As Vaughan concludes (ibid.: 201):

> The oral testimonies emphasise that whether or not women and their families suffered often depended on unquantifiable factors of marital breakdown, affection, reliability and so on. For instance, some of the women whose husbands were labour migrants were relatively privileged in having cash remittances at their disposal. Those women whose husbands sent nothing, however, were among the more vulnerable groups in the community when the famine struck.

In Vaughan's account, conjugal obligations stimulate men during famine to seek food through migration to less affected areas, and through labour and the exercise of kin-based entitlements, whilst women tend to remain with children within famine areas, and are thus dependent on the husband's commitments to conjugal obligations. When these break down, families fragment, men seek only individual survival, and then women are extremely vulnerable.[7] One might conclude that marriage itself is an important form of food security for women. A study of adult health and drought in Zimbabwe found that women's body mass index (BMI) fell during the 1994/5 drought, while men's did not, and that 'livestock held [by the household] in the year before the drought had a positive impact on the BMI of women who experienced drought (this relationship did not hold for men)' (Hoddinott and Kinsey, 2003: 132–3). Wives of men with livestock retained their BMIs during drought, as did daughters-in-law with (it is suggested) remitting husbands, but unmarried daughters did not. This suggests the real value of the conjugal contract in times of crisis. It also signals the gendered identities of men and how these affect their risk behaviour, both as individuals and in roles with responsibilities for others — a very neglected but clearly important topic, particularly in

---

7. However, overall mortality of men in times of famine tends to be greater than that of women as a result of the ability of women to survive at lower BMI, as well as other factors.

relation to the apparently increasing disengagement of men from domestic groups, discussed below.

What to make of this? This research seems to me to demonstrate a few points with broader relevance to the discussion of risk. Clearly, risk behaviour needs to be regarded with an intrahousehold perspective, rather than always treating households as undifferentiated units. Rosenzweig gives an economic analysis of how marriage exogamy may function as a risk insurance mechanism in rain dependent agro-ecosystems in south India, concluding that 'the common survey practice in which the household is the sampling unit... impede[s] tests of intrafamily and intrahousehold risk-sharing hypotheses' (Rozenzweig, 1988: 249).

Internal differentiation means that individuals within households are not uniform and substitutable, it means their well-being and their interests are both separate as well as shared, and that they conflict and co-operate in variable and changing ways over a life course. But this is emphatically *not* to suggest that households are composed of individuals with entirely separate interests, an assumption which seems to me to lie beneath the problematic treatment of women as a category. It is to recognize that the relations between women and men in households, for example of conjugality, are important mediating elements in the preferences and actions of individuals, constitute relations of power which frame the possibilities for such individuals, and are never simply oppositional but have varying degrees of solidarity inhering simultaneously in them.

For a woman who is a wife as well as a farmer, it matters a great deal what the cultural content of conjugal expectations is, and what are seen as legitimate grounds for deviation; it matters how one is placed in relation to a husband in terms of relative income control, status, social regard, role performance, and many other factors, and the balance between shared and separate interests matters too. Therefore I can envisage women being, as in the Zimbabwean example, individually willing to take crop risks in the judgement that for the household collectively there is insurance against failure — in the shape of a husband, with a set of resources that can be drawn down in these circumstances. And labour avoidance may be a more powerful influence on choices and actions than risk avoidance, where these are incompatible. In these circumstances one might hypothesize that secure marriage to a good provider spouse allows more risk taking by women, and risk aversion reflects the converse. This may be true up to a point, but the Zambian case below shows a further stage of risk taking, when women entrepreneurs can find that success places a severe strain on marriage. Gender differentials in risk behaviour are not an explanation of anything, nor can they be pinned to the categories women and men, but instead pose questions about the nature of social relations between the sexes.

It is not a good idea to either imagine that preferences and risk behaviour of male household heads can be taken to reflect that of all members within the household, or to separate out women from the context of household relations and suggest they are reliably risk averse and oriented to subsistence and food security in a narrow sense of food production. A husband may be food security personified. Women make investments which are geared to insurance against divorce, which signals the value of marriage, a point to which I return below. For example, amongst the Hausa women the institution of *biki* (bond friendship) unites two women in repeated gift giving and receiving, which endures over long periods, often much longer than marriages which are notoriously unstable in Hausaland (Jackson, 1996; see also Hill, 1972). Relations with kin, both natal and marital, can serve the same purpose — for example, the practice of wives secretly siphoning off food and other resources from husbands to parents and siblings is a very common phenomenon, effectively maintaining the support of natal kin in the event of marital failure.

Does it matter that women are assumed to be more risk averse than men? One study of the supposed greater risk aversion of women investment managers makes the comment that, '[A]lthough the precise reason for this gender difference in risk taking is unknown, it appears to be related to evolutionary and social factors' (Olsen and Cox, 2001: 29), which shows how neatly this stereotype naturalizes gender difference. It is then a small step for these 'natural' differences to be used to justify discrimination. Schubert et al. (2000) point out that female investment managers face glass ceilings in promotion since it is widely believed that women are incapable of taking the risks that bring high returns in financial management (see also McDowell, 1997).

The implication of the idea that women are risk averse is that women are less innovative and entrepreneurial than men, since both innovation and enterprise require a degree of risk taking. This vision is all of a piece with other stereotypes of rural women, for example, that they are confined to subsistence production rather than 'cash' cropping. Despite contending voices (Guyer, 1988b; Whitehead, 1991b), Boserupian stereotypes remain pervasive, in which 'population growth, colonial rule, migration, urban employment, the introduction of the plough, the penetration of capitalism, or the development of, or access to, productive resources — have the marginalisation of women as their final and inevitable outcome', and 'all innovations are devoted to cash crops which are cultivated by men' (Seur, 1992: 228).

By contrast, Seur's study of enterprising women farmers in Serenje District of Zambia finds the majority of women growing hybrid maize and runner beans for sale in town: between 1985 and 1988 the proportion of marketed hybrid maize cultivated by women on their own fields rose from 19 per cent to 34 per cent (ibid.: 262), despite markedly lower levels of plough and oxen ownership by women. When Seur reads translated passages of Boserup's book to his respondents, they disagree strongly: Mrs Yumba comments 'nowadays a man, he is still a *sulutan* (the head of a village or farm); but he is a halfway *sulutani* now, because his wife is independent. She sells her own maize, so she has her own money. Therefore she cannot respect her husband because of his money. Women now consider themselves to be men' (ibid.: 293). Her son comments that '[Boserup] also says that when people start growing crops for money, a woman becomes the helper of her husband. Ah, no, most women here do not want to become helpers, they have their own fields of maize here' (ibid.: 294).

One such woman farmer bought oxen and plough and expanded her hybrid maize cultivation from 194 bags in 1984, to 270 bags in 1986 and nearly 500 bags in 1988 (ibid.: 243). Others experimented with a number of crops produced for sale in urban markets and made a great success of runner beans. Whilst these women farmers faced some formidable gender-based obstacles (witchcraft accusations, reluctance of male labourers to work for women, disadvantages in borrowing money), and complained about 'the fact that their husbands forced them to spend a relatively large part of their personal income for the benefit of the whole household [which] was delaying their emergence as commercially oriented farmers' (ibid.: 311), they nevertheless have continued to take risks, innovate and adopt new technologies. Incidentally, it is worth noting their somewhat different take on women's family-oriented expenditure to that commonly encountered in development literature, where the belief that women *choose* to spend money on family is one to which some feminists and development economists are firmly attached. Seur's accounts of how these successful commercial women farmers emerged, highlights many factors common to business success anywhere for either gender, but all of them had difficulties sustaining marriages in situations where they 'overtook' their spouses, and ended up single or in semi-separate arrangements. In the Zambian case we see a pattern of change over some decades in which a small number of early innovators, who experienced considerable marital instability, are named as role models by a large number of the next generation of married women farmers who follow their example by moving into beans and hybrid maize production on various scales.

I am, therefore, far from convinced that women are necessarily more risk averse than men and believe that any such generalizations are unwise. The examples above suggest that the character of conjugality and other intra-household relations mediate behaviour in relation to risk in ways that may encourage risk taking, as in the Zimbabwean case, or inhibit it as in the Zambian case. The Zimbabwean example was one of risk-taking women within an area of marginal agricultural production and subsistence production, where the nature of conjugality allowed women to exercise their preferences for labour-saving staple crops despite their greater uncertainty. Here the conjugal contract operates in ways that may be considered perverse if food security is seen as simply production of staples, but not if food security is envisaged with an entitlements perspective (Sen, 1981), where one set of entitlements are those derived from marriage. Conjugal entitlements, and conjugal entitlement failures, are important in the experience of food insecurity and famine, and in understanding how risk behaviour is gendered.

The Zambian case, by contrast, showed risk-taking women in a more favourable agro-ecological environment. Conjugality had become highly contested, and the subject of ongoing public and private debate, and the expectations of husbands and wives in relation to divisions of labour, divisions of responsibility and divisions of consumption are discursively and practically shifting. Men feel anxious and defensive about women's growing independence, but the establishment of independent farming by women is accepted to a degree which facilitates their increasing involvement in hybrid maize production — although male tolerance of the reshaping of conjugality does have limits and very successful women farmers find it hard to sustain marriage.

If beliefs about women as risk averse play into the naturalization of gendered disadvantage in the financial investment sector, this matters even more pressingly in relation to development studies and practice for two reasons: first, because we have yet to see a proper recognition of the significant mediating role of intrahousehold relations in debates about food security or risk behaviour; and second, because general assumptions about women easily become an unquestioned basis for policy, and the view of women as the bastion of food security, risk averse and disinterested in cash crops or production for markets, implicitly reinforces the focus of support for innovation and adoption of new technology on men, who by contrast appear, as a category, more likely to make effective use of such support. Attaching characteristics to social categories, such as women, is dangerous because development practice has to identify participants and beneficiaries, and categories all too easily become target groups.

INSURANCE, MARRIAGE AND HOUSEHOLDS

Is it the case that women are more exposed to risk than men because they are excluded from social security institutions which insure against risk? This may be true if one excludes kinship and marriage from these institutions, but otherwise I think one could argue that women enjoy particular advantage in relation to legitimate claims on others. Discourses of dependence in many cultures affirm the right of women as daughters, mothers and wives to rely on fathers, sons and husbands for support, provision and protection. This is not to suggest that women are necessarily 'dependants' in any practical or material sense, just that ideas of legitimate dependence can be discursive resources. These latent entitlements have practical value when men are enabled, by employment or agrarian economies, to meet these ideals, but they lose this value when high male unemployment and/or agrarian crises occur. Risk then entails the risk of reliance on a husband of uncertain qualities and in uncertain times, and the danger that by building a conjugal relationship with unquestionable entitlements, by conformity to gender ideals, a woman may have to forego certain actions geared towards autonomy which would otherwise stand her in good stead in the event of a failure in that relationship, or a failure in what Jane Guyer (1988a), in her study of transfers between men and women in marriage in Cameroon, calls the male economy.

Marriage can be seen as a set of (variably conditional) entitlements of value to women, and not only as a relationship of power and inequality which disadvantages them. This section therefore makes some blindingly obvious points, which nevertheless tend to be backgrounded in our efforts to disaggregate the household and forensically uncover women's disadvantages. In making them, I resile from any implication that conventional forms of household organization, kinship and marriage are anywhere gender equitable or desirable, but I do think that these are forms of social co-operation which women participate in, not as gender dupes, but because they have real and perceived attractions. It is important to focus on the ways in which women's agency is directed less to the rejection of these institutions and more towards reforming the terms of such co-operation. This is not a separatist agenda, aimed at individual autonomy, but one focused on remaking gender *relations* in ways more favourable to women.

This section will elaborate the following points. First, marriage is an attractive form of co-operation for many women, with evident potential material advantages. Second, if this is the case, then perhaps the suggestion that the degree of separation in conjugal relations is an index of women's power within that relationship and well-being derived from it deserves examination. Third, conjugality is a more historically changing, dynamic and open field for contestation of the terms of marital co-operation than has perhaps been acknowledged. Last, understanding marriage as a gendered institution must involve situating it within a broader frame of social relations, particularly between generations and siblings, to grasp its meanings and value for women.

The Value of Marriage to Women

The now extensive debate about female headed households and poverty (see for example Chant, 2004; Jackson, 1996) has revealed the variation in the experience of poverty in male and female headed households, which even the conventional *de facto/de jure* distinction fails to capture, and the fallacy of the idea that they represent the poorest of the poor. However, it is also certainly the case that female headed households are generally less likely to be rich than male headed ones, and opting out of conventional male headed households does not offer the reliable route to prosperity which might be expected if patriarchal exploitation of women within the household was quite as effective as supposed. In their work on Botswana, Kossoudji and Mueller (1983) show that the absence of men disadvantages the household, and although female headed households are not always and everywhere poorer than male headed households, they are not always and everywhere richer either. In her analysis of the large and growing numbers of female headed households in Botswana, Bridget O'Laughlin (1998) shows how in recent decades the link between marriage and childbearing has loosened, and increasing numbers of women never marry at all. They do, however, form domestic groups, and '[t]he more dramatic change in the organisation of rural livelihoods is thus the existence of a substantial group of men who, unlike women, never form domestic groups at all' (ibid: 21). Where wage income is critical to livelihoods and survival, growing unemployment has undermined marriage, and 'many men and women do not marry and establish common households because they cannot, not because they do not wish to do so. Their inability to marry both reflects and contributes to the erosion of diffuse bonds of intergenerational and communal solidarity' (ibid.: 24). O'Laughlin argues that '[c]hanges in the organisation of rural families and households reflect the sustained social exclusion of men from provisioning for their children and consequently. . . from any expectation of support from them in old age' (ibid.: 37). Sharp and Spiegel (1990), in work on South Africa, also show how, in circumstances of male unemployment and destitution, gender confrontation develops and marriage collapses.

The focus in gender analysis on intrahousehold inequality has overshadowed the idea of marriage as a form of gender co-operation which can be beneficial to women. Ann Whitehead has, in an extended body of work, pointed to the complex dependencies and interdependencies in marriage, the incentives for women, deriving from household consumption, to work on male controlled household production, and the deeper mutuality of shared interests which confound analysis of women's interests as only separate and individual (Whitehead, 1990, 1991a, 1991b; Whitehead and Kabeer, 2001). But the predominant approach has been to document women's experience of inequality within marriage, and very few gender studies have addressed the question of what was favourable about marriage for women. In a rare exception, Jane Guyer (1988a) examined the declining incidence of marriage amongst Beti women as a result of bridewealth inflation and decline in widow inheritance or remarriage; she found that unmarried women have smaller incomes than married women who gain from transfers from husbands, and that — although they managed to cover basic expenses and routine consumption through more farming and trade — unmarried women were unable to raise the 'relatively large sums of money needed to pay major medical costs, bridewealth for sons, and children's school fees' (Guyer, 1988a: 167). Guyer was interested in income transfers between men and women and argues that 'it is untenable to claim that male and female expenditure patterns do not interrelate at all' (ibid.: 160). During the cocoa season when men have money from cocoa sales, women 'explicitly discuss and assess the various means of tapping men's incomes ... [Women] look for a variety of ways to redistribute male income, and their success depends on the general state of the male economy' (ibid.: 168). For Yoruba women in Nigeria, Cornwall (2002) also shows how, in a context of a contracting male economy, women are finding ways to tap into this economy through extra-marital sexual relations to sustain livelihoods by accessing the resources of men other than husbands.

Thus the critique of the household, revealing the extent of intrahousehold inequalities, should not imply that women's well-being has no relationship at all to the well-being of their husbands. For example, Dercon and Krishnan (2000: 721), in a study of risk sharing in Ethiopian households, find that amongst southern groups risk sharing was incomplete and women bore the brunt of health shocks, but the factor most likely to positively affect risk-sharing behaviour was the extent of male landholdings; those with more land were much less likely to exhibit consumption patterns skewed against women.

Of course the politics of entitlements to support are such that one needs to be a deserving woman, a compliant woman, who performs her gender roles with socially acknowledged success, to be certain of support in the event of unforeseen shocks. By contrast husbands rarely have such recognized claims on wives. The insurance against shocks available to women as wives is arguably greater than many men can call upon, but it is a conditional insurance, and one that is tied to gender ideologies of subordination. The point about women and risk is not that they are fundamentally risk averse because of either their essential natures, or their commitments to children, but that risks are underwritten by symbolic capital, which may only be achieved at a high price. The moral approval earned by the status of 'wife' is necessary to varying degrees; amongst the women brickmakers in Rwanda studied by Jefremovas (1991), an unmarried woman was hounded out of business by mocking and harassment, a married woman brickmaker had to hide to a large extent behind a husband as a sleeping partner, and a widowed brickmaker maintained the ghostly presence of her dead husband as the head of the business. In all cases marriage was necessary to avoid the crippling moral disapproval of female livelihoods independent of men. Of course, married women do not always bask in public approval. They may make discursive use of the moral low ground to gain intra-marital influence by comparatively greater willingness to lose public face, having less to lose in the first place.

To adapt the old saying about capitalism, is the one thing worse than having a husband, having no husband? Alongside the major critique of households and marriage which has defined gender analysis of development we need a counterpoint which recognizes the potential value of both household organization and conjugality to women. Where marriage collapses under pressure of male unemployment, changing reproductive rights and responsibilities, the outcomes are not necessarily advantageous to women. In a small Yoruba town, the declining ability of men to meet material expectations of them as husbands is the backdrop for changing conjugalities in which wives take gift-giving lovers, or invest in independent trading and income control, or choose to live outside marriage altogether. All these carry social vilification. The increasing immorality of women, expressed in a 'collective sigh of despair' (Cornwall, 2002: 964), and their slash and burn or 'eat and run' attitudes to marriage (ibid.: 965) in which they use up a man's resources and then either move on, if they have not got children, or remain and take paying lovers if they have, is the cause of general public criticism.

Sexuality becomes detached from reproduction in women's efforts to compensate for the failures of 'useless' men to provide within marriage. Where confidence in male sharing is dwindling, women use their resources to extend their autonomy by investing in housing and individualized assets; survival pathways for women are shifting from the social (successful motherhood and wifery, and joint consumption) to the individual and the commoditized (individual sexuality, trade and investment). Women's waywardness is tolerated so long as it remains within marriage but independent women are subject to deep disapproval, labelled as voracious *ilemosu*, the contemporary scourge of troublesome wives who abandon children and husbands, and have insatiable appetites for men and money.

Marital meltdown certainly seems to be taking place in many diverse settings. The feminization of poverty in the USA, with mothers and children in poverty traps and 'deadbeat dads', has been recently analysed in relation to the changes that ensued with contraception and abortion in the 1970s. Akerlof et al. (1996) argue that these technologies led to a shift from accepted male responsibility in the event of pre-marital pregnancy (the shotgun marriage), to a denial by men of responsibility for pre-marital pregnancy in circumstances where it is the woman who is responsible for contraception and able to choose abortion if the need arises. They argue that the apparent power accorded to women over reproduction undermined male responsibility, and left those women whose contraception failed, or who rejected abortion, literally holding the baby — alone. Although their analysis is open to debate (see Bledsoe and Guyer, 2000) this may be an example of negative unintended consequences of a positive gender relational shift; the costs to women (as well as children and men) of male disengagement from parenting can be high.

Marriage also has a value beyond the direct material benefits it may offer to women as wives. Even after the death of a husband, a woman may be able to make use of her status as a once-married woman with not only legitimated, if variable, access to marital resources but also a particular social role with performative possibilities. In her analysis of widows in western Kenya, Mutongi (1999) shows how they consciously represent themselves as suffering females, and develop effective narratives designed to elicit sympathy by playing on male notions of ideal masculinity and manliness. Widows make use of their marital status (grief-stricken, helpless, emotional widow) through determined use of public displays of vulnerability. Being an elderly widow is a preferable location to being an elderly single woman, since it allows deployment of ideals of motherhood and marital achievements, and networks of marital kin, with associated obligations, as potential support.

There is one final point on the emotional value of conjugality. Elsewhere I have discussed the significance of patrilocal marriage, as a prevalent social form in rural societies, for women's subjectivities, that is, the experience of departure from natal families, the perpetual stranger status of in-marrying women within the husband's lineage group, and therefore the emotional investments in conjugality, and increasingly in explicit discourses of love, as a kind of gender struggle of younger women (Jackson, 2003). Cornwall (2002) also shows how love talk can be the refuge of men when harking back to an earlier era when marriage meant more than money to women. Perhaps discourses of love are generally promoted by the gender which feels disadvantaged by the power balances within conjugality, a weapon of the (self-perceived) weak in struggles to insist on the value of emotional 'work', loyalty, commitment and affection, beyond material exchanges. But whatever the discursive workings of love talk, there is a reality of emotional exchanges and support within intimate relations, whatever you call it, which marriage can offer. Strong relations with husbands can counter the power of mothers-in-law and fill some of the personal spaces left by distance (social and spatial) from the intimacies of natal kin. It is unwise to imagine that poor women would not find the same enjoyments of conjugality — friendship, sex, commitment, shared parenting pains and pleasures — that people everywhere can experience. The growing emphasis on the conjugal unit rather than the lineage unit, in a number of recent African ethnographies, can be seen as an outcome of women's agency. How then can we see it as just an institution designed by the invisible hand of patriarchy to give men control of women's reproductive bodies and labour power?

Degrees of Separation and Subordination

If marriage has indeed been rather negatively portrayed in gender analysis of development, then is the treatment of the co-operative element of household production and conjugality in danger of being misunderstood through simplifying intrahousehold relations into sets of opposing and individual interests of women and men? This tendency is grounded not only in the feminist work on disaggregating the household and identifying separate gender interests, but also in the myth of the African family which emphasizes descent and lineage groups over marriage and conjugal groups (O'Laughlin, 1995) and thus the belief that African societies are characterized by 'weak conjugal bonds'. O'Laughlin argues that 'we miss important determinants of women's farming strategies if we assume that conjugal relations are unimportant, or if we assume one particular variant of conjugal relations, i.e. the weak conjugal bond' (ibid.: 77).

West African households were the basis of the feminist deconstruction of joint households with pooled incomes, coterminous production, consumption, residence and reproduction functions, and shared utility, and the apparently dramatic separations of members were startling and thrilling in equal measure.[8] For example, in my research in Hausaland in the late 1970s, I

---

8. The model of the unitary household was the focus of enormous and effective gender critique and research from the 1970s, and it has stimulated the development of other models in economics (see, for example, Folbre, 1986; Hart, 1995; Kabeer, 1994) and the testing of these alternatives (Quisumbing, 2003).

encountered households described for the early decades of the twentieth century (with horror by contemporary male observers in the traces left in the Kaduna archives) in which women sold goat manure to their husbands for use on family farms, bought groundnut oil from themselves for cooking family meals, bought grain from husbands at harvest time and resold it to them when prices had risen, and loaned money to husbands (with interest, naturally) when it was required. Conjugal contracts had changed little by the time of my research, and like many others, I found that separate streams of income and clear divisions of gender interests, production and consumption were evident, and unsettling for development studies and economic theory. However, we now seem to have a set of counter-assumptions about households, conjugality and gender, that emphasize the separate over the shared interests in marriage, and conflict over co-operation.

Which particular marriages exhibit high levels of separation of income and activities (where these are found), in the continuum of conjugal practice? O'Laughlin, in her account of control of cotton incomes in Chad, points out that those married women who kept back their cotton incomes and paid their own taxes were 'considered perilously close to breaking the cooking pots, the last thing a woman did before leaving her husband. It was an option most often exercised by childless women or those whose children were already grown' (O'Laughlin, 1995: 78). Similarly, van den Berg (1997) finds for Cameroon that independent clearing of land by women to make their own fields signals marital discord, and separate women's fields can signify trajectories towards divorce in Seur's Zambian study (1992). I think we need to try to take a reflexive step back from the politics of autonomy, to consider rebalancing the treatment of shared and separate interests in marriage, so that we do not assume that shared is bad and separate is good.

Over-disaggregation within the household is difficult and can produce distortions and confusion, for example, over income contribution and control, where researchers seek to attribute income, decision making and consumption to discrete individuals, and a raised feminist eyebrow generally accompanies statements about joint decisions. Naila Kabeer comments on the tendency for gender analysts to read 'jointness' as evidence of male dominance (1998: 14) and the importance of not expecting empowerment to always be associated with individualization. Kabeer's study also demonstrates the complexity of transfers within households and their consequences — symbolic, material and discursive. It is methodologically very difficult to meaningfully individualize income contributions and control (parties earn as individuals and jointly, transfer between themselves, consume individually and jointly, and profound ambiguity surrounds what income control actually means) and such efforts may obscure genuinely joint projects. Guyer (1988a) shows the complexity of understanding patterns of expenditure by women and men within households and discusses how, beneath apparent female expenditure poverty, women and men may be jointly engaged in managing household finance for the education of children. Seur (1992) comments on how wives and husbands collude to establish joint conjugal interests under cover of apparently separate interests, in this case to limit the demands of matri-kin. Separate and shared interests are cultural representations and social acts, and not simply conjugal rules which equate the shared with patriarchy and the separate with women's gender interests.

Creative Conjugality

> It seems analytically valuable to consider all forms of conjugal relations ... as representing a bundle of interactional possibilities ... How these interactional possibilities are utilised by male and female actors is a central, if very complex, question for future research. (Burnham, 1987: 50)

The third point of this section is that conjugality is a performance, and an institution bearing many traces of women's agency, as well as male attempts at control. Change and choice have been increasingly recognized in anthropological approaches to marriage, and 'though women have often been depicted as ... the subordinate bearers of men's children, they have also been shown ... as the primary agents of change in marriage and the family' (Parkin and Nyamwaya, 1987: 16). A Zimbabwean example (Jackson, 1995) illustrates some of this.[9] Zimbabwe exhibits multiple forms of marriage, at least two bodies of law concerned with marriages, and a history of contestation since colonial occupation (Jeater, 1993; Schmidt, 1991). Despite the invention of marriage customs by the rural gerontocracy, women themselves shaped the forms of conjugality which emerged during the colonial period through opportunistic use of the marriage laws and the gender ideologies of settlers as well as missionaries, by the commoditization of sex, by resisting marriage to old men and by marrying young migrant workers who could afford bridewealth.

In Chivi by the mid 1980s, marriage had changed significantly from the supposedly traditional pattern, and many of these changes were beneficial to women, such as the falling age gap between spouses. Being marriageable was easier for women than men, since men expressed the wish for hardworking and respectful wives, whilst women increasingly demanded husbands with employment who were capable of supporting them. Having a job had become a prerequisite for men to be able to marry, not because of rising costs of bridewealth (see also Vijfhuizen, 1998) but due to a marriageability criterion established by women. Bridewealth had become very attenuated with many never paying, and here too women were implicated — many thought little or no payment a good thing since it allowed easier exit from an unhappy marriage, shifted rights in children towards their mothers, and conserved male incomes for the use of the conjugal unit.

---

9. This study was situated in two contrasting villages in Chivi Communal Area over eighteen months in 1987–8, and involved, amongst other things, a series of marital histories of thirty households in each location.

In Chivi, marriage had become individualized in many ways; it was no longer a contract between two lineage groups but between two men,[10] and the period of patrilocal residence of newly married couples had shortened very dramatically, with household fission occurring after only a year or two of co-residence. The reasons for this were consistently put down to the wishes of the in-marrying daughter-in-law, in relation to both friction with her mother-in-law, and the desire to gain control of migrant remittances. It used to be the case that migrants remitted to their parents, but increasingly they were remitting to their wives, and separate residence of the conjugal pair (that is, virilocal rather than patrilocal residence) makes wives' claims on remittances stronger. In this case, there are thus many aspects of what marriage now means that are the outcome of women's struggles to reshape conjugality, to establish the conjugal unit against the lineage group, and to access male incomes (see also Cornwall, 2002).

Women's agency is part of a recursive process with intended and unintended effects on conjugality. When women vegetable growers in The Gambia experienced a surge in their incomes in the early 1990s, via income-generating projects for women, 45–80 per cent of women in horticultural areas were earning more than their husbands (Schroeder, 1996: 70), unleashing a 'bitter war of words' in which men accused women of treating their gardens as their 'second husbands' (ibid.). Gardening women have had to avoid being demonized as bad wives, by sustaining rituals of greeting and respect, the care of husbands' egos, and compliance with male strategies to access female incomes through requests for 'loans' without intention of repayment, and sometimes theft. Counter strategies by women to protect their incomes include spending their money as quickly as possible to limit demands, concealment, marketing through intermediaries and without bringing produce home, wearing money belts, saving with older women relatives outside the household or trusted shopkeepers monitored by civil servants, and giving smaller uninvited gifts to husbands to inoculate themselves against bigger 'loan' demands. The inverted fortunes of women and men has led to new forms of conjugality through women defaulting on domestic labour duties, men defaulting on provisioning responsibilities, and — inverting the Guyer scenario — men attempting to tap into the female cash economy. Women have had to both shoulder greater financial responsibility for household expenses and transfer more to husbands; their increased incomes have brought greater personal autonomy but only at a price. 'Women in The Gambia's garden districts have succeeded in producing a striking new social landscape — by embracing the challenge of the garden boom, they have placed themselves in a position to carefully extricate themselves from some of the more onerous demands of marital obligations . . . and won for themselves "second husbands" by rewriting the rules governing the conjugal contract' (ibid.: 84)

---

10. But note that women do contribute to bridewealth payments.

Part of my uneasiness with assumptions about marriage as a manifesta-
tion of patriarchy is that they rule out the possibility that it is also an arena
for a significant exercise of women's power. The term 'patriarchal bargain'
(Kandiyoti, 1998) suggests that it involves the bartering of power and person-
hood for material security and protection in a world where these are essential
for survival. This has a great deal of truth in it, as the material above would
suggest. But there is more. Conjugality also offers possibilities for women
to manipulate discourses of respectability, manage ironic performances of
compliance, and engage in cultural inversions and mimicry of the gender
order (Boddy, 1989).

Conjugality in Context

The final point I wish to make here is the significance of wider institutions and
processes to the forms and character of conjugalities. Guyer (1988a: 170)
argues that differentiation in rural areas emerges between the children of
married and unmarried women on the basis of their differential access to
the only resources which count — education and land. Like O'Laughlin, she
emphasizes the interactions of familial relations with historical conditions,
in this case those that determine both the marriage rate and the costs and
returns to education. In her account of the centrality of conjugal relations to
women's farming strategies in Chad and Mozambique, O'Laughlin (1995)
shows how social differentiation and broader political economy (for instance,
of migrant labour systems in southern Africa) shape the character and the
value of conjugality. Moreover, marriage does not change in a vacuum, but
alongside other shifts in kinship. It is possible to somewhat ethnocentrically
overemphasize the significance of the conjugal as essentially a relationship
between husband and wife, and Vijfhuizen (1998: 53) argues persuasively
for the importance of sibling relationships within the practices of marriage.
Townsend, for Botswana, also emphasizes the importance of sibling relationships, commenting that being a deadbeat brother is as problematic as being
a deadbeat dad. He cautions against 'the imposition of a model of paternal
responsibility derived from Western patterns' and shows how a lifecourse
perspective is needed to understand fathering, which extends over long periods in Botswana, and involves parenting grandchildren and siblings' children,
spread across multiple domestic groups at the same time (Townsend, 2000:
343). O'Laughlin argues that 'maintenance of conjugal ties is often advantageous to all members of the household. Among other things, it permits
access to the wider web of non-conjugal support that each partner's ties of
kinship, friendship and clientage weave' (1995: 76). Although I think that
women often exercise agency towards clearer and deeper conjugal commitments, rather than wider commitments to alliance, this is possibly related
to particular socio-economic circumstances in which transfers from spouses
are valuable and competed for, and a scenario which could easily change
if more diversified relational investments make more sense, for example

with widespread male unemployment. The attractiveness of Christianity to African women (especially the evangelical and pentecostal variants), with its emphasis on the conjugal bond, also may speak of an increasing desire by women for more exclusive conjugality.

To return to the question of insurance, a (risky?) hypothesis might be that marriage works as a safety net for women in many contexts, as a form of insurance, but should women's enterprises threaten to outstrip husbands' incomes it becomes an impediment to accumulation — a feature shared with other social security institutions (Platteau, 1991).

CONCLUSIONS

This chapter has considered two interconnected gender 'myths'. It began with the idea that women are more risk averse and less insured than men, and argued that marriage may constitute a form of insurance against risk; in the process, this argument opened up a second idea for scrutiny, that marriage is essentially a social relationship through which men exploit women. I am not seeking to substitute one generalization, that women are more risk averse than men, with another, that they are less so, but to argue that any such generalizations are meaningless, and that we should instead treat risk and gender as an open question requiring analysis of specific contexts and institutions that configure the risk and insurance environment faced by individuals. Risk behaviour of women and men is mediated by marriage in important ways which are little recognized in risk literatures; a prerequisite for thinking about how women may be insured through conjugal entitlements is to open up a potentially more positive approach to co-operation and sharing between spouses. This is done through considering the value of marriage to women, through recognizing the problem with individualizing well-being and empowerment to the extent that conjugal well-being and empowerment become invisible, and through seeing marriage as a more open and dynamic terrain of change deriving from both historical circumstances and the everyday pressure of women's agency and their performance of conjugality.

This is not a pessimistic view of the essential rightness of the status quo of marriage, given the abundant evidence of the constant remaking of the meanings of marriage by women. In this regard the term 'conjugal contract' has an unfortunately static feel to it, since the terms of contracts are agreed in advance and hold for their duration. Marriage, on the other hand, is a shifting terrain in which ambiguity, particular (re)interpretations of norms, exceptions and special circumstances, changing positions with ageing and with external conditions, and the ever-present yawning gap between stated and actual practice, offer fertile ground for 'creative conjugality' .

A critical consideration of risk behaviour and gender leads me to reflect on how often the prism of marriage and conjugal relations serves to alter the ways in which women and men experience unpredictable environments, are enabled to experiment and innovate, and experience, and cope with, 'vulnerability' in profoundly different ways. If marriage has value as a legitimate form of dependence and insurance for women, should this not make us — as gender analysts — look again at the balance sheet of intrahousehold relations and wonder whether we have been a little too ready to dismiss as mystifications expressions of solidarity between genders within households, to reject subjectivities which emphasize jointness of well-being, as Sen so famously did (1987), and to assume that intrahousehold ill-being and inequity signals patriarchal compulsion alone? An approach which sees marriage as offering a deal that has variable room for manoeuvre, is less a conjugal contract and more a conjugal performance, with a much larger cast than only spouses, and a valuable co-operative dividend for those who can manage to limit the sacrifices, may bring us closer to understanding women's subjectivities and agency. A properly contextualized analysis would also seek to understand the changing value of marriage and domestic co-operation under conditions of broader social change, and to consider why marriage has been fairly enduring in many kinds of gender order, and what the fragmentation of domestic groups, appearing in diverse settings, might mean.

REFERENCES

Akerlof, G., J. Yellen and M. Katz (1996) 'An Analysis of Out-of-Wedlock Childbearing in the United States', *Quarterly Journal of Economics* CXI(2): 277–315.

Balderrama et al. (1987) 'Farming System Dynamics and Risk in a Low Potential Area: Chivi South, Masvingo Province, Zimbabwe'. International Course for Development Oriented Research in Agriculture (ICRA), Wageningen University, The Netherlands.

van den Berg, A. (1997) 'Land Right, Marriage Left: Women's Management of Insecurity in North Cameroon'. Leiden: Research School CNWS, Leiden University.

Bledsoe, C. and J. Guyer (2000) 'Introduction', in C. Bledsoe, S. Lerner and J. Guyer (eds) *Fertility and the Male Life Cycle in the Era of Fertility Decline*, pp. 1–26. Oxford: Clarendon Press.

Boddy, J. (1989) *Wombs and Alien Spirits*. Princeton, NJ: Princeton University Press.

Burnham, P. (1987) 'Changing Themes in African Marriage', in D. Parkin and D. Nyamwaya (eds) *Transformations of African Marriage*, pp. 37–54. Manchester: Manchester University Press.

Carlsson, F. D. Daruvala and O. Johansson-Stenman (2001) 'Are People Inequality Averse or Just Risk Averse?'. Working Papers in Economics no 43. Gothenburg: Göteborg University, Department of Economics.

Chant, S. (2004) 'Dangerous Equations? How Female-headed Households Became the Poorest of the Poor: Causes, Consequences and Cautions', *IDS Bulletin* 35(4): 19–26.

Cooper, B. (1997) *Marriage in Maradi: Gender and Culture in a Hausa Society in Niger 1900–1989*. Oxford: James Currey.

Cornwall, A. (2002) 'Spending Power: Love, Money, and the Reconfiguration of Gender Relations in Ado-Odo, Southwestern Nigeria', *American Ethnologist* 29(4): 963–80.

Dercon, S. and P. Krishnan (2000) 'In Sickness and in Health: Risk Sharing within Households in Rural Ethiopia', *Journal of Political Economy* 108(4): 688–727.

Eckel, C. and P. Grossman (2003) 'Forecasting Risk Attitudes: An Experimental Study of Actual and Forecast Risk Attitudes of Women and Men'. Virginia Tech Discussion Paper. Blacksburg, VA: Virginia Polytechnic Institute and State University.

Folbre, N. (1986) 'Hearts and Spades: Paradigms of Household Economics', *World Development* 14(2): 245–55.

Guyer, J. (1988a) 'Dynamic Approaches to Domestic Budgeting: Cases and Methods from Africa', in D. Dwyer and J. Bruce (eds) *A Home Divided: Women and Income in the Third World*, pp. 155–72. Stanford, CA: Stanford University Press.

Guyer, J. (1988b) 'The Multiplication of Labor: Historical Methods in the Study of Gender and Agricultural Change in Modern Africa', *Current Anthropology* 29(2): 247–272.

Hart, G. (1995) 'Gender and Household Dynamics: Recent Theories and their Implications', in M. Quibria (ed.) *Critical Issues in Asian Development: Theories, Experiences and Policies*, pp. 39–74. Hong Kong: Oxford University Press.

Hill, P. (1972) *Rural Hausa: A Village and a Setting*. Cambridge: Cambridge University Press.

Hoddinott, J. and B. Kinsey (2003) 'Adult Health in the Time of Drought', in A. Quisumbing (ed.) *Household Decisions, Gender and Development: A Synthesis of Recent Research*, pp. 131–8. Washington, DC: IFPRI/Johns Hopkins University Press.

IFPRI (2002) *Sustainable Food Security for All by 2020*. Proceedings of International Conference, Bonn, Germany (4–6 September 2001). Available online: http://www.ifpri.org/pubs/books/2020conpro.htm#about

Jackson, C. (1995) 'Conjugal Contracts and Agency in Rural Zimbabwean Environments'. Unpublished conference paper, available from author.

Jackson, C. (1996) 'Rescuing Gender from the Poverty Trap', *World Development* 24(3): 489–504.

Jackson, C. (2003) 'Gender Analysis of Land: Beyond Land Rights for Women?', *Journal of Agrarian Change* 3(4): 453–80.

Jeater, D. (1993) *Marriage, Perversion and Power: The Construction of Moral Discourse in Southern Rhodesia 1894–1930*. Oxford: Clarendon Press.

Jefremovas, V. (1991) 'Loose Women, Virtuous Wives, and Timid Virgins: Gender and the Control of Resources in Rwanda', *Canadian Journal of African Affairs* 25(3): 378–95.

Kabeer, N. (1994) *Reversed Realities: Gender Hierarchies in Development Thought*. London: Verso.

Kabeer, N. (1998) '"Money Can't Buy Me Love?" Re-evaluating Gender, Credit and Empowerment in Rural Bangladesh'. IDS Discussion Paper 363. Brighton: University of Sussex, Institute of Development Studies.

Kandiyoti, D. (1998) 'Gender Power and Contestation: Rethinking "Bargaining with Patriarchy"', in C. Jackson and R. Pearson (eds) *Feminist Visions of Development: Gender Analysis and Policy*, pp. 135–52. London: Routledge.

Kossoudji, S. and E. Mueller (1983) 'The Economic and Demographic Status of Female-headed Households in Rural Botswana', *Economic Development and Cultural Change* 31(4): 831–59.

McDowell, L. (1997) *Capital Culture: Gender at Work in the City*. Oxford: Blackwell Publishers.

Mutongi, K. (1999) '"Worries of the Heart": Widowed Mothers, Daughters and Masculinities in Maragoli, Western Kenya 1940–60', *Journal of African History* 40(1): 67–86.

O'Laughlin, B. (1995) 'Myth of the African Family in the World of Development', in D. Bryceson (ed.) *Women Wielding the Hoe: Lessons from Rural Africa for Feminist Theory and Development Practice*, pp. 63–92. Oxford: Berg Publishers.

O'Laughlin, B. (1998) 'Missing Men? The Debate over Rural Poverty and Women-headed Households in Southern Africa', *Journal of Peasant Studies* 25(2): 1–48.

Olsen, R. and C. Cox (2001) 'The Influence of Gender on the Perception and Response to Investment Risk: The Case of Professional Investors', *Journal of Psychology and Financial Markets* 2(1): 29–36.

Parkin, D. and D. Nyamwaya (1987) 'Transformations of African Marriage: Change and Choice', in D. Parkin and D. Nyamwaya (eds) *Transformations of African Marriage*, pp. 1–36. Manchester: Manchester University Press.

Platteau, J-P. (1991) 'Traditional Systems of Social Security and Hunger Insurance: Past Achievements and Modern Challenges', in E. Ahmad (ed.) *Social Security in Developing Countries*, pp. 112–70. Oxford: Oxford University Press.

Price Gittinger, J., with S. Chernick, N. Horenstein and K. Saito (1990) 'Household Food Security and the Role of Women'. World Bank Discussion Paper 96. Washington, DC: The World Bank.

Quisumbing, A. (ed.) (2003) *Household Decisions, Gender and Development: A Synthesis of Recent Research*. Washington, DC: IFPRI/Johns Hopkins University Press.

Quisumbing, A., L. Brown, H. S. Feldstein, L. Haddad and C. Peña (1995) *Women: The Key to Food Security*. Food Policy Report. Washington, DC: IFPRI.

Rosen, A., J. Tsai and S. Downs (2003) 'Variations in Risk Attitude across Race, Gender and Education', *Medical Decision Making* 23(6): 511–17.

Rosenzweig, M. (1988) 'Risk, Private Information and the Family', *American Economic Review Papers and Proceedings of the 100th Annual Meeting* 78(2): 245–50.

Schmidt, E. (1991) 'Patriarchy, Capitalism, and the Colonial State in Zimbabwe', *Signs* 16(4): 732–56.

Schroeder, R. (1996) '"Gone to their Second Husbands": Marital Metaphors and Conjugal Contracts in The Gambia's Female Garden Sector', *Canadian Journal of African Studies* 30(1): 69–97.

Schubert, R., M. Brown, M. Gysler and H. W. Brachinger (1999) 'Financial Decision-making: Are Women Really More Risk Averse?', *American Economic Review* 89(2): 381–5.

Schubert, R., M. Gysler, M. Brown and H. W. Brachinger (2000) 'Gender Specific Attitudes towards Risk and Ambiguity: An Experimental Investigation'. Zurich: Centre for Economic Research, Swiss Federal Institute of Technology.

Sen, A. (1981) *Poverty and Famines: An Essay on Entitlement and Deprivation*. Oxford: Clarendon Press.

Sen, A. (1987) *Gender and Cooperative Conflicts*. Helsinki: World Institute for Development Economics Research.

Seur, H. (1992) 'Sowing the Good Seed: The Interweaving of Agricultural Change, Gender Relations and Religion in Serenie District, Zambia'. PhD thesis, Agricultural University Wageningen, The Netherlands.

Sharp, J. and A. Spiegel (1990) 'Women and Wages: Gender and Control of Income in Farm and Bantustan Households', *Journal of Southern African Studies* 16(3): 527–49.

Townsend, N. (2000) 'Male Fertility as a Lifetime of Relationships: Contextualising Men's Biological Reproduction in Botswana', in C. Bledsoe, S. Lerner and J. Guyer (eds) *Fertility and the Male Life Cycle in the Era of Fertility Decline*, pp. 343–64. Oxford: Clarendon Press.

Vaughan, M. (1985) 'Famine Analysis and Family Relations: 1949 in Nyasaland', *Past and Present* 108: 177–205.

Vijfhuizen, K. (1998) 'The People You Live With: Gender Identities and Social Practices, Beliefs and Power in the Livelihoods of Ndau Women and Men in a Village with an Irrigation Scheme in Zimbabwe'. PhD thesis, Agricultural University Wageningen, The Netherlands.

Whitehead, A. (1990) 'Wives and Mothers: Female Farmers in Africa'. ILO World Employment Programme Research Working Papers. Geneva: ILO.

Whitehead, A. (1991a) 'Rural Women and Food Production in Sub-Saharan Africa', in J. Dreze and A. Sen (eds) *Political Economy of Hunger*, pp. 425–73. Oxford: Clarendon Press.

Whitehead, A. (1991b) 'Food Crisis and Gender Conflict in the African Countryside', in H. Bernstein et al. (eds) *The Food Question*, pp. 54–68. London: Earthscan.

Whitehead, A. and N. Kabeer (2001) 'Living with Uncertainty: Gender, Livelihoods and Pro-poor Growth in Rural Sub-Saharan Africa'. IDS Working Paper 134. Brighton: University of Sussex, Institute of Development Studies.

Wik, M., T. A. Kebede, O. Bergland and S. Holden (2004) 'On the Measurement of Risk Aversion from Experimental Data'. Discussion Paper D 16. Äs: Agricultural University of Norway, Department of Economics and Resource Management.

7

Feminism, Gender, and Women's Peace Activism

Judy El-Bushra

INTRODUCTION

This contribution explores 'different feminisms' as they are manifested in the field of peace building — a field which has experienced a growth spurt since the end of the cold war, and in which women's activism has likewise gained an increasingly high and respected profile. There is no doubt that women, and women's organizations, are increasingly being called on to intervene not only in mediation and peace negotiations, but also (and perhaps particularly) in the various processes of post-conflict reconstruction. 'Women and peace-building' is a rapidly evolving field, in both policy and practical terms. However, this chapter will argue that differences of approach between different feminisms are in danger of confusing the women's peace-building agenda, and hence of diluting the efforts of an incipient global women's peace movement.

On 31 October 2000, the United Nations Security Council adopted Resolution 1325, which enjoins member states to provide protection for women and girls in war and to ensure the full participation of women in humanitarian, conflict resolution, peace-building and post-conflict reconstruction initiatives.[1] Alongside the Beijing Conference on Women of 1995[2] and the ratification of the Rome Statute of the International Criminal Court,[3] Resolution 1325 is a key milestone in the international recognition of women's rights in policy and in international human rights and humanitarian law. The

Thanks are due to Ancil Adrian-Paul and Judith Gardner, who made comments on previous drafts of this chapter.
1. The text of UNSC Resolution 1325 can be found at: http://www.un.org/events/res_1325e.pdf (accessed 20 June 2005).
2. The Beijing Platform for Action — a document agreed by representatives from every government in the world — identified twelve 'critical areas of concern' about women's status and rights, with specific action points for each critical area. The UN General Assembly required each member state to submit a progress report on the 5th anniversary of the Conference in 2000, and further reviews in 2005. The text of the Platform for Action can be found at http://www.un.org/womenwatch/daw/beijing/platform/plat1.htm (accessed 20 June 2005).
3. Article 7 of the Rome Statute of the International Criminal Court declares that crimes against humanity include, 'when conducted as part of a widespread or systematic attack directed against any civilian population, with knowledge of the attack ... rape, sexual slavery, enforced prostitution, forced pregnancy, enforced sterilization, or any other form of sexual violence of comparable gravity' (see http://www.un.org/law/icc/statute/romefra.htm, accessed 9 June 2005).

Resolution resulted in large part from concerted lobbying by a consortium of international women's organizations (Adrian-Paul, 2004). These in turn reflect the growth and increasing profile of women and women's organizations working for peace, in various guises, and at many levels from the local to the global. Now that the Resolution has been unanimously adopted, these same organizations are critical to the next stage, that of ensuring its implementation through awareness raising and lobbying in specific contexts (Anderlini, 2000; International Alert and Women Waging Peace, 2004). Many organizations are contributing to this task, whether or not they are consciously and deliberately focusing their campaigning activities on Resolution 1325. Given the significant number of wars currently or recently taking place on the African continent, it is unsurprising that African women's organizations are well represented within this 'movement'.[4]

Behind this growth of peace activist women's organizations are a number of theoretical positions and assumptions (often implicit) about the relationship between women, war and peace. With more and more documentation building up around women's peace-oriented activities, it is becoming possible to examine what these experiences can contribute to feminist perspectives on conflict, violence and peace, and to assess how well-founded their assumptions are. From the point of view of feminist theory, part of the importance of linking armed conflict with gender identity and gender relations lies in the opportunity it creates to explore questions about men, and about violence, which gender analysts have in the past tended to sidestep. Much of the emerging debate about men, women, violence and war can be related to earlier and wider struggles within feminism about the nature of patriarchy, and in particular those between essentialist and social relations positions. Are men inherently territorial and aggressive, and women inherently nurturing and peaceable? Or are their roles in war explainable entirely in relation to the social and cultural context? Do we have to choose between these positions, or can we accept both as containing elements of truth?

In attempting to answer these questions, I draw on recent documentation about women's experiences of war and of their involvement in peace activism, and in particular, on three NGO investigations in which I have participated over the last seven years: assessing the impact of war on gender relations (El-Bushra and Sahl, 2005), the strengths and weaknesses of women's peace organizations (El-Bushra, 2003), and the role of women in peace building in Somalia and Somaliland (Gardner and El-Bushra, 2004). I start by assessing evidence of how women experience war, and the extent to which this experience has driven a growth of women's organizations. I then summarize evidence on the what, why and how of women's peace organizations, before attempting to clarify some of the conceptual issues involved. I

---

4. It is perhaps too early to talk of a women's peace movement in a formal or organized sense. However, the growing number of organizations undertaking peace-related roles, and the increasingly strong networks they are developing, suggest that such a time is not far off.

argue that conceptual confusion around women's role in peace building might negatively affect the work that women's peace organizations do and the potential for a global women's peace movement to emerge. 'Women and peace' is a field where everyone can and does claim the moral high ground, a fact which is ultimately detrimental to the analysis of problems and hence to achieving progress.

WOMEN'S EXPERIENCES OF WAR

Development organizations became aware of armed and violent conflict as a major contextual dynamic to their work in the late 1980s (Roche, 1996), as the end of the cold war brought many latent conflicts into the open. Early attempts to conceptualize the implications of violent conflict for development were based on assumptions of war as an activity carried out by male armies on far-away battlefields, with minimal involvement of or impact on women. With growing numbers of non-formalized wars, generally taking place within the territory contested by the active protagonists, the recognition grew that there were direct and terrible implications for 'ordinary' citizens — men, women and children — within whose homes and fields wars were being fought, and that the differential impacts on these groups needed to be better understood by humanitarian and other assistance providers (El-Bushra and Piza-Lopez, 1993). This understanding later encompassed the recognition that those often considered to be disinterested bystanders — 'ordinary citizens' or the 'international community' for example — do in fact contribute both directly and indirectly to peace/war through their everyday decisions and actions (Anderson, 1999).

Accounts of the impacts on women of post-cold war conflicts, and other forms of mass violence,[5] show that the direct physical impacts on women are serious in the extreme. Rehn and Sirleaf, for example, introducing a global survey carried out for UNIFEM, express shock at their findings, in spite of their previous exposure to the issues:

> knowing all this did not prepare us for the horrors women described. Wombs punctured with guns. Women raped and tortured in front of their husbands and children. Rifles forced into vaginas. Pregnant women beaten to induce miscarriages. Foetuses ripped from wombs. Women kidnapped, blindfolded and beaten on their way to work or school. We saw the scars, the pain and the humiliation. We heard accounts of gang rapes, rape camps and mutilation. Of murder and sexual slavery. We saw the scars of brutality so extreme that survival seemed for some a worse fate than death. (Rehn and Sirleaf, 2002: 9)

Moreover, the impacts are not only seen in women's physical security but in all aspects of their lives. They encompass direct targeting of women as victims of rape and other forms of violence (sexual, physical and psychological),

---

5. Without digressing here into the fraught arena of defining 'war', we can nevertheless add that events and trends such as genocides and states of raised insecurity exhibit many of the same features as war.

as well as more indirect impacts such as the destruction of environmental resources from which women gain their livelihoods, the breakdown of health, education, financial and legal services, loss of markets, the physical and mental traumas of displacement and refuge, and the impact on women of these same disasters being visited on their families and communities. They include the many sacrifices, stresses and indignities which women have to resort to as coping strategies in order to ensure their continuing roles in maintaining their families and communities.[6] In addition, war entails far-reaching social changes such as demographic imbalances and the restructuring of the gender division of labour, which tend to have the overall effect of increasing women's family responsibilities and burden of work, while failing to provide them with commensurate increases in respect, recognition or resources. In short, war threatens women's security at the deepest levels and in the broadest ways (Bennett et al., 1995; El-Bushra, 2003; International Alert and Women Waging Peace, 2004; Kelly, 2000; Sorensen, 1998; Turshen, 2001; Turshen and Twagiramariya, 1998).

Despite this catalogue of both deliberately targeted and incidental disasters which are visited on women during and after wartime, the notion of women as 'victims' of war needs questioning, on several grounds. First, there is a substantial amount of evidence that women often support war, whether they are directly engaged in fighting or providing other types of inputs into war efforts. They may take part in armed movements as soldiers, messengers, carriers of ammunition, nurses or camp followers (African Rights, 1995; Bennett et al., 1995 on Liberia; Ibanez, 2001; Sharoni, 2001). Women encourage their menfolk to commit violence when they see fit, often by ridiculing the faint-hearted (Kanogo, 1987), through their participation in nationalist political movements (Gautam, 2001; Mukta, 2000; Ridd and Callaway, 1987), or through ritual activities which provide political and religious legitimacy to warfare (Lumoro, 2002).

Women do not necessarily speak with one voice on issues of war and peace. Clearly they are divided by political identities and allegiances, just as men are. Women involved in reconciliation work may be derided by other women, as Dahabo Isse, a relief worker in Mogadishu in 1992, describes (Isse, 2004) and often cite the lack of unity among women as a major impediment to this work (El-Bushra, 2003). Women may also respond differently at different points in time, as did women in Somaliland who, after supporting the war of liberation from the Barre regime, balked at the violence which later broke out between clans previously united in that struggle (Gardner and El-Bushra, 2004). Where women do undertake peace initiatives, these are often based

---

6. Studies such as Bennett et al. (1995) and El-Bushra and Sahl (2005) provide ample illustration of the truism that in many war situations, men tend to lose motivation and self-respect while women gain these qualities, since women take over many of men's responsibilities, exerting extraordinary efforts to maintain provision of food, shelter and security for their families.

on a pragmatic response to desperate situations rather than on an inherently pacifist orientation.

These examples suggest that to cast women as 'victims' of male violence in war ignores the complex realities of women's experience, denying them agency and negating the spirit with which women have responded to crises. Women's testimonies and other evidence from around the world paint a pattern whereby women tend to withstand the personal agonies they have undergone with resilience, commit themselves to maintaining their households with energy and inventiveness, and make active decisions about shaping their political realities. These two marked features of women's experience of war — the trauma and the resilience — are prominent among explanations for the growth of women's organizations in response to post-cold war warfare in Africa. These are not the only factors of course: it is undeniable, for example, that changing patterns of funding also offer partial explanation.[7] However, women involved in such organizations themselves testify that their commitment to peace activism is borne out of their experience in and after war. While the initial impetus for organizing may be the immediate need to pool resources to meet the survival requirements of families and communities, many organizations are later sustained by the sense of empowerment that women gain in this process, as well as by a frustration with the 'failed politics of violence' (El-Bushra, 2003).[8]

Men's experiences of war appear to be similarly ambiguous. Although 'men predominate across the spectrum of violence' (Connell, 2000: 33, citing men's preponderance in armies and other enforcement agencies such as the police and security firms, as perpetrators of violent crime and domestic violence, and in violence-like conduct such as extreme sports), there is no neat polarity to be distinguished around men–women, violence–caring. At a fundamental human level, war is indiscriminate in its capacity to kill, maim, and destroy property and livelihoods. It accentuates existing differences of power and access to resources, weakening the position of those who are already without power, whether they are men, women or children.[9] Women suffer through the violence and deprivation imposed on their men folk, just as men are affronted and emasculated through the abuse and humiliation of their wives, mothers and daughters. Within the household, both men and women struggle to fulfil their social roles of providing for and protecting family members, in circumstances of extreme difficulty. Sexual violence against men, though less common than that against women, is also a feature of warfare, and its consequences may be just as devastating to

---

7. USAID reports that reliance on donors is a factor in the weakness of some such organizations (Kumar et al., 2000).

8. Such were the origins of Pro-Femmes Twesehamwe, the Rwandan women's umbrella organization, which has developed as a major political player through a combination of women's commitment and government support (UNIFEM, 2003).

9. However, there are cases when war can be said to advance social justice, as can be seen in Mali (El-Bushra and Sahl, 2005) and in the case of the Rwanda genocide (Prunier, 1995).

the individuals concerned and to their families and communities (Zarkov, 2001). Men are often discouraged — by formally imposed legal measures as well as by conventional values — from resisting organized violence or from working for peace. It is rare to find policy documents that acknowledge the gendered constraints on men who take part in, are victims of, or resist war.[10]

WOMEN'S PEACE ORGANIZATIONS

In the last ten years there has been increasing interest among academic and policy communities in documenting the peace-building work of women's organizations. Studies such as the Aftermath project of USAID (Kumar, 2001) have assessed women's organizations in particular countries (Cambodia, Bosnia, Guatemala, El Salvador, Georgia and Rwanda) according to criteria such as management and financial efficiency. Initiatives such as International Alert's Women Building Peace campaign, and a number of in-depth studies in individual countries, have attempted to document women's experience of peace activism from their own perspectives and in their own words.[11]

There are now a considerable number of women's peace activist organizations operating in every continent.[12] While many operate at a grass-roots community level, others have a national, regional or international profile, acting as umbrella organizations for local groups or providing training and support to them, while at the same time taking part in international networking and campaigning. Activism is directed both towards specific conflicts and towards global issues of war and peace. Two African regional women's peace activist organizations are illustrative:

- ISIS/WICCE is the international cross-cultural exchange office of an international organization dedicated to the promotion of women's human rights. Based in Uganda, ISIS/WICCE has developed an exchange, training and women's leadership programme covering Burundi, DRC, Kenya, Rwanda, Sudan and Tanzania, with the intention of helping women

10. For two notable exceptions, see the work of Gendercide Watch at http://www.gendercide.org (accessed 9 November 2005) and the OECD DAC Guidelines (OECD, 2001).

11. See, for example: Abdo and Lentin (2002) on Israel/Palestine; Cockburn (2004) on Cyprus; El-Bushra (2003) and El-Bushra et al. (2005); Gardner and El-Bushra (2004) on Somalia; International Alert (1999); International Alert and AAWORD (2000).

12. There appears to be no co-ordinated attempt at drawing up a directory, although several organizations have produced lists using a variety of criteria. For example, the website of Women Waging Peace lists fifty-one organizations operating in Africa, at a regional level and in six countries. (<http://www.womenwagingpeace.net/content/links/af.asp> accessed 27 June 2005). This does not include the other forty-nine countries, nor the myriad local and community-based women's associations with conflict mitigation agendas operating in virtually every African country.

from those countries build relationships across conflict divides and providing them with the skills to participate in peace-building initiatives (El-Bushra, 2003).

- Femmes Africa Solidarité (FAS) is a Geneva-based organization promoting women's leadership in conflict prevention, management and resolution. FAS, through its regional office in Dakar, promoted the establishment of the Mano River Women's Peace Network (MARWOPNET), which in turn co-ordinates a network of local and national organizations throughout Sierra Leone, Guinea and Liberia (El-Bushra et al., 2005).

International Alert's project, 'Women Building Peace: Sharing Know-how' has designed a 'Framework for Documentation' aimed at synthesizing what women's peace-building organizations do into five categories of activities (El-Bushra, 2003):

1. Survival and basic needs: for example, providing food, shelter, welcome, health care, etc. to individuals and families that have been attacked or displaced; caring for vulnerable individuals such as pregnant mothers or orphans during conflict; organizing communal agricultural work to ensure food production; running food kitchens; providing such support to diverse communities across political divides.
2. Peace building and mediation at different levels, including (in rare cases) taking part in formal peace negotiations; interceding with warlords; taking part in local mediation teams; demonstrating and campaigning in favour of peace and against violence; putting pressure on men generally, and on own men folk, to reach agreement.
3. Advocacy: working with civil society, government and the media to raise awareness of human rights issues in general and around specific policy goals such as reintegration of refugees or the holding of elections.
4. Promoting women's inclusion in decision-making and leadership: promoting women's rights to political participation and security in policy and practice, through civic and rights education; women's leadership training; training and support to women parliamentarians.
5. Community outreach and rebuilding: carrying out projects to integrate demobilized soldiers, trauma counselling, peace education, justice and reconciliation work, lobbying for equal access to services, etc.

This and other typologies of women's conflict transformation work (see, for example, Bouta et al., 2005; Cockburn, 2000; Mazurana and McKay, 1999) illustrate not only the range of activities which women peace activists view as falling within their scope, but also the difficulty of trying to categorize these activities. As Mazurana and McKay point out, the issue is not simply that women's work in conflict transformation and peace building needs to be acknowledged, but that women's experiences expand the scope of peace making itself, since their activism addresses the psychosocial, relational and spiritual as well as the political and economic dimensions of conflict transformation. Moreover, unlike the mainstream of formal peace and reconciliation work, women's peace activist organizations tend to have deep roots in the local context and in cultural specificity (Mazurana and McKay, 1999). These are among the main factors to have encouraged policy makers such as the UN Security Council members to promote women's inclusion in peace and reconciliation initiatives (Bouta et al., 2005).

Assessing the impact of women's peace organizations, either in specific cases or in general, is extremely difficult (as it is for any organization with peace-related aims). Women's peace groups point to a variety of specific, localized practical achievements such as negotiating safe passage with warlords, calming tensions between market-sellers, or providing employment opportunities to demobilized ex-soldiers, and through these achievements they may be beginning to 'develop an alternative, gendered view of society that will lead to the transformation at all levels of structures, practices and social relations, including gender relations' (Ndeye Sow, in El-Bushra, 2003: 5). At the level of peace negotiations and mediation, women have played an important and increasingly acknowledged, but essentially 'back-room' role by bridging divides and by providing encouragement.

Many women's organizations themselves consider organizational capacity to be one of their main weaknesses. This is partly because of their relative newness and what tends to be a separation from mainstream civil society, so there is little experience of organizational management. Debates about separatism versus integration (what sort of alliances to form with other civil society groupings, for example) often reflect a fear that women's organizations will be vulnerable to domination by more established groups, unless they strengthen their organizational management skills and their technical knowledge, for instance, of women's civic and political rights or of nonviolent communication (El-Bushra, 2003).

However, they also perceive differences of philosophy and style between women's (feminist) and other types of organization, which make it difficult for women's organizations to 'speak the language' of the mainstream development world and hence access its financial and networking resources. Within women's peace organizations there is often a desire to become proficient in, for example, strategic planning or logframes, but at the same time a resistance to using such mechanisms, which are often seen as being inconsistent with the ethos of women's organizations.

For example, a group of women activists attending an International Alert workshop on monitoring and evaluation in 2004 identified a distinction between 'results-driven' and 'process-driven' organizations (both being represented at the workshop). 'Results-driven' organizations planned their work systematically according to defined indicators, carried out regular workplan reviews, documented their activities exhaustively, and used this documentation as a basis for lobbying work. They saw scrupulous political neutrality as a key feature of their capacity to influence others. 'Process-driven' organizations, on the other hand, valued intuition in their analysis and flexibility in their planning, made use of symbols and metaphors in their communications work, and sought to identify women's own styles of expression and communication. They saw these as being based on mutual acknowledgement, commitment to values, and on solidarity, that is, on women's capacity to reach out across barriers to other women (El-Bushra et al., 2005).[13]

Women's peace initiatives often tend to be ignored by mainstream actors in conflict resolution, especially in the area of peace negotiations. In Somalia and Somaliland, for example, where women have a strong record of organizing against the divisiveness and violence of clan politics, men appear to have mixed views on women's role. In this particular social setting women have much weaker clan allegiances than men since they have close links both with their own, natal clan and with that of their husbands. This means, on the one hand, that in wartime they are able to use these cross-cutting linkages for protection (of themselves and others) and to promote reconciliation, and on the other that when it comes to the hard-nosed business of inter-clan decision making, women have until recently been excluded. One Somaliland observer at the Sheikh reconciliation and peace conference in 1992 described women as 'the wind behind the peace conference ... in terms of mobilizing the elders, in preparing the venue, the food, and in encouraging the participants to keep going until the final peace accord was reached' (Dr Adan Yousef Abokor, quoted in Gardner and El-Bushra, 2004: 147). Yet although women had contributed all this and more, at the moment of the final decision making they were asked to leave the room. Similarly in Somalia, women's activism round the idea of a 'sixth clan' (the notion that women form a clan of their own with a non-partisan agenda) led to a quota of thirty-three reserved seats for women (12 per cent) being agreed in the transitional parliament. This was, however, later reduced to twenty-two (*The Nation*, 2004).

Elsewhere too, male power structures may be willing to acknowledge women's role in the maintenance and rebuilding of society during and after war, but are slow to welcome them into the political arena. Post-conflict societies administered by the international community have not shown themselves to be immune to such problems (Abdela, 2003); the passing of Resolution 1325 has not been followed by any notable progress in this matter in, say, Iraq. Moreover, women are not always sure that they want to enter this arena. In Sierra Leone, for example, their analysis has been that after initially being a major force in the peace movement, women's organizations declined in significance because they failed to capitalize on this experience by developing their own political analysis (Eno, 2000; Jusu-Sheriff, 2000). However, the pattern is not universal: examples such as South Africa (Modise, 2000) and Rwanda (UNIFEM, 2003) illustrate the difference that can be made when

---

13. The workshop recognized the value in both approaches and concluded that both types of organization should try to learn from each other, so as to be able to 'plan for miracles'.

political will at the highest level is prepared to pursue actively the need for restructuring gender relations in the post-conflict environment, and to insist on the inclusion of women's voices in national reconstruction processes.

To gauge the effectiveness of women's peace-building activities, it is first necessary to be clear what they are trying to achieve. Are they aiming to encourage a cessation of violence? To achieve parity in representation in peace negotiation teams? To establish women's rights? Or to promote broader qualitative transformations in relationships and structures which benefit all members of society? The problem is that women's role as mothers provides them with a platform on which to approach and appeal to powerful men (an example perhaps of 'the power of the powerless'), but it simultaneously undermines their desire to be taken seriously as political players. The goal of establishing women's rights in post-conflict societies is similarly caught between the need to establish a distinctive women's agenda on the one hand and the need to engage with an alien and potentially oppressive politics on the other.

DISCUSSION

Descriptions and analyses of women's peace activism display a range of theoretical frameworks which broadly lie between two poles. The first could be termed the essentialist position, which understands the innate violence of males as being at the root of war. In this view, the violence of war and that of the domestic arena are linked: war is effectively war on women (Kelly, 2000). Turshen suggests that violence directed towards women in war, far from being incidental, reflects a concern by male militias to possess both women's property and women *as* property, bearing in mind the resources they represent in terms of both productive and reproductive labour (Turshen, 2001). In this interpretation, war impacts women on two levels: not only do they suffer the most severe direct impacts in terms of physical and psychological affronts, but they also carry the main burden of mending broken bodies, relationships and societies through the exercise of their caring and nurturing functions.

The second view is a 'social analysis' critique, which suggests that the essentialist conflation of womanhood with motherhood (and similar caring, nurturing roles) not only seems remote from the reality of many women's and men's lives and outlooks, but also fails to challenge the very stereotypes of masculinity and femininity which may need to be transformed if conflict is to be managed non-violently. In the words of Vincent (2001: 5): 'To the extent that peace-builders draw on stereotypes of women's "natural" capacities and assumed biological traits, they are reinforcing rather than assisting the fundamental revisioning of prevailing relations of gender dominance which justify women's exclusion from the public sphere of work and politics on the basis of their putative special responsibilities and proficiencies as mothers'. A central problem noted by this critique is the conflation of 'gender' with 'women', and the concomitant failure to engage in political analysis by teasing out the specific forms of oppression women face in particular contexts. In this view, a gendered analysis of war requires us to look beyond women as victims to the social structures and mechanisms that shape and reinforce — and in some cases undermine — their vulnerability in times of crisis. It also requires us to consider the possibility that vulnerability applies to men too, not necessarily (but sometimes) in the same ways.

Of course, similar, and broadly parallel, contentions have existed within feminism for decades, and have also recently been evident in the development arena.[14] Where do women's peace organizations place themselves in this debate? Here we find a mixture of positions. Some reflect an essentialist approach in the imagery with which they describe their work, speaking for example of women peace builders as 'weaving' peace or as providing a 'warm blanket' of peace (El-Bushra et al., 2005). Others would see their role as working within mixed organizations or mixed alliances, with the aim of challenging both the oppression of a particular group and unequal gender relations within it. However, in general one can say that few fall unequivocally into one camp or the other, and many adopt elements of both.

For example, the women who took part in International Alert's workshops were generally struck by the commonality of experiences among women from different communities and different continents, while at the same time recognizing the complexities of their differing contexts. Indeed, this commonality is one of the main planks of their belief in women's capacity for peace building. Their belief is that women peace activists are united by several factors, including: a capacity to build bridges across political divides on the basis of shared experience; an interest, borne of their caring and social service roles, in the restoration of security; a shared experience of oppression which encourages in them an appreciation of the value of peace; their capacity as wives and mothers to influence other family members; and the fact that in many societies women have traditionally played mediation roles in violent conflict (El-Bushra, 2003). This list illustrates a strong belief in women's solidarity, while still recognizing the influence of context in determining women's responses to violence.

Moreover, participants identified a number of dilemmas faced by women's peace organizations, dilemmas which tend to illustrate the contradictions inherent in much of the policy discourse about women and peace. Does a common women's agenda really exist? How do activists deal — theoretically and practically — with the fact that women are divided by the same political schisms that have generated war as well as by differences of status, ideology, and so on? If women's activism takes the nurturing, motherhood role as its common platform, does this not foreclose options for re-envisaging women's roles and position? If, as a broad strategy for guaranteeing real change, women engage in mainstream politics, what compromises can they

---

14. Baden and Goetz (1998) describe similar debates at the Beijing Conference on Women of 1995.

acceptably make in the process? Are the efforts of politicians and policy makers to involve women in peace building based on a commitment to transformed gender relations, or are they mere tokenism, and, if the latter, what should women's response be? And should women activists aim to promote their own interests and rights, or to promote the rights of all subordinate groups? How will they promote the rights of women who may not be part either of women's movements or of other organized categories?

Activists and policy makers alike share a view of 'womenandpeace'[15] which, in terms of the global policy agenda, finds its most potent expression in Resolution 1325. This view owes much to the language of the essentialist position. Yet its adherents often deny the essentialist label, holding instead that gender differences are indeed culturally and socially conditioned rather than innate. Elaborating further, they explain that it is society which shapes women's lives, but that women's oppression is a universal characteristic of society — a view which one might describe as a sort of 'cultural essentialism'. Women peace activists are not alone in holding this view: it has become a pervasive one within the development profession at large and has been adopted, at least at the level of rhetoric, by institutions and individuals whose general orientation is very far from being inspired by feminism of any persuasion.[16]

This 'cultural essentialism' may be conceptually inconsistent, but it has been responsible for some remarkable advances in development policy and practice. This is not the place to describe the progress of 'gender and development': suffice it to say that the increased awareness of women's rights and contributions to development has had a radical impact in many quarters, shaking up patterns of dominance within institutions of many sorts, and rendering those institutions more responsive to the needs of many marginalized categories, women and others. Moreover, the 'cultural essentialism' view of women's position and condition reflects a substantial degree of truth, since women's oppression is a demonstrable reality in myriad contexts. The debate about the universality of women's oppression is therefore a critical one, as it strikes at the heart of feminist struggles and of gender politics in institutions. If we cannot say with absolute certainty that women are oppressed everywhere, but are fairly sure that it is a reasonable generalization to make, shouldn't we be using all means at our disposal to combat that oppression, even if that means ironing out awkward exceptions in generalities?

---

15. I am grateful to Ruth Jacobson for this formulation.
16. The racist undertow beneath this position is sometimes quite near the surface: the (not always unspoken) implication is that, in relation to Africa for example, it is African men who oppress African women, but that the gender policies of development agencies, in contrast, represent a more civilized, modern and egalitarian approach. Thus Connell's assertion that colonialism laid the foundation for the globally hegemonic version of masculinity to incorporate 'soft' values, while 'violence and licence were, symbolically and to so some extent actually, pushed out to the colonies' (Connell, 1995: 194) finds a latter-day expression in the development and peace-building professions.

In the field of peace building and post-conflict social reconstruction, there are huge risks in over-generalizing and thereby failing to understand the dynamics of power inherent in each situation. For women, the main risk is that they will be stereotyped as victims and/or politically neutral carers, and that in practice the political and financial support they receive will be based on conformity with these stereotypes. While for some this is an acceptable risk, a first step on the ladder towards accessing larger fields of influence, others consider that accepting support for women's 'practical needs' will effectively sideline their key 'strategic interests', most particularly their interest in being taken seriously as players in the political arena. Moreover, there is a thin line to be trodden between claiming the space and time for women activists to work out their own analysis and agenda on the one hand, and pursuing a separatist strategy on the other, thereby failing to influence the wider civil society and hence the dominant power structures.[17]

In the long run, policy conditionalities in favour of women may lead to cosmetic changes designed to impress funders, while restricting the possibility of real debate and grounded progress.[18] Blanket prescriptions to involve women in project management can generate a backlash or other forms of resistance from men (which development and humanitarian agencies are usually not sufficiently tuned into the community to be aware of) while still failing to address the realities of women's subordination in the particular circumstances. Conflict and post-conflict situations do hold some prospect of social change, but managing this change effectively and sustainably is a key skill in which agencies working in this field are still novices (El-Bushra, 2000). The stereotype of 'women as victims of war' rather than resourceful survivors with potential for leadership reflects nothing so much as a view of the humanitarian assistance profession as twenty-first century Sir Galahad.

There are further, broader risks for men, for conflict-affected societies generally, and for the development community itself. NGO projects which provide priority assistance or encouragement to women sometimes unjustly exclude men who are vulnerable to violence and poverty, or exclude them by default by failing to address their specific needs. Men who have been raped may be even more reluctant to come forward for treatment than women are.[19] In situations where men's access to productive resources has been stripped away as a result of war, to prioritize women in, for example, animal restocking projects can exacerbate the psychological pressures on men, ultimately to the detriment of both men and women (Dolan, 2002).

17. Contexts such as eastern DR Congo, for example, display a substantial separation between women's and men's civil society organizations, a situation which benefits neither. International Alert's Women's Peace Programme is unusual in operating simultaneously at different levels, supporting both grassroots women's organizations which address local practical concerns and those that aim to enlarge women's political space at a provincial and national level.
18. For example, Somali women have long been frustrated by male politicians agreeing to women's participation in politics in principle, and blocking it in practice.
19. Although in eastern DRC, for example, women's rape crisis centres are beginning to see men seeking help.

Development workers in the field, daily confronted with critical decisions to make about who to support and how, are often bewildered by this confusion. Torn between policy orthodoxy on the one hand and reality on the other, they may have to resort to tokenism while privately writing off gender equality policy as irrelevant.

CONCLUSIONS

Clearly women's peace activist organizations are widespread, and are working hard to achieve a better society for themselves and for others. Their work is important and deserves support and recognition. It is undeniable that women's solidarity plays a major part in cementing and dynamizing this movement. Indeed, the range of activities in which women's peace organizations engage, all of which appear to them to fall under the heading of 'peace building', suggests the need to adopt a definition of 'peace' which encompasses the totality of women's needs and interests and which puts the accent on structural change towards justice and towards representativity in political decision making. What needs to be understood is that, to the extent that women have organized to resist violence and claim their right to a political voice, they have been spurred on to do this by their context-specific experiences rather than through an innately peace-loving nature.

Identifying the convergences between 'gender' and 'violent conflict' raises a number of questions for feminism. In my view, reviewing the evidence reveals that rather than seeing war as the violation of women by men, we should recognize that men and women are 'differently violated' by war (El-Jack, 2003). Consigning women to the status of victim represents a sort of secondary violation. Essentializing their roles as wives, mothers and nurses is not only unrealistic but also tends to blind us to the injustice of women's exclusion from the world of active players and decision makers. Feminism may be a project to promote women, but it is much more than that, encompassing a way of viewing the world, of putting the accent on the defence of rights, not the defence of women alone.

The development community is starting, albeit slowly, to embrace some of the lessons of women organizing for peace. However, in pursuing these lessons, it must recognize that there are no right answers and no generalized prescriptions to be made. 'Women and war' is too complex a topic in which to promote the politics of the sound bite.

REFERENCES

Abdela, L. (2003) 'Kosovo: Missed Opportunities, Lessons for the Future', *Development in Practice* 13(2/3): 208–16.

Abdo, N. and R. Lentin (eds) (2002) *Women and the Politics of Military Confrontation: Palestinian and Israeli Gendered Narratives of Dislocation.* New York and Oxford: Berghan Books.

Adrian-Paul, A. (2004) 'Legitimising the Role of Women in Peace-building in the United Nations: A Campaign Approach', in M. Fitzduff and C. Church (eds) *NGOs at the Table: Strategies for Influencing Policy in Areas of Conflict*. Lanham, MD: Rowman & Littlefield for INCORE, Belfast.

African Rights (1995) *Rwanda. Not So Innocent: When Women Become Killers*. Kigali and London: African Rights.

Anderlini, S. (2000) 'United Nations Security Council Resolution 1325: Summary, Implications and Actions to be Taken'. Women Building Peace Campaign. London: International Alert.

Anderson, M. (1999) *Do No Harm: How Aid Can Support Peace — Or War*. Boulder, CO, and London: Lynne Reinner.

Baden, S. and A. Goetz (1998) '"Who Needs (Sex) When You Can Have (Gender)?": Conflicting Discourses on Gender at Beijing', in C. Jackson and R. Pearson (eds) *Feminist Visions of Development: Gender Analysis and Policy*, pp. 19–38. London and New York: Routledge.

Bennett, O., J. Bexley and K. Warnock (eds) (1995) *Arms to Fight, Arms to Protect: Women Speak Out about Conflict*. London: Panos Institute.

Bouta, T., G. Frerks and I. Bannon (2005) *Gender, Conflict and Development*. Washington, DC: The World Bank.

Cockburn, C. (2000) 'Women's Organisation in the Rebuilding of Postwar Bosnia-Herzegovina', in C. Cockburn and D. Zarkov (eds) *The Postwar Moment: Militaries, Masculinities and International Peacekeeping*, pp. 68–84. London: Lawrence and Wishart.

Cockburn, C. (2004) *The Line: Women, Partition and the Gender Order in Cyprus*. London: Zed Press.

Connell, R. W. (1995) *Masculinities*. Polity Press.

Connell, R. W. (2000) 'Masculinities, the Reduction of Violence and the Pursuit of Peace', in C. Cockburn and D. Zarkov (eds) *The Postwar Moment: Militaries, Masculinities and International Peacekeeping*, pp. 33–40. London: Lawrence and Wishart.

Dolan, C. (2002) 'Collapsing Masculinities and Weak States: A Case Study of Northern Uganda', in F. Cleaver (ed.) *Masculinities Matter! Men, Gender and Development*, pp. 57–83. London: Zed Press.

El-Bushra, J. (2000) 'Editorial: Gender and Forced Migration', *Forced Migration Review Vol 9: Gender and Displacement*, pp. 4–7 Oxford: Refugee Studies Centre, University of Oxford.

El-Bushra, J. (2003) 'Women Building Peace: Sharing Know-how'. Gender and Peace-building Programme. London: International Alert.

El-Bushra, J. and E. Piza-Lopez (1993) *Development in Conflict: The Gender Dimension*. Oxford: Oxfam/ACORD.

El-Bushra, J. and I. Sahl (2005) *Cycles of Violence: Gender Relations and Armed Conflict*. Nairobi: ACORD.

El-Bushra, J. with A. Adrian-Paul and M. Olson (2005) *Assessing Impact: Planning for Miracles*. London: International Alert.

El-Jack (2003) 'Gender and Armed Conflict: Overview Report'. BRIDGE Cutting Edge Packs. Brighton: University of Sussex, Institute of Development Studies.

Eno, J. (2000) 'Sierra Leone', in International Alert and AAWORD *Conflict Transformation in Africa: African Women's Perspectives*, p. 15. Report of the workshop in Dakar (May). London: International Alert/AAWORD.

Gardner, J. and J. El-Bushra (eds) (2004) *Somalia, the Untold Story: The War through the Eyes of Women*. London: CIIR/Pluto Press.

Gautam, S. (2001) 'Women and Children in the Periphery of the People's War'. Kathmandu: Institute of Human Rights Communication.

Ibanez, A. (2001) 'El Salvador: War and Untold Stories: Women Guerrillas', in C. Moser and Clark (eds) *Victims, Perpetrators or Actors? Gender, Armed Conflict and Political Violence*, pp. 117–30. London: Zed Books.

International Alert (1999) *Women, Violent Conflict and Peace-building: Global Perspectives*. Report of the international conference, London (May). London: International Alert.

International Alert and AAWORD (2000) *Conflict Transformation in Africa: African Women's Perspectives*. Report of the workshop in Dakar (May). London: International Alert/AAWORD.

International Alert and Women Waging Peace (2004) *Inclusive Security: Sustainable Peace — A Toolkit for Advocacy and Action*. London: International Alert; Boston, MA: Women Waging Peace.

Isse, D. (2004) 'Testimony 6: Dahabo Isse', in J. Gardner and J. El-Bushra (eds) *Somalia, the Untold Story: The War through the Eyes of Women*, pp. 179–86. London: CIIR/Pluto Press.

Jusu-Sheriff, J. (2000) 'Sierra Leonean Women and the Peace Process', in D. Lord (ed.) *Paying the Price: The Sierra Leone Peace Process*. Accord Conciliation Resources, no 9. London: Conciliation Resources.

Kanogo, T. (1987) 'Kikuyu Women and the Politics of Protest: Mau Mau', in S. Ardener, P. Holden and S. Macdonald (eds) *Images of Women in Peace and War: Cross-cultural and Historical Perspectives*, pp. 78–99. Macmillan.

Kelly, L. (2000) 'Wars Against Women: Sexual Violence, Sexual Politics and the Militarised State', in S. Jacobs, R. Jacobson and J. Marchbank (eds) *States of Conflict: Gender, Violence and Resistance*, pp. 45–65. London: Zed Books.

Kumar, K. (2001) 'Aftermath: Women and Women's Organizations in Postconflict Societies'. USAID Evaluation Highlights no 74, Centre for Development Information and Evaluation. Washington, DC: USAID

Kumar, K., H. Baldwin and J. Benjamin (2000) 'Aftermath: Women and Women's Organizations in Post-Conflict Cambodia'. CDIE Working Paper no 307. Washington, DC: USAID.

Lumoro, I. (2002) 'Uganda Case Study', in ACORD (ed.) *Gender-sensitive Design and Planning in Conflict-affected Situations*. Available online: http://www.acord.org.uk/Publications/G&CResearch/annex1ugandaeng.pdf (accessed 13 June 2005).

Mazurana, D. and S. McKay (1999) *Women and Peace-building*. Montreal: International Centre for Human Rights and Democratic Development.

Modise, T. (2000) 'Human Security meets Military Security: South Africa's Experience', in International Alert (ed.) *Women, Violent Conflict and Peace-building: Global Perspectives*, pp. 23–4. London: International Alert.

Mukta, P. (2000) 'Gender, Community, Nation: The Myth of Innocence', in S. Jacobs, R. Jacobson and J. Marchbank (eds) *States of Conflict: Gender, Violence and Resistance*, pp. 163–78. London: Zed Books.

The Nation (2004) 'We've Been Cheated, Say Somalia Women', *The Nation*, Nairobi (13 September).

OECD (2001) 'Helping Prevent Violent Conflict'. DAC Guidelines. Paris: OECD.

Prunier, G. (1995) *The Rwanda Crisis: History of a Genocide*. London: Hurst.

Rehn, E. and E. J. Sirleaf (2002) *Women, War and Peace: The Independent Experts' Assessment on the Impact of Armed Conflict on Women and Women's Role in Peace-building*. New York: UNIFEM.

Ridd, R. and H. Callaway (1987) *Women and Political Conflict: Portraits of Struggle in Times of Crisis*. New York: New York University Press.

Roche, C. (1996) 'Operationality in Turbulence: The Need for Change', in D. Eade (series ed.) *Development in States of War*, pp. 15–25. Oxford: Oxfam.

Sharoni, S. (2001) 'Rethinking Women's Struggles in Israel–Palestine and in the North of Ireland', in C. Moser and F. Clark (eds) *Victims, Perpetrators or Actors? Gender, Armed Conflict and Political Violence*, pp. 85–98. London: Zed Books.

Sorensen, B. (1998) 'Women and Post-conflict Reconstruction: Issues and Sources'. UNRISD War-torn Societies Project Occasional Paper no 3. Geneva: UNRISD.

Turshen, M. (2001) 'The Political Economy of Rape: An Analysis of Systematic Rape and Sexual Abuse of Women during Armed Conflict in Africa', in C. Moser and F. Clark (eds) *Victims,*

Perpetrators or Actors? Gender, Armed Conflict and Political Violence, pp. 55–68. London: Zed Books.

Turshen, M. and C. Twagiramariya (1998) *What Women do in Wartime: Gender and Conflict in Africa*. London: Zed Books.

UNIFEM (2003) 'Report of the Learning Oriented Assessment of Gender Mainstreaming and Women's Empowerment Strategies in Rwanda, 2–12 September 2002'. New York: UNIFEM.

Vincent, L. (2001) 'Engendering Peace in Africa: A Critical Inquiry into Some Current Thinking on the Role of African Women in Peace-building'. Available online: http://www.accord.org.za/ajcr/2001-1/accordr_v2_n1_a4.html (accessed 12 May 2005).

Zarkov, D. (2001) 'The Body of the Other Man: Sexual Violence and the Construction of Masculinity, Sexuality and Ethnicity in the Croatian Media', in C. Moser and F. Clark (eds) *Victims, Perpetrators or Actors: Gender, Armed Conflict and Political Violence*, pp. 69–82. London and New York: Zed Books.

8

Myths To Live By? Female Solidarity and Female Autonomy Reconsidered

Andrea Cornwall

INTRODUCTION

Feminist engagement with development has long sought to challenge the myths created and sustained by pervasive male bias. Images of harmonious unitary households dissolve in feminist analyses of the realities of intrahousehold inequity and far-from-benevolent patriarchs (Folbre, 1994; Kandiyoti, 1988; Whitehead, 1981). The inequities of dominant models of economic development clearly emerge as the spotlight is placed on the assumptions that drive them, as on those who stand to gain or lose (Evans, 1991; Kabeer, 1994). And yet amidst the feminist critique of orthodoxies, exposure of prejudices and assumptions, and efforts to put right the 'gender blindness' of development, reside potent gender myths in which idealized representations of women, and of their relationships with men and with each other, gain a life of their own.

In this chapter, my focus is on these idealized representations and on two of the key supportive elements in feminist fables of women's liberation from male oppression. The first element is the powerful social imagery of women's solidarity. This is underpinned by assumptions of women's inherent co-operativeness with each other and the belief that if only they were to recognize their collective interests and oppression by men, they would be able to mobilize *as women* to seek greater social justice. The second element is the notion that if only women had greater access to and control over money, they would exercise economic autonomy in ways that would free them from the shackles of subordination to men, achieving with this the freedom to make their own choices, which many development actors regard as the fundamental ingredients of empowerment (Alsop et al., 2006).

I begin by taking a closer look at these ideals of solidarity and autonomy. My starting point is not conceptual but personal: how I as a 'Western feminist' came to relate to these ideals, and the readings of African women's lives

I am profoundly grateful to all the women and men in Ado-Odo who shared their experiences with me, not knowing quite what would become of their confidences. I would especially like to thank Mary Akinsowon, Baba Yemisi Akinsowon and Dorcas Odu for all they taught me about gender relations in Ado. I thank Jo Doezema from whom I learnt so much about the uses of myth; and, for their critical engagement with the ideas expressed here, I am grateful to Rosalind Eyben, Ann Whitehead and Buzz Harrison.

that they led me towards — and away from. I then go on to explore how an analysis of gender and development narratives as myth and fable might help explain the purchase that certain ideas about women gain in policy and practice. My own ethnographic fieldwork in a small southern Nigerian town is used to juxtapose Western feminist visions of women's solidarity and autonomy against women's lived experiences of relationships with other women and with their husbands and lovers in this cultural context. I highlight the extent to which prevalent understandings of the nature and scope of 'gender relations' in gender and development narratives occlude other gendered power relationships experienced by women in this, as in other settings. I conclude with reflections on the implications of revisiting the salience of the myths of female solidarity and female autonomy for feminist engagement with development.

SOLIDARITY AND AUTONOMY: IDEALS IN PRACTICE?

Ideas about female solidarity and female autonomy appear in many, if not most, gender and development interventions. They underpin the promotion of self-help and savings and credit groups; and they inform a host of 'women's projects', as well as mainstream interventions that seek to enhance women's participation in the public sphere. Get women into groups, the development mantra goes, and they will be transformed into social, economic and political actors. Get women into parliament, and they will represent women's interests. Give women access to independent incomes, and they will be freed from dependency on men. From the popularization of focus group discussions in applied research, to PRA exercises aimed at seeking the perceptions and perspectives of 'women' as a social group, sex-segregated spaces are seen as those in which women will feel able to be vocal, authentic and find the confidence and support to express themselves, and to act.

These representations, I suggest here, might be usefully characterized as myths, as much for the work they do, as for their actual narrative content. In using the concept of myth as a device to explore how assumptions of solidarity and autonomy feature in gender and development narratives, I am not suggesting for a minute that female solidarity or female autonomy do not exist. Although the popular understanding of the term 'myth' is that it can be counter-posed to 'reality', myths are neither true nor false. To see them in these terms is to miss the point, and misunderstand their social and cultural salience (Cassirer, 1946; Laclau, 1996; Sorel, 1908/1941). Myths are narratives that do more than tell a good story. They are composed of a series of familiar images and devices, and work to produce an order-of-things that takes shape and has its effects through resonance with the affective dimensions of deeply held values and norms. As Cassirer contends: 'Myth does not arise solely from intellectual processes; it sprouts forth from deep human emotions . . . it is the *expression* of emotion . . . emotion turned into an image' (Cassirer, 1946: 43, emphasis in original). Myths may disturb, but they also assuage; they may question, but they do so in order to reaffirm and reassure.[1]

What has this got to do with development? Albert Hirschmann recognized the role that myths play in animating development actors in his 1967 book *Development Projects Observed*. He cites Georges Sorel, whose analysis of myth remains as salient now as when it was written almost a hundred years ago: 'Myths are not descriptions of things, but expressions of a determination to act ... A myth cannot be refuted since it is, at bottom, *identical with the convictions of a group*' (Sorel, 1908/1941: 33, my emphasis). Where Sorel highlights the identifications that can mobilize myths, Laclau (1996) emphasizes the political salience of the ideological, as well as affective, character of myth. Doezema's (2004) powerful analysis of the ideological uses made of the myth of the innocent trafficking victim draws on the work of Laclau and other political theorists to demonstrate the extent to which myths infuse politicized agendas with moral purpose.

Drawing on these theorists, it is my contention that female solidarity and female autonomy might be usefully seen as gender myths that many feminists — myself included — like to live by. I suggest that the dissonance between idealized representations of women's solidarity and autonomy and the complex contours of women's relationships with men and with each other provides a set of tensions that gender and development has struggled, and largely failed, to contend with. These tensions have often been resolved by simply air-brushing away conflicts and contradictions in women's relationships with each other and women's identifications with the men in their lives. The reason that these relationships remain poorly addressed is precisely because of the power that idealized notions of female solidarity and autonomy hold, as myths. My intention here is not to break with what might be regarded as the wellspring of what Sorel terms 'expressions of a determination to act'. Rather, it is to suggest that for development to make a meaningful difference to the relations of power that are such a potent source of gender injustice, we need to recognize the other stories that might be told about women's relationships with other women, and with men.

OF IDEALS AND MISRECOGNITION

The stories we tell have always served the dual purpose of explaining an otherwise incomprehensible world and creating and sustaining the world in our own likeness. (Busia, 1990: 93)

Female solidarity and female autonomy represent two ideals that I would not wish to live without. They have such a powerful grip on me that it is

---

1. There is of course a huge anthropological literature on myth, growing out of the foundational work of Claude Levi-Strauss (1963). Providing an adequate account and critique of this literature goes beyond the scope of this chapter.

difficult to even countenance questioning them. Even as I recognize that they are fragile and flawed, and that the category 'woman' that they are premised upon is deeply problematic, they are still ideals in which I have considerable personal investment. Feminist fables, didactic tales that deploy and resignify elements of gender myths, embed particular readings of gender relations and women's agency in injunctions to act. I grew up the UK, in an era where second-wave feminism was to transform the perspectives of middle-class women, like my mother. She raised me with a series of feminist injunctions: don't ever let yourself be dependent on a man; don't have children without having secured yourself a good career; women are powerful, women are good, women are right. Less visible to me were her identification with my father or the tensions she may have experienced with the expectations of his female relatives, in her subject position as a wife and mother, or indeed her investment in maintaining a position of respectability by remaining married.

In the mid-1980s, I went to Zimbabwe, and stayed on there to work as a teacher. My feminist ideals took a beating as I wrestled to make sense of how women were regarded and treated by men, and the tense and distrustful relationships that women seemed to have with each other. I was guilty of all that Chandra Mohanty (1987) says about Western feminists' representations of the Other: I simply didn't understand what was going on, and in my attempts to make sense of it, read Zimbabwean women's lives through my own Western eyes. I constructed them as victims of male oppression and of the embedded structural dynamics of patriarchy that pitted mothers-in-law against their daughters-in-law in competition for affective and economic resources (cf. Kandiyoti, 1988). And I saw as heroines those who escaped, who defied their husbands, who used *mupfuwira* (a magical medicine to delight many a feminist, which turns men into putty in a woman's hands and makes them do whatever they can to please women, including domestic work), who took lovers to match their husbands' philandering, and who gave as good as they got.

My beliefs in sisterhood and solidarity remained unscathed by my experiences in Zimbabwe. Women's hostility to other women could easily be explained away with recourse to ideas such as structural tensions residing in kinship systems — an old anthropological chestnut. The relative absence of close female friendships could also be explained by the pressure on women's time, the organization of production and so on. Women's suspicions of each other could be accounted for by the extensive sexual networking that was so much part of the social fabric, and which has caused such tragedy and loss in the years since then. And apart from those men who had been modified by *mupfuwira*, it was easy enough to read off from men's attitudes towards women as sexual partners and wives, a generalized notion of men-are-bastards that served the feminists of my generation well.

The very partiality of my understanding of gender relations in Zimbabwe — polarized, incomplete, read from my particular position as a white, middle-class, Western feminist — was to inform my choice of a field site for my PhD. I wanted to work somewhere where women were not dependent on men for their fortunes, where they were able to successfully balance motherhood and career, where strong women's organizations existed and where cultural and religious notions of femaleness were of power rather than weakness, agency rather than passivity, where women were respected *as women*. It was, in many respects, a quest for the feminist equivalent of the Holy Grail: for a place in which it was possible for women to really experience the solidarity and autonomy I regarded as fundamental to women's struggles against gender injustice.

It was a lavishly illustrated art history book bursting with images of women's power, autonomy and presence amongst the southwestern Nigerian Yoruba peoples that first captured my attention (Drewal and Drewal, 1983). The more I read about Yoruba women, the more fascinated I became. Accounts spoke of the legendary economic prowess of the market woman, source of an iconic image that conjures up a spatial and representational domain of female power *par excellence* (Belasco, 1980; Matory, 1994). I read about households in which men's and women's contributions were quite separate, and in which women exercised considerable *de facto* decision-making power (Fapohunda, 1988; Sudarkasa, 1973). I devoured tales of women balancing own-account income-generating work with child-rearing, helped out by other women and by older children (Dwyer and Bruce, 1988). I delighted in finding out about women doing very little domestic work, buying in meals and paying others to do their washing (Oyewumi, 1997; Sudarkasa, 1973). And the stories about the numerous and vibrant women's trade and social associations, and of women's protests and political mobilization (Mba, 1980) were a source of inspiration. More inspiring still were accounts of Yoruba religion, some of which include tales from the area in which I was to work of a female goddess Odudua,[2] from whom the entire Yoruba peoples originated, and characters like the strong and stroppy goddess Oya (Gleason, 1987).

I had a million questions about the more mundane aspects of women's lives: about how they got by and got on in their work and with their children and husbands, and about the contingencies of their struggles for money, children and peace (Cornwall, 1996). My research journey, pitted with all manner of epistemological and personal-political obstacles, was one that revealed to me the power of my own longing for something to be different. The difficulties I initially had in hearing what women and men had to say about each other and themselves threw up some of the potent challenges which theorizing gender in this African context represented for me. In the account that follows, I weave together personal narrative with ethnographic

---

2. The town in which I worked, Ado-Odo in Ogun State, is home to a major shrine of some antiquity to the goddess Odudua; Odudua (also known as Oduduwa) takes on a male form in much of the rest of the Yoruba sub-groups to the north and east of this region (Peel, 2000).

evidence culled from intensive participant observation and interviews,[3] to reflect on the power of the myths of female solidarity and autonomy and on the implications of the dissonance between lived experience and idealized representations of women's identifications and relationships for gender and development practice.

FEMALE SOLIDARITY IN ADO-ODO

Once a thriving agricultural centre at the heart of the trade routes running through the far southwestern corner of Nigeria, recent decades have seen Ado-Odo's fortunes change and the town revert to a rather sleepy backwater. With a population of over 40,000 people, an approximately equal number of Muslims and Christians and a small residue of adherents to the Yoruba deities whose shrines remain in the town, Ado has a huge array of social institutions. These range from associations of women who save together, called *egbe*, with names like 'friends become an association', to church and mosque societies, to trades associations and unions, to vigilante and community development groups. A central market that bursts into life every four days brings women from the villages in the hinterland and from adjacent markets into town, many of whom organize themselves into associations to maintain harmony and save together. Although men have long been a minor part of the market, it is mainly a female arena and certain commodities are only sold by women — notably those of least value such as leaf vegetables, as well as those associated with the highest turnover and most prestige, such as cloth and kola nut. Female market-sellers come to be known by the name of their commodity and gain prestige from their prowess within this domain.

The main road through the town is dotted with small shop-based businesses, many of which are owned by women. In hairdressing and tailoring salons, bands of female apprentices dressed in identical uniforms spend their days together learning their craft. Near the river and along the minor roads that run in all directions, groups of women gather to process palm and cassava, to pack pats of *fufu* (fermented, ground cassava flour made into a stiff porridge) for sale in the ring of markets that supply the Lagos metropolis. Some of these processing stalls are adjacent to clusters of houses in which co-wives and the wives of brothers and sons live and work together, others are sites in which neighbours come together to work. At church and in the mosque, women pray together, meet to plan activities to further the fortunes of their places of worship and extend invitations to the naming ceremonies, weddings or funerals of each others' families.

In most of the arenas in which women live their everyday lives, they interact primarily with other women. Some of these relationships might be chosen,

---

3. This chapter draws on anthropological fieldwork conducted over the course of eighteen months from 1992 to 1994 (Cornwall, 1996), and two subsequent shorter periods of research in 1997 and 2000.

others might come about because of a woman's line of business, the man she married or the religion with which she came to be involved, either by choice or through marriage. Mapping women's social networks, I found them to span multiple domains of association in which one woman may have very different relational identities — as the mother of twins, as Iya Alata the successful pepper trader, as the faithful supplicant on whom blessings are bestowed, or as the client of herbalists in search of magical medicine (*juju*) to keep enemies at bay. I found some women to have diffuse, generalized social networks, and some to have remarkably constricted ones that consisted of a few trusted associates.

When it came to asking women about their close friendships, the people they really felt they could confide in, many said there were no such people: only their children. One of the women who said 'my children are my friends' claimed that she passed the time of day with women who went past the porch of her house, from which she ran a petty trading business, but never got into chat because 'you never know what people will do with the things that you tell them'. Women would laugh loudly when I asked if they were close to their husbands or able to talk to them about their worries, explaining the ideal of companionate marriage that the British like to entertain, and that some Nigerian Christians have adopted, although with rather limited reach beyond the elite (Mann, 1985).

In all of the sites in which women gathered and spent their everyday lives, there was a current of mild suspicion that would sometimes swell into outright hostility. Women spoke a lot of having enemies, *ọta*, people who were out to do them harm, undermine their businesses, stop them getting pregnant or carrying a child to term, or cause them a lingering sickness that would drain away all their resources. Those enemies, often the reason why blessings and magical means of protection are sought, are commonly of a female provenance. There is a Yoruba proverb that vividly conveys the haunting sense of enemies all around, none more potent or potentially harmful than those within the house itself: *Ẹhinkule lọta wa, ile ni asẹni igbe; bi iku ile ko pani, ti ode ko rini gbe ṣe* — the enemy is in the backyard, the plotter against you is in the house; if death does not come from inside the house, that from outside will do nothing to you. As the proverb suggests, enemies outside — in the market, in rotating credit associations, in the church or mosque — are one thing. Those within the household are another again.

Feminists have long remarked on the sources of conflict within the household, and some have highlighted the divided, and divisive, loyalties of household members with different interests and investments in men as husbands, brothers or sons (Kandiyoti, 1988; Whitehead, 1981). But few have been able to acknowledge quite how difficult women can make the lives of other women. This is not surprising; exposure of this kind obviously detracts from the building of conviction to act that is so much at the heart of feminist myth-making. As I was tersely cautioned by a senior feminist colleague when I went in search of literature on gender relations amongst women that would help make sense of what I was finding out, 'we don't write about these things'. Nor could I really take it in at first, when women and men in Ado began to tell me tales of co-wives poisoning each others' children or causing sterility, of mothers-in-law plotting to get rid of daughters-in-law their sons seemed to love too much, or of sisters-in-law or even women's own sisters visiting healers to buy *juju* to make the thriving businesses or multiple pregnancies that they so envied fail. Women, I was constantly told, are 'the death of the world' (*obinrin iku aiye*).

It was perhaps to be expected that tensions between women within the compound might turn into suspicion and conflict. But what of other sites in which women came together? What of women's associations in the market, at first glance an optimal site for female solidarity? Observation of the myriad market and trades associations in the town showed that they often did act collectively in the interests of their members, and provided a space for women to develop their leadership abilities as well as to network and build relationships with other women. But they did so despite and because of otherwise potentially fractious relationships between women. Functionalist as it seems, market associations appeared to serve less as spaces for solidarity than as mechanisms to avoid overt conflict. Women sitting side by side selling the same commodity were in direct competition with each other, a recipe for trouble. Herbalists reported a steady flow of market women coming to them to seek a range of protective measures to gird them against the interference of those who may wish a person ill. The marketplace is, after all, a place where friends, relatives and strangers mix: a place of power, and of potential danger from those enemies who might wish to bring a woman down and put her in her place (Belasco, 1980; Matory, 1994).

Women's savings and credit groups in Ado often had an instrumentality about them, functioning less to build group-based identifications as women than to administer loans. Some groups went as far as bringing men in to do the actual administration of money, 'because women always quarrel with each other' and because 'women cannot be trusted/are not trustworthy' (*obrinrin ko şe gbękęle*). The shift from group-based savings and credit to the patronage of individual — almost all male — 'collectors', who creamed off a proportion of women's savings in exchange for keeping it safe, reflected the fracturing of trust that was a consequence of a string of disaster stories, where women failed to honour their turns to contribute once they had benefited from a payout, or disappeared with all the money. As Colette Solomon (2003) shows for Ghana, savings and credit groups may often be spaces simply for transactions rather than for anything resembling solidarity. The pervasive sense that to share personal information with others is to lend them power that can be used against you meant that in many of these spaces, women simply would not divulge if they were experiencing difficulties, let alone gain 'empowerment' through group-based solidarity.

These were not the stories I wanted to hear, but I wrote them down as a good anthropologist is supposed to, then struggled with how I was going to tell them, as a white outsider tangling with representations of the Other. That they were fables of another kind, stories encoding cautionary tales about women's power, only became evident to me when I sought out actual examples. Their effects on consciousness and behaviour were real enough, but closer investigation showed that some at least were 'urban myths' — eponymous tales of a 'friend of a friend of a friend'. The occasions on which these stories came to be told and the editorializing that accompanied them provoked me to reflect: why is it that these narratives, retold in myriad forms but based on a similar core storyline, capture women's imaginations to such a degree? What is it about the ways in which they represent other women that resonates? Why was I never hearing anything but negativity about women, even from the younger women whose behaviour was so often a cause for moralizing commentary? What was in it for the women who told these tales?

FEMALE AUTONOMY IN ADO-ODO

If these stories disrupted my beliefs about female solidarity, how did my ideals of female autonomy fare in this context? On the face of it, Yoruba women would seem to be admirable feminist role models when it comes to autonomy. Joint household budgets are something so rare as to be exceptional and it is virtually unthinkable for a woman not to generate her own independent income (Fapohunda, 1988). The subject positions of wife, worker and mother are configured in very different ways in this context, enabling women to find ways of combining them in which there appear to be few of the tensions and trade-offs experienced by women like those of my mother's generation in the UK, and indeed many of my peers. This very multiplicity of possibilities poses problems, however, for singular notions of empowerment and autonomy. A woman may be more autonomous or empowered in respect to one area of her life, without any necessary congruence or mutual impingement on other everyday relationships.

Many of the women I knew in Ado were financially independent. Some were even in a position where they were effectively supporting their families unaided by their husbands; and some confessed in private to buying their husbands smart clothes so that they could maintain the status of the family in the public eye. Financial autonomy does not translate so easily, however, into the ability to 'do and undo' that women would speak of when they described the exercise of agency in everyday life. Seeing poor women as individuals who pursue entirely independent and goal-oriented strategies, as is often the case in discourses on 'empowerment' and 'choice' in development, is to deny the complexities of their relational ties and the contingencies of lived experience. As members of families, associations and compounds, women's claims and entitlements are constantly reconfigured in relation to these others (Petchesky, 1998; Strathern, 1991). Making clear-cut, strategic choices is dependent on having the power to realize them: power that many of the women in Ado, including those with considerable buying and spending power, were not in a position to fully exercise (Cornwall, 2002).

Making it for themselves enables women to establish sources of security beyond their marriages; but, importantly, it also sustains marriages. As one trader confided:

> When I was in money, my husband treated me well. He used to come to me to ask me this and that about how he was going on. Now I have no money, he just does whatever he likes without even coming to me to inform me. Some men do this. They will start making a misunderstanding every time and report you here and there [i.e. complain about you to relatives and elders]. They use this as a way of marrying another wife.

Contrasting perspectives on the way women use money gained from micro-credit shed light on some of the complexities at stake here. Goetz and Sen Gupta (1996) suggest that in handing over their loans to their husbands, women may end up doubly vulnerable and with dubious gains to empower-ment; yet, Kabeer (1998) suggests, money can buy love, keep relationships afloat, enable women to maintain the peace and their respectability, and keep their families intact. Contingent circumstances make both of these readings a possibility in this context. The role financial autonomy plays in maintaining otherwise unstable relationships is significant. Yet this puts women in a del-icate position precisely because of the uncertainties involved in maintaining wealth if they acquire it. Given that the majority of women in the town are engaged in the informal economy, the vagaries of the market pose one set of challenges. But, or so women's narratives suggest, far more potent obstacles to security were seen to reside not in women's relationships with men, but in the agency of other women.

One day I was chatting with a couple of women my age about co-wives. They asked me what women do in London. Restraining myself from spinning a feminist fable or two, I told them that it was against the law for a man to marry two wives, but that some married men have secret mistresses. I then told them the story of a relative of mine who did this for many years. When his wife found out, she was angry and threatened him with divorce. Eventually, she decided not to go. She had told me, I recounted to them, that if she had been able to get a reasonable job, she would have left. The women nodded, using this as an opportunity to caution the two teenage girls sitting with us to get their own jobs as 'men are useless'. But, they said, her reaction was too extreme. 'That's what men do here in Nigeria', said one of them with a sigh of resignation. The real problem starts, they said, when the husband's relatives or his other wives begin to make trouble.

Ado women's narratives on intrahousehold relations dwelt less on the classic concerns of feminist economists with the misleading presumptions about benevolent patriarchs and the inequities of intrahousehold allocation (Evans, 1991); rather, they were preoccupied with trouble, and with a very particular kind of trouble, that brought about and experienced by women. Talk of 'women's wars' and of ill-defined but menacing 'trouble' peppered herbalists' accounts of what brought women to seek their assistance. Women told me stories of how friends of friends had mysteriously swelled until limbs were so heavy or bodies so wasted they could scarcely move, upon which they would flee for their natal compounds in fear of their lives. Those who stayed in their natal homes thereafter, either to pursue their marital relationship in peace or seek someone new, were maligned by other women as *ilemoṣu* — literally women who return home without a good reason (such as illness or domestic violence), figuratively women who went astray and who, as women would be fond of telling me, 'useless themselves [i.e. behave with 'improper' sexual licence] here and there running after men'. As I narrate elsewhere (Cornwall, 2002), tracking down women who were labelled *ilemoṣu* was a real eye-opener: they included many older women who had moved out when co-wives got vicious, and maintained their marriages from a distance; and others who recounted a string of mysterious illnesses caused, they thought, by other women in their husband's compound.

'Women's wars' within the household are considered to be some of the most dangerous. For many of the women I spoke with about their experiences of this kind of trouble, their reaction had been to try to keep the peace as far as possible, and only when things got intolerable to consider 'packing out'. Their husbands seemed to have very little part in the whole thing, and often barely featured in accounts of why women left their marital homes. Women's responses ranged from pleading for mercy, enlisting supporters from among their marital kin to defend them, and fighting back by using 'weapons of the weak' (Scott, 1985) such as songs. Women would recount these songs to me to illustrate why women needed to watch their backs. One, sung by a gutsy junior wife, gives a flavour of these forms of resistance:

> The senior wife abused me that I stole locust bean
> The senior wife abused me that I stole salt
> How shall I spoil her name
> The one with a hanging lip
> The one with a hanging lip
> I shall make *buba* and *agbada* from her mouth [i.e. she's got such a big mouth, it's big enough to sew an outfit from] (translated from the Yoruba).

What drives women to leave, then, is less having acquired economic autonomy or even being sick of their husband — unless he is violent and openly abusive to her and his male elders' attempts to chastise him for this behaviour fail. It is more often that trouble with other women in the compound makes life so intolerable that women risk the reprobation of other women, and the damage to their reputation that the label of *ilemoṣu* can pose, and 'pack out'. In doing so, they jeopardize their relationships with those whom, for many women, are their closest friends — their children — who, regarded as the 'property' of the man, are often forced to remain at home, subject to the mercies of future stepmothers.

PUTTING 'GENDER RELATIONS' IN PERSPECTIVE

'Gender relations' are generally conceived in gender and development as referring not to *any* gendered power relationship, but to a particular kind of relationship between men and women: that of the heterosexual dyad (Moore, 1994; Tcherzekoff, 1993). In this context, as the account given in this chapter suggests, it seems that the kind of 'gender relations' that mattered more to women's prospects and well-being were the kind that barely feature in gender and development narratives: relations between women (Peters, 1995). Chantal Mouffe (1992) argues that the category 'women' consists of a collection of contingent, positional identifications that only gain salience or stability in particular configurations, for particular purposes. As I suggest earlier, women have multiple identifications in this setting; not all of them are framed as subject positions that are the kind of relational identities such as wives, wards and daughters that are often the substantive focus for gender analysis in development. As competitors in the marketplace, supplicants in religious settings, members of associations and, arguably, as those who cohabit compounds structured as much around women-centred 'hearth-holds' (Ekejiuba, 1995) as around male-anchored households, these other gender relations — relations amongst women — are vital when considering the complexities of gender and power.

The significance of this type of gender relations is put into relief by looking more closely at the particular kinds of relations on which analyses of gender relations depend — those between women and their husbands. Men as husbands or lovers are largely absent in much of women's everyday lives and interactions in Ado; and, as many of my women acquaintances and friends assured me, men are often the least of their problems. The phrase 'facing my children and my work' is one I heard used often when women talked about their intimate relationships with their husbands, years into a marriage. The feeling was less that these men were actively misusing or otherwise oppressing them, than that they were vaguely useless, and not really giving them much of anything — be it love or money (Cornwall, 2002, 2003).

Once I got to know the husbands of the women I spent time with, I came to recognize that for all the patriarchal prerogative they could have had access to, some were positively sheepish when it came to telling their wives what to do. One particular man, who was to become a dear friend (sadly now departed), lived in a neighbouring room in the old mud plaster family house we shared with other family members. Dependent on his trader wife for sustenance, and on alcohol for peace of mind, I saw him cowering as she bellowed his incompetence at him, and then living through the agony of her openly seeing another man, packing all their possessions into a truck and moving to another town, then taking him to court for divorce.

What was happening to this friend of mine was, in some respects, the stuff of feminist fables: an 'empowered' woman giving as good as she got, securing herself a sex life and a 'helper' to compensate for his shortcomings, and making use of her economic autonomy to free herself from a marriage that had become a millstone. I had told a few of these fables myself. But when I witnessed this scene it made me step back and reconsider. I had become locked into a circular version of a particularly embedded piece of feminist rhetoric: that marriage is an oppressive institution which places women in a position of subordination. My friend's situation did not seem to fit the bill at all. His wife flouted a lover in front of his nose, and he could do nothing about it; his economic impotence was exacerbated by his utter failure to exercise any control whatsoever over her, as prevailing norms dictated that he should do. He loved his wife and was outraged and hurt that she would treat him so badly.

This case might have been exceptional, but it made me look more care-fully at what was going on around me. There was a string of other cases in which it would be hard to describe the female half of a marital partnership as 'oppressed' in any respect. Granted, men like my friend were not the types who womanized, spent their earnings elsewhere and sought the easiest lives they could have, which represented very real dimensions of some hetero-sexual partnerships in this context. But, as I suggest elsewhere (Cornwall, 2003), seeing such behaviour as expressive of 'hegemonic masculinity' (Connell, 1995) leaves a number of questions unanswered, and obscures other masculinities that may be just as culturally salient.

As Jackson (this issue) argues, some feminist analyses of marriage have been blinkered to other dimensions of this particular 'gender relation'. These include relationships of care and co-operation, as well as a mutual dependency that goes beyond idealized narratives of complementarity. And, as O'Laughlin (1995) points out, conjugal relations are in any case only part of the complex relational ties within which women live their everyday lives, while — as I have suggested here — relations of conflict or co-operation with other women may come to play far more important a part in women's struggles to get on and get by.

RE-READING 'GENDER RELATIONS' IN ADO

African feminist scholars have critiqued the profound misreadings of gender in Africa by Western feminist researchers.[4] Challenging the polarities on which the kind of gender analysis that is prevalent in development tends to be based, they have highlighted the diversity of women's identifications and attachments. Ogundipe-Leslie, for example, argues that outsiders have failed

---

4. See Gaidzanwa (1982); Imam et al. (1997); Nnaemeka (1998); Ogundipe-Leslie (1994); Oyewumi (1997); Steady (1987). Like 'Western feminists', the category 'African feminists' is unstable, plural and dissonant; there is a rich debate on what 'feminism' might mean in Africa, including whether it has any salience at all (Gaizanwa, 1982; Steady, 1987), which includes important collections such as Nnaemeka (1998) and Imam et al. (1997).

to realize that relationships with men may well be peripheral to African women's self-perceptions, lives and desires. She contends: 'All African women have multiple identities, evolving and accreting over time, enmeshed in one individual. Yet African women continue to be looked at and looked for in their coital and conjugal sites which seem to be a preoccupation of many Western analysts and feminists' (Ogundipe-Leslie, 1994: 251).

Privileging conjugality over consanguinity leads, as Sudarkasa (1986) points out, to a tendency to almost completely overlook important relationships of support that exist between women and men and obscure culturally salient axes of difference such as seniority and wealth. It also works to disregard the significance of the other gender relations that this chapter has highlighted. Indeed, Oyewumi (1997) argues that the unitary construct 'woman' occludes the interests women have in common with some of the men in their lives, whether as members of generations, families or economic groups, as well as the lack of common interests women may experience with other women. It also, perhaps most potently of all, misrecognizes the power that women can and do exert — over men, as much as over women. Acholonu (1995: 28) goes further: 'those who present the notion that the African woman is suppressed and oppressed or is placed in an inferior position to men, have failed to realise that in many cases women are part and parcel of, if not the power behind, the scattered instances of male dominance'. This is an uncomfortable 'truth' for many of the varieties of feminism that have characterized gender and development; at the same time, it may well be 'part and parcel' of the very real experience of some of those women that gender and development interventions seek to 'empower'.

Casting gendered power relations into as restricted a frame as heterosexual partnerships between women and men not only fails to make analytical sense. It also shores up representations of women, as victims or as heroines, that fail to get to grips with the realities of women's lived experiences of power and powerlessness. By erasing significant aspects of these experiences, the gender myths that are pervasive in development discourse can end up reinforcing a 'determination to act' that reproduces the very inequities that Chandra Mohanty (1987) pinpointed in her critique of Western feminists' writings on 'Third World women'. Read through 'Western eyes', African women's relationships with men in 'coital and conjugal sites' come to represent in gender and development narratives the major challenge in overcoming their presumed subordination; and the complex power relations that sustain social injustice and inequity are effectively shut out of the frame.

MYTHS TO LIVE BY?

My aim in this chapter has not been to argue that gender myths of female solidarity and female autonomy are of no purpose in inspiring efforts to change the unfair gender order. Nor has it been to suggest that these myths and the representations of women that they encode do not continue to hold value in some cultural contexts and for some purposes, both as 'ways of worldmaking' (Goodman, 1978) and as 'expressions of a determination to act' (Sorel, 1908/1941). Rather, the argument I am making here is that the myths that animate gender and development interventions may hold little resonance with the lived experiences of the women whom gender and development interventions seek to empower.

Despite all the lipservice that has been paid to gender as socially constructed, mainstream development interventions aimed at empowering women are often based on gross essentialisms about women and men. For all the nuance feminist theory can offer, the translation of feminist thinking into development narratives has tended to produce social constructions that are remarkably singular and static. Narratives of gender in development often take little account of the complexity of women's relational subject positions, nor of the contingency of their identities and identifications. Simplification and sloganizing shears away the analytical potential of the concept of gender, reducing it to a catchphrase that connotes so limited a range of relational identities that it tells us little about the lived dynamics of gendered power relations.

Hirschmann (1967) cautions that to confuse the idealized prescriptions with which myths provide us with any actually existing reality is a grave mistake: myths serve, he argues, less to speak about what is really going on than to motivate action. It could, of course, be contended that to confuse the promotion of instruments such as the creation of women's groups with the existence of solidarity within them is to miss the point: such interventions often serve to *create* organization where it is lacking. But as Solomon's (2003) analysis of savings and credit groups in Ghana and Harrison's (1997) account of men in women's groups in Zambia show, this may be wishful thinking: women may simply use these institutions for their own projects, draw together members of their own kin and networks to constitute 'women's groups' so as to benefit from development assistance, and be puzzled as to why donors do not seem to want their menfolk to benefit from them too. Similarly, it can be argued that even if economic empowerment interventions stop short of dislodging embedded inequities, they do at least give women more choices — including the choice to use their gains to maintain their marriages and enhance their bargaining power within the domestic arena (Kabeer, 1998). Yet, as Cecilia Sardenberg's (2006) distinction between 'liberal' and 'liberating' empowerment suggests, to turn spending power into personal clout is one thing but to use that clout to lever gains for gender justice is another thing again.

Clearly, sustaining the myths that women are inherently co-operative and selfless on the one hand, and, on the other, that they would readily break out of the webs of social relations in which their lives are enmeshed and act as autonomous sovereign individuals if only they had the material means to do so, is not doing women — and particularly poor women — much of a service. For a start, it fails to acknowledge the gendered power relations that women themselves may experience as more of an obstacle to the exercise of their agency and pursuit of well-being than relations with their husbands or lovers. It also fails to appreciate the very real implications of social connectedness for any account of agency, and with it the limits of the form of liberal individualism that is so hegemonic in mainstream development thinking.

It is easy to explain away (and continue to disregard) the significance of the kinds of gender relations this chapter has placed at the centre of its analysis, and replace them with gender myths about female solidarity and autonomy. Indeed, it is safer to bury frictions between women in explanatory frameworks that place the blame with patriarchy than to acknowledge that not only are women's identifications contingent rather than fixed, stable or enduring, but so too are those of men (Connell, 1995; Cornwall and Lindisfarne, 1994). The implications for development practice are two-fold. First, short-cut, quick-fix empowerment solutions skimp on the kind of power analysis and the long, slow, processes of engagement that are needed to enable women to work together effectively to bring about change in their and other women's lives. Second, it suggests that zero-sum strategies that seek to enhance the power of women relative to that of men are too crude an instrument to redress prevailing injustice and inequity. Recognizing this calls for enquiring more deeply into and working with women's own sources of strength, solace and security rather than reading their situations through a set of institutionalized lenses that bring only one dimension of their gender relations into focus.

Acknowledging the limits of the gender myths that this chapter focuses on means going beyond a view in which giving women spending power is the way to tackle deep-seated social inequities in which these very women may have significant investments. It means going beyond the assumption that women are inherently more co-operative and if only women had a voice they would use it in favour of women as a group. This does not mean giving up on autonomy and solidarity as ideals that can guide and inspire action: it does, however, call for qualifying them. Autonomy can be cast in more relational terms as expanding the capacity 'to participate effectively in shaping the boundaries that define ... the field of what is possible' (Hayward, 1998: 12), rather than in terms of the unfettered acts of sovereign individuals. 'Empowerment' thus comes to constitute renegotiating and re-imagining the boundaries of the possible from within actually existing webs of sociality, not simply the act of making independent choices. And solidarity can be recast as something that can be actively constructed through identification with a shared concern about issues of social and gender injustice: it comes, thus, to reside in 'inter-est' (Arendt, 1958; see also Adams, 2002) — that which people find in common, which binds them together — rather than in a presumed commonality of interests.

Solidarity, autonomy and empowerment remain feminist keywords; they represent closely held ideals for many, capturing vital elements of the normative project of changing gendered power relations that lay at the heart of the original Gender and Development (GAD) agenda (Razavi and Miller, 1995). The gender myths associated with these ideals may have outlived their usefulness, but the overarching goal of transforming unequal and inequitable gender relations has not lost its salience. To address it, strategies are needed that can reanimate and repoliticize the gender agenda and lend it broader purchase and greater analytical and political bite. For this, new myths may be needed: narratives that speak about justice and equality in ways that both hold more resonance with women's everyday lives and can better serve to enlist broader constituencies in the struggle to bring about a fairer world.

REFERENCES

Acholonu, Catherine Obianuju (1995) *Motherism: The Afrocentric Alternative to Feminism*. Owerri, Nigeria: Afa.

Adams, Katherine (2002) 'At the Table with Arendt: Towards a Self-interested Practice of Coalition Discourse', *Hypatia* 17(1): 1–33.

Alsop, Ruth, Mette Bertelsen and Jeremy Holland (eds) (2006) *Empowerment in Practice: From Analysis to Implementation*. Washington, DC: The World Bank.

Arendt, Hannah (1958) *The Human Condition*. Chicago, IL: University of Chicago Press.

Belasco, Bernard (1980) *The Entrepreneur as Culture Hero: Preadaptations in Nigerian Economic Development*. New York: Praeger.

Busia, Abena (1990) 'Silencing Sycorax: On African Colonial Discourse and the Unvoiced Female', *Cultural Critique* 14 (Winter 1989–90): 81–104.

Cassirer, Ernst (1946) *The Myth of the State*. New Haven, CT: Yale University Press.

Connell, Robert (1995) *Masculinities*. Oxford: Polity.

Cornwall, Andrea (1996) 'For Money, Children and Peace: Everyday Lives in Changing Times in Ado-Odo, Southwestern Nigeria'. PhD Thesis, SOAS, University of London.

Cornwall, Andrea (2002) 'Spending Power: Love, Money and the Reconfiguration of Gender Relations in Ado-Odo, Southwestern Nigeria', *American Ethnologist* 29(4): 963–80.

Cornwall, Andrea (2003) '"To be a Man is More than a Day's Work": Shifting Ideals of Manliness in Ado-Odo, S. W. Nigeria', in L. Lindsay and S. Miescher (eds) *Men and Masculinities in Modern Africa*, pp. 230–48. Princeton, NJ: Heinemann.

Cornwall, Andrea and Nancy Lindisfarne (eds) (1994) *Dislocating Masculinity: Comparative Ethnographies*. London: Routledge.

Doezema, Jo (2004) 'Sex Slaves and Discourse Masters: The Historical Construction of Trafficking in Women'. DPhil Thesis, IDS, University of Sussex, Brighton.

Drewal, Henry and Margaret Drewal (1983) *Gelede: Art and Female Power amongst the Yoruba*. Bloomington, IN: Indiana University Press.

Dwyer, Daisy and Judith Bruce (eds) (1988) *A Home Divided: Women and Income in the Third World*. Stanford, CA: Stanford University Press.

Ekejiuba, Felicia (1995) 'Down to Fundamentals: Women-centred Hearth-holds in Rural West Africa', in Deborah Bryceson (ed.) *Women Wielding the Hoe: Lessons from Rural Africa for Feminist Theory and Development Practice*, pp. 47–63. Oxford: Berg.

Evans, Alison (1991) 'Gender Issues in Rural Household Economics', *IDS Bulletin* 22(1): 51–59.

Fapohunda, Eleanor (1988) 'The Non-pooling Household: A Challenge to Theory', in D. Dwyer and J. Bruce (eds) *A Home Divided: Women and Income in the Third World*, pp. 143–54. Stanford, CA: Stanford University Press.

Folbre, Nancy (1994) *Who Pays for the Kids? Gender and the Structures of Constraint.* London and New York: Routledge.

Gaidzanwa, Rudo (1982) 'Bourgeois Theories of Gender and Feminism and their Shortcomings with Reference to Southern African Countries', in Ruth Meena (ed.) *Gender in Southern Africa: Conceptual and Theoretical Issues*, pp. 92–125. Harare: SAPES.

Gleason, Judith (1987) *Oya: In Praise of the Goddess.* New York: Shambala Publications.

Goetz, Anne Marie and Reeta Sen Gupta (1996) 'Who Takes the Credit? Gender, Power and Control over Loan Use in Rural Credit Programmes in Bangladesh', *World Development* 24(1): 45–63.

Goodman, N. (1978) *Ways of Worldmaking.* Sussex, UK: Harvester.

Harrison, Elizabeth (1997) 'Men in Women's Groups: Interlopers or Allies?', *IDS Bulletin* 28(3): 122–32.

Hayward, Clarissa Ryle (1998) 'De-facing Power', *Polity* 31(1): 1–22.

Hirschmann, Albert (1967) *Development Projects Observed.* Washington, DC: Brookings Institution.

Imam, Ayesha, Amina Mama and Fatou Sow (eds) (1997) *Engendering African Social Sciences.* Dakar, Senegal: CODESRIA.

Kabeer, Naila (1994) *Reversed Realities: Gender Hierarchies in Development Thought.* London: Verso.

Kabeer, Naila (1998) 'Money Can't Buy me Love? Re-evaluating Gender, Credit and Empowerment in Rural Bangladesh'. IDS Discussion Paper 363. Brighton: University of Sussex, Institute of Development Studies.

Kandiyoti, Deniz (1988) 'Bargaining with Patriarchy', *Gender and Society* 2(3): 274–90.

Laclau, Ernesto (1996) 'The Death and Resurrection of the Theory of Ideology', *Journal of Political Ideologies* 1(3): 201–20.

Levi-Strauss, Claude (1963) *Structural Anthropology.* New York: Basic Books.

Mann, K. (1985) *Marrying Well: Marriage, Status and Social Change among the Educated Elite in Colonial Lagos.* Cambridge: Cambridge University Press.

Matory, James Lorand (1994) *Sex and the Empire that is No More: Gender and the Politics of Metaphor in Oyo Yoruba Religion.* Minneapolis, MN: University of Minnesota Press.

Mba, Nina (1980) *Nigerian Women Mobilized: Women's Political Activity in Southern Nigeria, 1900–1965.* Berkeley, CA: University of California Press.

Mohanty, Chandra (1987) 'Under Western Eyes: Feminist Scholarship and Colonial Discourses', *Feminist Review* 30: 61–88.

Moore, Henrietta (1994) *A Passion for Difference: Essays in Anthropology and Gender.* Cambridge: Polity.

Mouffe, Chantal (1992) 'Feminism, Citizenship and Radical Democratic Politics', in J. Butler and J. Scott (eds) *Feminists Theorize the Political*, pp. 369–84. New York: Routledge.

Nnaemeka, Obioma (ed.) (1998) *Sisterhood, Feminisms and Power: From Africa to the Diaspora.* Trenton, NJ: Africa World Press.

Ogundipe-Leslie, Molara (1994) *Re-creating Ourselves: African Women and Critical Transformation.* Trenton, NJ: Africa World Press.

O'Laughlin, Bridget (1995) 'Myth of the African Family in the World of Development', in Deborah Bryceson (ed.) *Women Wielding the Hoe: Lessons from Rural Africa for Feminist Theory and Development Practice*, pp. 63–92. Oxford: Berg.

Oyewumi, O. (1997) *The Invention of Women: Making an African Sense of Western Gender Discourses*, Minneapolis, MN: University of Minnesota Press.

Peel, J. D. Y. (2000) *Religious Encounter and the Making of the Yoruba.* Bloomington, IN: Indiana University Press.

Petchesky, Rosalind (1998) 'Introduction', in R. Petchesky and K. Judd (eds) *Negotiating Reproductive Rights: Women's Perspectives Across Countries and Cultures*, pp. 1–30. London: Zed Press.

Peters, Pauline (1995) 'Uses and Abuses of the Concept of "Female Headed Households" in Research on Agrarian Transformation and Policy', in Deborah Bryceson (ed.) *Women Wielding the Hoe: Lessons from Rural Africa for Feminist Theory and Development Practice*, pp. 93–108. Oxford: Berg.

Razavi, Shahra and Carol Miller (1995) 'From WID to GAD: Conceptual Shifts in the Women and Development Discourse'. UNRISD Occasional Paper. Geneva: United Nations Research Institute for Social Development.

Sardenberg, Cecilia (2006) 'Liberal vs Liberating Empowerment: Conceptualising Women's Empowerment from a Latin American Feminist Perspective'. Paper presented at the Inception Workshop, Pathways to Women's Empowerment RPC, Luxor, Egypt (13–18 September).

Scott, James (1985) *Weapons of the Weak: Everyday Forms of Peasant Resistance*. New Haven, CT: Yale University Press.

Solomon, Colette (2003) 'Giving Women Choices? Development Interfaces: Women and Credit in Tamale, Northern Ghana'. DPhil Thesis, Institute of Development Studies, University of Sussex, Brighton.

Sorel, Georges ([1908]1941) *Reflections on Violence*. New York: Peter Smith.

Steady, Filomena (1987) 'African Feminism: A Worldwide Perspective', in Rosalind Terborg-Penn, Sharon Harley and Andrea Benton Rushing (eds) *Women in Africa and the African Diaspora*, pp. 3–24. Washington, DC: Howard University Press.

Strathern, Marilyn (1991) *Partial Connections*. Savage, MD: Rowman & Littlefield.

Sudarkasa, Niara (1973) 'Where Women Work: Yoruba Women in the Marketplace and in the Home'. Anthropological Papers 53. Ann Arbor, MI: University of Michigan.

Sudarkasa, Naira (1986) '"The Status of Women" in Indigenous African Societies', *Feminist Studies* 12(1): 91–103.

Tcherzekoff, Sergio (1993) 'The Illusion of Dualism in Samoa: "Brothers-and-Sisters" are not "Men-and-Women"', in T. del Valle (ed.) *Gendered Anthropology*, pp. 54–87. London: Routledge.

Whitehead, Ann (1981) '"I'm Hungry Mum": The Politics of Domestic Budgeting', in K. Young, C. Wolkowitz and R. McCullagh (eds) *Of Marriage and the Market: Women's Subordination in International Perspective*, pp. 88–111. London: CSE Books.

Index